THE ARDEN SHAKESPEARE

GENERAL EDITOR: RICHARD PROUDFOOT

THE MERCHANT
OF VENICE

THE ARDEN SHAKESPEARE

All's Well That Ends Well: edited by G. K. Hunter
Antony and Cleopatra: edited by M. R. Ridley
As You Like It: edited by Agnes Latham
The Comedy of Errors: edited by R. A. Foakes
Coriolanus: edited by Philip Brockbank
Cymbeline: edited by J. M. Nosworthy
Hamlet: edited by Harold Jenkins
Julius Caesar: edited by T. S. Dorsch
King Henry IV, Parts 1 & 2: edited by A. R. Humphreys
King Henry V: edited by John H. Walter
King Henry VI, Parts 1, 2 & 3: edited by A. S. Cairncross
King Henry VIII: edited by R. A. Foakes
King John: edited by E. A. J. Honigmann
King Lear: edited by Kenneth Muir
King Richard II: edited by Peter Ure
King Richard III: edited by Antony Hammond
Love's Labour's Lost: edited by Richard David
Macbeth: edited by Kenneth Muir
Measure for Measure: edited by J. W. Lever
The Merchant of Venice: edited by John Russell Brown
The Merry Wives of Windsor: edited by H. J. Oliver
A Midsummer Night's Dream: edited by Harold F. Brooks
Much Ado About Nothing: edited by A. R. Humphreys
Othello: edited by M. R. Ridley
Pericles: edited by F. D. Hoeniger
The Poems: edited by F. T. Prince
Romeo and Juliet: edited by Brian Gibbons
The Taming of the Shrew: edited by Brian Morris
The Tempest: edited by Frank Kermode
Timon of Athens: edited by H. J. Oliver
Titus Andronicus: edited by J. C. Maxwell
Troilus and Cressida: edited by Kenneth Palmer
Twelfth Night: edited by J. M. Lothian and T. W. Craik
The Two Gentlemen of Verona: edited by Clifford Leech
The Winter's Tale: edited by J. H. P. Pafford

THE ARDEN EDITION OF THE
WORKS OF WILLIAM SHAKESPEARE

THE MERCHANT
OF VENICE

Edited by
JOHN RUSSELL BROWN

METHUEN

LONDON and NEW YORK

The general editors of the Arden Shakespeare have been
W. J. Craig (1899–1906), R. H. Case (1909–44),
Una Ellis-Fermor (1946–58), Harold F. Brooks (1952–82),
Harold Jenkins (1958–82) and Brian Morris (1975–82)

Present general editor: Richard Proudfoot

This edition of *The Merchant of Venice*, by John Russell Brown,
first published in 1955 by
Methuen & Co. Ltd
11 New Fetter Lane, London EC4P 4EE
Reprinted with minor corrections 1959
Reprinted 1961

First published as a University Paperback 1964
Reprinted ten times
Reprinted 1985

Published in the USA by
Methuen & Co.
in association with Methuen, Inc.
29 West 35th Street, New York, NY 10001

ISBN (hardbound) 0 416 47500 0
ISBN (paperback) 0 416 10180 1

Printed and bound in Great Britain by
Richard Clay (The Chaucer Press) Ltd,
Bungay, Suffolk

CONTENTS

PREFACE

THIS EDITION was prepared while I held a Fellowship at Birmingham University's Shakespeare Institute, Stratford-upon-Avon. I am much indebted to its Directors, Professor Allardyce Nicoll and Professor C. J. Sisson, for their advice and encouragement, and to my colleagues, Dr Reginald Foakes and Mr Ernst Honigmann, for their detailed criticism. My work was greatly facilitated by the Institute's microfilm collection of manuscripts and early printed books, and by the indices which it maintains.

My grateful thanks are also due to Mr David Borland for reading my manuscript and proofs, and saving me from many imprecisions and errors, to Miss Brunilde Sismondo for help with Italian works, and to Professor Clifford Leech, Professor Kenneth Muir, Mrs Corinne Rickert, and Mr David Brown.

The general editors of the Arden Shakespeare, Professor Una Ellis-Fermor and Dr Harold Brooks, have given generously of their time and knowledge; I thank them for understanding help on many occasions.

Rare early printed books in the Folger and Huntington Libraries are quoted from microfilm, by kind permission.

JOHN RUSSELL BROWN.

THE SHAKESPEARE INSTITUTE
STRATFORD-UPON-AVON
May 1954

I have taken advantage of reprinting to introduce some corrections and additions.

J. R. B.

THE UNIVERSITY OF BIRMINGHAM
March 1961

ABBREVIATIONS

Abbott	E. Abbott, *A Shakespearian Grammar* (ed. 1878).
Bullough	G. Bullough, *Narrative and Dramatic Sources of Shakespeare* (I, 1957; II, 1958).
Eliz. Stage	E. K. Chambers, *The Elizabethan Stage* (1923), 4 vols.
William Shakespeare	E. K. Chambers, *William Shakespeare: a Study of Facts and Problems* (1930), 2 vols.
Coryat	T. Coryat, *Coryat's Crudities* (ed. 1905), 2 vols.
Cotgrave	R. Cotgrave, *A Dictionary of the French and English Tongues* (1611).
Douce	F. Douce, *Illustrations of Shakespeare* (1807), 2 vols.
Greene, *Wks*	R. Greene, *Works*, ed. A. B. Grosart (1881-6), 15 vols.
Ed. Problem	W. W. Greg, *The Editorial Problem in Shakespeare* (ed. 1951).
Hunter	J. Hunter, *New Illustrations* (1845), 2 vols.
Kökeritz	H. Kökeritz, *Shakespeare's Pronunciation* (1953).
Lyly, *Wks*	J. Lyly, *Works*, ed. R. W. Bond (1902), 3 vols.
M.S.R.	Malone Society Reprint.
Nashe, *Wks*	T. Nashe, *Works*, ed. R. B. McKerrow (1904-8), 4 vols.
Dodsley	*Old English Plays*, ed. R. Dodsley and W. C. Hazlitt (ed. 1874-6), 15 vols.
Onions	C. T. Onions, *A Shakespeare Glossary* (ed. 1941).
Schmidt	A. Schmidt, *Shakespeare-Lexicon* (ed. 1874-5), 2 vols.
Tilley	M. P. Tilley, *A Dictionary of the Proverbs in England in the Sixteenth and Seventeenth Centuries* (1950).
Walker	W. S. Walker, *A Critical Examination of the Text of Shakespeare* (1860), 3 vols.
Discourse	Sir Thomas Wilson, *A Discourse upon Usury* (1572).

The customary abbreviations are used for periodicals.

Editions of Shakespeare and *The Merchant of Venice* from Rowe to the present day are referred to by the name of their editors, with the exception of the "Variorum" editions from 1773 to 1821 (Var. '73, etc.), the Cambridge (1863), Globe (1864), and Clarendon (1883) editions by W. G. Clark and W. A. Wright (Cambridge, Globe, and Clarendon, respectively), and the New Cambridge edition (1926) by Sir Arthur Quiller-Couch and J. Dover Wilson (*N.C.S.*).

The abbreviations of the titles of Shakespeare's plays and poems follow C. T. Onions, *A Shakespeare Glossary*, p. x.

All quotations from Shakespeare (except those from *The Merchant of Venice*) are from the Globe Shakespeare (ed. 1911), unless otherwise stated.

INTRODUCTION

I. THE PRINTER

The earliest text of *The Merchant of Venice* is a quarto dated 1600. The title-page reads:

The most excellent / Historie of the *Merchant* / *of Venice*. / VVith the extreame crueltie of *Shylocke* the Iewe / towards the sayd Merchant, in cutting a iust pound / of his flesh: and the obtayning of *Portia* / by the choyse of three / chests. / *As it hath beene diuers times acted by the Lord / Chamberlaine his Seruants.* / Written by William Shakespeare. // [type ornaments] // AT LONDON, / Printed by *I.R.* for Thomas Heyes, / and are to be sold in Paules Church-yard, at the / signe of the Greene Dragon. / 1600.

The initials I.R. stand for James Roberts, in whose name the play had been entered in the Stationers' Register two years previously:

xxij° Iulij [1598]
Iames Robertes. / Entred for his copie vnder the handes of bothe the wardens, a booke of the Marchaunt of Venyce or otherwise called the Iewe of Venyce. / Prouided that yt bee not prynted by the said Iames Robertes; or anye other whatsoeuer w^{th}out lycence first had from the Right honorable the lord Chamberlen   vj^d

By this means, Roberts secured the printing rights of the play, but he did not publish it himself; in 1600 he transferred his rights to Thomas Heyes, for whom he printed the quarto:

28 octobr' [1600]
Tho. haies Entred for his copie vnder the handes of the Wardens & by Consent of m^r Robertes. A booke called the booke of the m'chant of Venyce   vj^d

The full story of the transactions which lie behind these entries will probably never be known, but there are some more clues. Roberts printed very few plays and it is noteworthy that all those which he entered in the Stationers' Register were from the repertory of the Chamberlain's Men. Besides *The Merchant*, he entered *A Moral of Cloth Breeches and Velvet Hose* (27 May 1600), *A Larum for London* (29 May 1600), *Hamlet* (26 July 1602), and *Troilus and*

Cressida (7 Feb. 1603). Of the first of these, no copy has survived,
A Larum and *Troilus* were printed and published by other members
of the Stationers' Company, and *Hamlet* was printed by Roberts for
Nicholas Ling in 1604/5, after a very imperfect text had appeared
in 1603.

Professor Pollard suggested that Roberts acted as an agent for
the Chamberlain's Men, and made the entries, including that of
The Merchant, at their instigation, in order to prevent unauthorized
publication by anyone else.[1] This might explain the unusual pro-
viso about the Lord Chamberlain's licence in the original entry for
The Merchant, and the fact that the entries for *A Moral* and *A Larum*
were associated with a note, made on a fly-leaf of the Register, to
the effect that four other Chamberlain's plays had to be "staied".
However, as Sir E. K. Chambers pointed out,[2] the original entry
for *The Merchant* does not suggest that the players put any special
trust in Roberts, and, if the plan was tried with *Hamlet*, it was far
from successful. It seems more probable that Roberts made the
entries entirely on his own account. He was more printer than publisher, and transferred his rights on other occasions; Markham's
Sir Richard Grenville (1595) and Munday's translation of *III, Pal-
merin of England* (1602) were entered in his name but he printed
them for other publishers.[3] Roberts held the privilege of printing
"all manner of billes" for the players,[4] and he seems to have used
this connection to secure the rights to more plays than he had
money or time to print.

The wording of the entries for *The Merchant* may give a further
clue to Roberts' actions. On the outside of prompt-books used in
an Elizabethan theatre, the title of the play was usually preceded
by the words "The Book of", as "The Book of The Merchant of
Venice". The 1600 entry suggests that the scribe of the Stationers'
Company had such a prompt copy before him, and so wrote "A
booke called the booke of . . ."; the 1598 entry was simply "a
booke of . . ." Perhaps Roberts used his special contact with the
players to obtain a copy of *The Merchant* which could be spared
from the theatre while the play was in the regular repertory—the
author's foul papers, or fair copy, from which the prompt-book had
been prepared—and was allowed to enter it at the Stationers' Hall

1. Cf. W. W. Greg, *Some Aspects and Problems of London Publishing* (1956),
pp. 112–22, for a general review of this theory.

2. Cf. *William Shakespeare*, I. 146.

3. *Orlando Furioso* (1594) and *King Leir* (1605) more fully exemplify this fairly
widespread practice; the ownerships of these plays were transferred in the
Register and each time it stipulates that the original owner should undertake
the printing.

4. Cf. A. W. Pollard, *Shakespeare Folios and Quartos* (1909), p. 67.

on the strict understanding that he would not print it until the players, in the name of their patron, gave further permission. When that permission was granted, the prompt-book might have been taken to the Stationers as incontrovertible evidence of the players' consent. There is reason to think that plays were not always printed from the manuscripts presented for entry in the Register,[1] so Roberts may have printed from his first copy and returned the prompt-book to the players. This procedure would explain the different forms of entry, the special licence required by the first entry and the lack of interest in it in the second, and the fact that, despite the form of the second entry, the play seems to have been printed from a copy which was more like an author's papers than a theatrical prompt-book.[2]

II. THE PRINTING

Two compositors were responsible for setting *The Merchant of Venice*, probably the same two who set *Titus Andronicus* (1600) and *Hamlet* (1604/5).[3] All that is known of their work suggests that they were competent and careful workmen. From *Hamlet*, it is clear that when faced with a difficult passage, they would often set down exactly what they saw, rather than try to provide some easy reading of their own. *Titus Andronicus*, which was a reprint of the 1594 quarto, shows that they would often reproduce odd arrangements in their copy (such as centred speech prefixes), and tended to reproduce punctuation faithfully, correcting only a few obvious errors and occasionally making it slightly heavier. In non-Shakespeare texts, their punctuation varies considerably from book to book, showing that they made no great attempt to impose a "style" of their own but were content to represent the punctuation of their copy. Judging from *Titus Andronicus*, they also reproduced the elisions of their copy.

An examination of the six copies of *The Merchant* which are at present in England[4] has revealed no variant reading besides the one on G4 (IV. i. 73) which has been known for some time, and is obviously due to a technical slip. Dr McManaway has noted that

1. Cf. *Ed. Problem*, p. 107, and F. P. Wilson, 'Shakespeare and the "New Bibliography" ', *The Bibliographical Society, 1892–1942* (1945), p. 109.

2. Roberts' quarto of *Hamlet* was probably printed from Shakespeare's own manuscript; cf. *Ed. Problem*, p. 64.

3. Cf. J. R. Brown, *S.B.*, VII (1955), p. 31. They probably divided the work on *The Merchant* as follows: Compositor "X", title-page, II. i. 18 to II. v. 3, II. ix. 29 to III. ii. 102, III. iv. 19 to IV. i. 141, and IV. i. 423 to the end; Compositor "Y" set the remainder.

4. I.e., at the British Museum (C.12.g.11, C.12.g.32, and C.34.k.22), Bodleian, Dyce Collection, and Trinity College, Cambridge.

the copy in the Huntington Library has a variant on K2 (v. i. 300) which is probably another printer's slip.

III. THE COPY

Sir E. K. Chambers and Sir Walter Greg both believed that the copy from which Roberts printed the first quarto was very close to Shakespeare's own manuscript.[1] This is shown most clearly in some stage directions. Several do not specify the number of entrants, as in "three or foure followers accordingly, . . . and their traine", or "*a follower or two*".[2] Other entry directions fail to mention characters who are obviously required by the dialogue.[3] From the study of Elizabethan manuscript plays, it is known that copies for use in a theatre were usually precise and accurate in these matters;[4] an author's manuscript, on the other hand, might well leave the number of supernumeraries to be decided in the playhouse, and give incomplete or uncorrected entry directions—such inaccuracies might be expected in the course of composition.

There are some directions which probably only Shakespeare could have written. A book-keeper in the theatre would not think of adding that a servant came "*from* Anthonio", or that Bassanio comments on the caskets "*to himselfe*".[5] A prompter would not allow his page to be cluttered up with the description of a "tawnie Moore all in white", nor would he risk confusing himself with the name Balthazar, which Portia assumes in disguise but by which she is never addressed.[6] Such literary directions sometimes survived in theatrical manuscripts, but their presence in the text of *The Merchant* strengthens the probability that its copy was close to Shakespeare's own manuscript.

Similar theories are tenable for the other eleven quartos "that can without qualification be classed as 'good'."[7] For several of these quartos, the copy was probably Shakespeare's "foul papers", or working manuscript, but the text of *The Merchant* is remarkably free from obvious errors and must represent a fairer copy. Nevertheless there is good hope that it was autograph, for the quarto's lining, punctuation, and use of elision are remarkably sensitive,[8]

1. Cf. *William Shakespeare*, I. 370, and *The Shakespeare First Folio* (1955), pp. 256–9.

2. II. i Entry, and II. ii. 108. See also II. vii Entry, II. ix. 3, III. ii Entry, IV. i Entry, 403, and V. i. 126.

3. II. ii. 108, II. ix. 3, III. ii Entry, IV. i Entry, and IV. ii Entry. An entry for musicians is omitted V. i. 65.

4. See *William Shakespeare*, I. 117–21, and *Ed. Problem*, pp. 34–42.

5. III. i. 66 and III. ii. 62. See also II. v Entry, III. ii. 218, and III. iv Entry.

6. II. i Entry, and IV. i. 162.   7. *Ed. Problem*, p. 129.

8. Cf. *N.C.S.*, p. 122, and *William Shakespeare*, I. 370.

and it can be shown that its copy probably had several spelling characteristics in common with the foul-paper copy for *Hamlet*.[1]

It has been suggested that the manuscript which Roberts used had been slightly "corrected" in the theatre.[2] For instance, the direction "*Enter Iewe and his man that was the Clowne*" (II. v Entry) may have been written in two parts, the explanatory words "*the Clowne*" being added from a prompt-book or as a step towards compiling one.[3] But even if the explanatory words were an addition, there is nothing to say where or when they were written; a literary editor might have been responsible, or Shakespeare himself, during composition. The latter seems probable for there are other directions with similar explanatory phrases; twice they precede the proper names, as in "the maskers, *Gratiano* and *Saleri[o]*", but at other times they follow, as in "*Salerio* a messenger from Venice".[4] It is simplest to suppose that Shakespeare was not always economical in phrasing stage directions; comparable explanatory phrases are found elsewhere, as in the second quarto of *Hamlet*, "*Polonius, and his Sonne Laertes*" (I. ii Entry). Imperative stage directions, "*Iessica aboue*", "*A Song the whilst...*", "*open the letter*", and "*play Musique*",[5] have also suggested that the copy for *The Merchant* was connected with a prompt-book. But authors as well as book-keepers used the imperative,[6] and similar ones are found in *Romeo* and *Much Ado*, texts printed from foul papers. A duplicate entry for Tubal (III. i) appears to be a more definite sign of prompt-book correction, for a prompter sometimes re-wrote entries a few lines in advance of the correct places.[7] But this is an isolated example in the text, the redundant entry probably follows the correct one, the duplication occurs during prose dialogue where a compositor was especially liable to misplace directions,[8] and the context is such that the error might arise through a change of intention in writing the scene.[9]

Some scholars have thought that the copy for *The Merchant* was

1. Cf. J. R. Brown, *S.B.*, VII (1955), p. 38.

2. Cf. *William Shakespeare*, I. 370, and *The Shakespeare First Folio*, p. 257.

3. Cf. *N.C.S.*, p. 105. In the annotations to the text I suggest another way of reading this direction.

4. II. vi Entry (see note, ll. 1–2), and III. ii. 218. See also I. ii Entry, I. iii Entry, and II. i Entry.

5. II. vi. 25, III. ii. 62, 235, and v. i. 68.

6. Cf. *William Shakespeare*, I. 118, and *Ed. Problem*, p. 36.

7. Cf. W. W. Greg, *Dramatic Documents from the Elizabethan Playhouses . . . Commentary* (1931), pp. 217–19.

8. Four entries may be placed late during prose dialogue; I. ii. 115, I. iii. 34, II. ii. 108, and III. i. 20.

9. Cf. III. i. 69, note. A somewhat similar duplication is found in the "good" quarto of *R 2* (I. iv).

not merely "corrected" from a prompt-book, but was ultimately
derived from one. But in the course of time, their evidence for this
has proved equivocal. Sir Walter Greg showed that the "sweete
soule" of v. i. 49 was probably given to Launcelot (instead of
Lorenzo) because the preceding passage was an interpolation in the
manuscript and these words were a "key" to show where the connection was to be made; Professor Dover Wilson thought this was
clear evidence of a prompt-book copy, but later, Sir Walter pointed
out that Shakespeare might have made the interpolation in his own
foul papers.[1] Professor Wilson also drew attention to half lines of
verse, mixtures of prose and verse, confusions of fact, and lines
which seem to be added to make a better role for the clown; all
these he took as evidence of cutting and revision in the theatre.
Shakespeare's responsibility for the clown scenes is partly a matter
for subjective judgement, but it should be noted that they do echo
other clown scenes in Shakespeare and are closely interwoven with
the main structure of the play.[2] The other details noted by Professor Wilson could equally well be explained as imperfections left
by the author in his own papers. For instance, he laid special stress
on divergent conceptions of the Venetian state in III. ii. 277–8,
III. iii. 27–31, and IV. i. 38–9; the second passage he considered un-
Shakespearian. But Shakespeare was not always consistent in such
details and, as Mr Middleton Murry pointed out, the similarities of
phrasing between the first and second passages suggest that they
were written by the same hand.[3] Other "imperfections", like
Antonio's sudden entry to prevent the masque (II. vi. 59), can be
defended as astute stagecraft, in this example inducing anticipa-
tion and a sense of pace, and preventing subsidiary action from
usurping too much attention.

In elaborating his theory about the copy for *The Merchant*, Professor Wilson concluded that it was "assembled" from players'
parts and a "plot" of the play. It is now doubted whether a text
could be made up in this way,[4] and the evidence for "assembling"
The Merchant has not stood the test of time. On several occasions
when a character reads from a letter or scroll, the quarto has a
second speech prefix before he resumes speaking in his own person,

1. Cf. *N.C.S.*, pp. 106–7, and *Ed. Problem*, p. 123; this point is more fully discussed in the annotations.

2. Cf. annotations to III. v, and to v. i. 49.

3. Cf. *Shakespeare* (1936), p. 208. See also, E. K. Chambers, review of *N.C.S.*,
M.L.R., XXII (1927), 221–2.

4. See F. P. Wilson, 'Shakespeare and the "New Bibliography"', *The Bibliographical Society, 1892–1942* (1945), pp. 110–11 for a survey of the work done on
this problem.

and, on the grounds that the manuscript of Alleyn's part of Orlando
in *Orlando Furioso* omits the text of the verses read by Orlando, Professor Wilson took this as evidence for an "assembled" copy. Later,
when he was editing *Hamlet*, he withdrew this evidence for, in the
"good" quarto of that play (which he himself thought was based on
foul papers), there are similar repetitions of speech prefixes.[1] Professor Wilson also thought that the "entry-directions have obviously not been taken from the same source as the dialogue" because they do not give the names Leonardo, Stephano, and Balthazar which appear in the dialogue.[2] He thought too that
"Gobbo", which is found only in stage directions, was a "correction" of "Iobbe", the form used in the dialogue. He accounted for
these differences by arguing for an "assembled" text. But such
variations are common in the "good" quartos; in *Much Ado*, for
example, George and Francis Seacole, Hugh Oatcake, and Antonio
are named only in the dialogue, and Don Pedro is also called Don
Peter in the dialogue. Such variations are more readily explained
as the inaccuracies and inconsistencies of an author's manuscript.
They are akin to the variations between Shylock and Jew, and
Launcelot and Clown which are found in stage directions and
speech prefixes. Since Professor Wilson wrote, this last kind of vari-
ation has been taken as a sign of foul papers behind a printed text,
for "a copy intended for use in the theatre would surely, of necessity, be accurate and unambiguous in the matter of the character-
names."[3] For *The Merchant*, this is not strong evidence because variations between character name and character *genre* would not be
such a difficulty to a prompter as the variations in name or title
which are found in other texts based on foul papers.[4] Nevertheless,

1. Cf. *N.C.S.*, pp. 96–9, and *The Manuscript of Shakespeare's* Hamlet (1934), II.
229. The references are, *Mer. V.*, II. vii. 74, II. ix. 73, III. ii. 139 (as catchword on
F1 only), and IV. i. 163; *Ham.*, II. ii. 125, and IV. vii. 50.
2. *N.C.S.*, p. 99. The entries are II. ii. 108, III. iv Entry, and v. i. 24.
3. R. B. McKerrow, *R.E.S.*, XI (1935), 464.
4. This point was made by F. P. Wilson, *op. cit.*, p. 108. Professor J. D. Wilson
suggested (*N.C.S.*, p. 95) that the variations in *The Merchant* were caused by a
shortage of italic capitals. "*Iew*" may have changed to "*Shyl*" on B2ᵛ because,
at this point, a shortage of capitals had led the compositor to use italic *I*s and
roman *Y*s in the place of roman *I*s in the dialogue. Elsewhere, however, Shylock
is found in speech prefixes and stage directions where there were many italic *S*s
in use and no immediate shortage of *I*s (i.e., E2; III. i. 20 ff.). Later, a change
was made to "*Iew*" when *I*s were much in demand but few *S*s needed (F4; III. iii.
Entry and 1 ff). Professor J. D. Wilson also suggested that Clown was used
occasionally because of the run on italic *L*s, but this will not explain the frequent
"*Clowne*" of III. v (G1ᵛ–2ᵛ); in Sigs. F, G, and H only 27 italic *L*s were used in
all, but 63 had been available for Sig. C alone—clearly there was no shortage
when III. v was set up.

the occasional imprecision in nomenclature,[1] far from suggesting an "assembled" text, may rather support the contention that the copy for *The Merchant* was very close to Shakespeare's own manuscript.

IV. EARLY EDITIONS AND REPRINTS

As far as we know, *The Merchant of Venice* was not reprinted until 1619 when a second quarto was published with the simple but deceptive imprint, "Printed by *J. Roberts*, 1600." Until comparatively recently this was called the first quarto, but Professor A. W. Pollard and others have proved that it was, in fact, printed by William Jaggard for Thomas Pavier in 1619, along with other Shakespeare and pseudo-Shakespeare plays.[2] Proof of this depends on the use of standing type, linking all but one of the 1619 quartos, and on the type, devices, ornaments, and paper used; a technical but entirely convincing argument has restored the true sequence of editions. Pavier probably intended to print a collection of Shakespeare plays, but the news seems to have spread and on 3 May 1619 the Lord Chamberlain wrote to the Stationers directing that no play from the repertory of the King's Men should be printed "without their consents."[3] In the eyes of the Stationers, Pavier and Jaggard had no right to reprint *The Merchant*, and Laurence Heyes, son of the first publisher, put in a claim which was upheld in a full court of the Company.

The quarto of 1619 inherited many orthographical peculiarities from its predecessor and is clearly a reprint of it. Professor Pollard demonstrated the dependence of the new edition by one typographical point: Roberts' compositor had printed "GOD" (II. ii. 68) in capitals as if in a devotional work, and Jaggard's copied this.[4] Likewise, the form "coster" (IV. i. 350) in Q2 is most easily explained by the damaged ligature *ff* used in the "coffer" of Q1. Although the reprint introduced many new errors, Jaggard did attempt to edit the text; the metre is sometimes regularized, and obscure or unusual phrasing emended. This editing had little principle and, as might be expected in a semi-underhand edition, no special authority; it could have been undertaken in the printing

1. There are further confusions between Salerio and Solanio, but the compositors may have been responsible for these.

2. Cf. A. W. Pollard, *Shakespeare Folios and Quartos* (1909), ch. IV, and W. J. Neidig, 'The Shakespeare Quartos of 1619', *M.P.*, VIII (1910), 145–63.

3. Malone recorded this from the Stationers' Court Book in his annotated Shakespeare (Bodleian, Malone 1046); cf. *William Shakespeare*, I. 136, n. 1.

4. *Shakespeare Folios and Quartos* (1909), p. 98, n. *.

house without access to any secondary authority.[1] The same is true of all Jaggard's 1619 reprints.

The Merchant was printed a third time in 1623, in the folio collected works, and again the text was set from a copy of Q1. That Q1 and not Q2 was used for the copy is shown by details of orthography and typography,[2] by the return to Q1 where Q2 had introduced errors,[3] and by the reading of IV. i. 73–4 which shows that a copy of Q1 with G4 in the incorrect state was used for F, whereas one with G4 in the correct state was used for Q2. Besides modernizing the spelling of Q1 and clarifying its punctuation, someone "edited" the text so that with the new errors normal to a reprint, there are some corrections.

Some of the new readings in F had already occurred in Q2; the two texts often modernize the spelling in the same way and occasionally make the same errors or corrections. The most remarkable similarities are "Slubber" (II. viii. 39), "gossips" (III. i. 6), and "in it" (V. i. 65); the first is now an accepted reading, the others are probably errors.[4] These coincidences between the two texts suggest that their "editors" had access to a similar lost manuscript or quarto, or that Q2 was occasionally consulted for F. There is no single argument against these possibilities, but rather, a strong probability; Q1 is such a good text that there was little reason to collate it with another for minor details only. Moreover, on several occasions where the text is obscure or obviously faulty, either Q2 alone emends, or else Q2 and F have different solutions; for instance, Q2 alone meddles with the confusions of Launcelot's dialogue in II. ii.[5] There is strong reason to agree with Sir Walter Greg in thinking that the coincidences are accidental.[6]

The "editor" of F probably consulted a play-house manuscript

1. The most considerable readings accepted from Q2 are found at II. ii. 94, II. v. 8–9 and 52–3, II. viii. 39, III. ii. 101, III. v. 20, IV. i. 30, 31, 100, 226, 394, and v. i. 51 and 152.

2. E.g., F sometimes retains Q1's "than" for *then* and "ile" for *Ile* (i.e., I'll) where Q2 normalizes them.

3. For example, the restoration of II. vi. 66, a line entirely missing from Q2. Other omitted words were restored as "Why" and "you" (I. i. 46), "marke" (III. ii. 82), and "Doctors" (V. i. 305).

4. For other similarities see especially, II. ii. 169, II. vii. 4, III. v. 20, IV. i. 65, 100, 226, and 394.

5. I.e., ll. 21, 26, and 35; see also, for example, I. ii. 31–2, I. iii. 59–60, III. ii. 62, III. iv. 50, III. v. 71, IV. i. 342, and V. i. 305, and six of the emendations quoted in note 1, above.

6. Cf. *The Shakespeare First Folio* (1955), p. 261. Both Q2 and F were printed by Jaggard; perhaps the same "editor" was used, and while working on F he remembered some of his alterations of three years before.

for he added act-divisions and new directions, chiefly for music, as
"*Flo. Cornets*" (II. i Entry) or "*Musicke ceases*" (v. i. 110).[1] For Act III,
Sc. iii, he directed Solanio to enter instead of Salerio, and so helped
to disentangle the identities of these two characters. But, whatever
source he used, he worked carelessly; there is a direction for music
when it is already playing (v. i. 97) and a flourish of cornets which
ushers in a conversational scene (II. viii) instead of the preceding
stately one. The elimination of a few references to the deity and the
concealment of one to Scotsmen (I. ii. 74) was a tactful piece of
Jacobean expurgation which might well have been done in the
printing house;[2] one would expect a prompt-book to be more
thorough. The corrections to the dialogue in F would not command much respect on their own account,[3] but the possibility that
another manuscript was consulted gives an interest to them beyond
that proper to Q2's corrections.

During the seventeenth century *The Merchant of Venice* was reprinted in the folios of 1632, 1663, and 1685 and in a quarto
dated 1637. Some sheets of this quarto were issued with a new
title-page in 1652. None of these reprints has any special authority.

V. THIS EDITION

The Text

I have based my text on the first quarto, which in future I shall
call Q.

The few stage directions which I have added are printed within
square brackets. Act and scene divisions, and place locations are
marked in the same way. I have regularized speech prefixes, and
Q's inconsistent use of capitals and italic type. The spelling is
modernized, but, following earlier volumes in the New Arden
series, I have retained some forms which were probably more than
mere variations in spelling; for example, vildly, cur'sy, and
burthens.

Since the compositors of Q were conservative workmen and possibly had Shakespeare's manuscript before them, I have made very
few changes in their punctuation. If the dialogue is read with the
pauses which they have marked, good dramatic sense nearly always
results. Elizabethan punctuation was not so fully grammatical as
ours, and so, to help the modern reader, I have occasionally added
dashes or brackets; these are not meant to indicate pauses, but to

1. See also II. i. 45, II. iv. 9, II. ix. 3, III. ii. 62, IV. ii Entry, and 19, and v. i. 121.

2. Cf *Ed. Problem*, p. 155, n. 1 and Dr Alice Walker on the folio text of *R 3*,
in *Textual Problems of the First Folio* (1953), p. 31.

3. Those which are usually accepted are simple enough, as I. ii. 16, III. ii. 67,
III. ii. 297–8, III. iv. 50, III. v. 78, and IV. i. 75 and 123.

clarify the sentence structure and so help in phrasing. I hope that this procedure will retain the right pulse in Shakespeare's dialogue. For similar reasons, I have kept almost all the elided forms in Q, clarifying them where necessary by introducing apostrophes.

The Collation

Q, as the copy text, is fully collated with the printed text. All changes in punctuation are noted with the exception of inverted commas, dashes, and brackets; these are my own additions unless the collation notes otherwise. The introduction or deletion of hyphens and changes in the way of printing compound words are noted only where the metre or sense seems to be affected. Q's spelling is noted only where the modern form is in doubt, or where the original is specially significant. I have not usually recorded changes in the use of upper case or italic type.

Because a theatrical manuscript was possibly consulted in preparing the 1623 folio (which I shall call F), this text is more fully collated than any other derivative text; I have noted all significant variations from Q, and also the readings in which it agrees with Q or Q2 against the printed text or some commonly accepted reading. I have treated Qq2–3 and Ff 2–4 as reprints with no independent authority. From these, and subsequent modern editions, I note readings which differ from the printed text only when I see some reason for thinking they might be correct, or when they have some special textual interest. I give only the first known authority for each reading.

Unless the sense is in question, I do not give authority for changes in Q's punctuation; I have exempted Q2 and F from this rule, for their compositors have a special claim to an understanding of Elizabethan punctuation.

The text is quoted in the collation in the same type form (i.e., roman for roman and italic for italic) and is followed by its authority. Other readings are quoted in their original spelling but in the same type as the relevant quotation from the text. Where more than one authority is given, the spelling is that of the first authority quoted. For collating Qq2–3 and Ff1–4, I have used the copies at the Shakespeare Birthplace Library, Stratford-upon-Avon.

2. THE DATE

The Merchant of Venice must be dated earlier than the summer of 1598; it was entered in the Stationers' Register on 22 July, and it must have been known to the public before the entry of Francis Meres' *Palladis Tamia* on 7 September. Meres lists six comedies by Shakespeare:

his *Gentlemen of Verona*, his *Errors*, his *Loue labors lost*, his *Loue labours wonne*, his *Midsummers night dreame*, & his *Merchant of Venice*.[1]

The first three are acknowledged to be early plays, but as Meres' knowledge of current literature was very much up-to-date—he noted Edward Guilpin's *Skialetheia* which was not entered until 15 September 1598—*The Merchant*, the last in his list, may well have been a very recent play.

Sir E. K. Chambers suggested that the latest possible date for *The Merchant* was as early as autumn 1596; he thought that

the Gobbo of the play seems likely to have inspired two malicious references by Francis Davison in letters of 1596 to an unnamed enemy of the Earl of Essex, who can only be the hunch-backed Robert Cecil.[2]

In these letters, Cecil is alluded to as "St Gobbo" but this is readily explicable without reference to *The Merchant of Venice*. John Florio's Italian dictionary, *A World of Words* (1598), gave "*Gobbo*, crook-backt. Also a kind of faulkon", and this was probably the whole point of the nick-name; Davison travelled in Italy and could have learned the word there. There is no allusion to Cecil in *The Merchant*, and no hint that the two Gobbos, father and son, were crook-backed. The quarto's repeated "*Iobbe*" (II. ii. 3 ff.) suggests that Shakespeare intended to use the Italianized form of Job. The latest date for *The Merchant* must remain the summer of 1598.[3]

It is not so easy to fix the earliest possible date. Some scholars, such as the Clarendon editors and Professor J. D. Wilson,[4] have found traces of re-writing and wished to date Shakespeare's original draft from 1594. Much of their evidence for this depends on confused details in the structure of the play which are not remarkable if the author's manuscript was used as the printer's copy.[5] Other evidence has been found in the variety of styles in the dialogue. But there is variety in most plays by Shakespeare and the dramatic unity of *The Merchant* has had many defenders. Strong factual evidence would be needed to show that Shakespeare first wrote the play as early as 1594.

1. *Francis Meres's Treatise "Poetrie"*, ed. D. C. Allen (Univ. of Illinois, 1933), p. 76.
2. *William Shakespeare*, I. 372.
3. It used to be thought that *Wily Beguiled* which obviously imitates *The Merchant* (cf. v. i. 1, note) might date from 1596, but Professor Baldwin Maxwell has now shown that it must be dated *c.* 1601; cf. *S.P.*, XIX (1922), 206–37, and *Studies in Honor of Hardin Craig* (1941), pp. 142–7.
4. Cf. *N.C.S.*, pp. 108–19. But see also a review of *N.C.S.* by E. K. Chambers, *M.L.R.*, XXII (1927), 220–4.   5. See above, pp. xiv–xviii.

Such evidence has been seen in a connection with the execution of Roderigo Lopez for high treason. Lopez was a Portuguese Jew who, professing Christianity, became physician, first to the Earl of Leicester and then to Queen Elizabeth. When Don Antonio, a claimant to the Portuguese throne, came to London in 1592, Lopez engaged in political intrigue on his behalf.[1] He seems to have played a dangerous and self-interested part, and he soon fell foul of the Earl of Essex, who denounced him as a traitor seeking to poison both Antonio and Elizabeth. He stood his trial in February 1594 and was executed on 7 June. It was in Essex's interest to give notoriety to the proceedings, and many allusions to them in literature of the time show how successful he was in doing so. Marlowe's *The Jew of Malta* gained a gratuitous topicality and was played fifteen times between 4 February and the end of 1594. *The Merchant of Venice* is probably indebted to Marlowe's play which seems to have been printed for the first time in 1633, and Sir Sidney Lee suggested that Shakespeare took a hint from its popularity and wrote another "play of the hour", for his own company.[2] Dr Furness thought he saw a direct allusion to Lopez in IV. i. 133–7:

> thy currish spirit
> Govern'd a wolf, who hang'd for human slaughter—
> Even from the gallows did his fell soul fleet,
> And whilst thou layest in thy unhallowed dam,
> Infus'd itself in thee.

Although Gratiano speaks of a wolf, he may be thinking of a man, and Professor Wilson capped the suggestion by adding that "'Wolf' (the Q. capital is noteworthy) is a kind of translated pun on the name Lopez."

This identification seemed to provide factual evidence for dating *The Merchant*, but on further consideration the theory is insecure. The allusion in IV. i may be considered first. Wolves may well have been hung for slaughter as dogs certainly were: it was a practice that,

He that hath a dogge that is a sheepe biter, must by lawe either hang him vp, or else pay for the sheepe he hath wearied.[3]

Shakespeare alludes to the hanging of dogs in *Henry V*, where "gallows" are specifically mentioned:

---

1. Cf. C. Roth, *A History of the Jews in England* (1941), p. 141.
2. Cf. *The Gentleman's Magazine* (Feb. 1880), pp. 185–200. See also A. Dimock, *E.H.R.*, IX (1894), 440–72.
3. L. Wright, *A Summons for Sleepers* (1589), D1. I owe this reference to Mr Ernst Honigmann.

> ... he hath stolen a pax, and hanged must a'be:
> A damned death!
> Let gallows gape for dog; let man go free ... (III. vi. 42–4)

Moreover, usurers, such as Shylock, were often likened to wolves, as in Sir T. Wilson, *A Discourse upon Usury* (1572), where they are described as

greedie cormoraunte wolfes in deede, that rauyn vp both beaste and man, ...[1]

In this passage, Wilson also alludes to the killing of wolves, as if they were dogs, for slaughter: King Edgar ordered

al the wolfes [to be] killed in Englande and Wales, because they were rauenouse beastes, and deuourers of sheepe and other cattell, ...

The capital for "wolf" in the quarto adds nothing to the argument; about fifty lines earlier, there are capitals for "ewe", "lamb", "asses", "dogs", and "mules". Clearly the passage can be interpreted without any reference to Lopez.[2] But even if a secondary, punning allusion is admitted, it would not imply any definite date for the play. Lopez made such an impression on his contemporaries that authors could refer casually to him at any time before the end of the century; an example is found in Thomas Nashe's *Lenten Stuff* of 1599.[3]

    The more general theory that Shakespeare wrote *The Merchant* as a response to the Lopez case and the renewed success of *The Jew of Malta*, is likewise insecure: Shakespeare could have seen Marlowe's play in 1596 when it was again revived eight times between 9 January and 23 June by the Admiral's Men; there is little resemblance, besides that of race, between Shylock and Lopez, and none at all between Don Antonio and Shakespeare's Antonio; and, as a play on the Jewish question, *The Merchant* is very equivocal and has many irrelevances.[4]

---

1. ¶7. The point was made by E. Honigmann (*M.L.R.*, XLIX (1954), 293–307) who quoted P. Caesar, *A General Discourse against ... Usurers* (tr. 1578), *4ᵛ. Cf. also, M. Mosse, *The Arraignment and Conviction of Usury* (1595), L3.

2. Massinger made a similar allusion without explanation in *The Parliament of Love* (1624):

> Look not on me
> As I am Cleremond; I have parted with
> The essence that was his, and entertain'd
> The soul of some fierce tigress, or a wolf's
> New-hang'd for human slaughter. (ed. Gifford (1840), p. 163)

3. *Works*, ed. R. B. McKerrow, III (1905), 215–16.

4. For further study of the Lopez case see J. W. Hales, *E.H.R.*, IX (1894), 652–61.

Another possible allusion was found by Malone in III. ii. 48–50:

> Then music is
> Even as the flourish, when true subjects bow
> To a new-crowned monarch.

This might allude to the coronation of Henry IV of France at Chartres on 27 February 1594; the coronation was before "true subjects" because Rheims, where the ceremony ought to have taken place, was in the possession of rebels. A contemporary English pamphlet (*The Order of Ceremonies observed in the Coronation of Henry the IV* (1594), *S.T.C.* 13138) described the shout of the people and the flourish and salute of guns. But "true subjects" is a common phrase of no special significance,[1] and it is by no means certain that Shakespeare had any specific coronation in mind—if he did, it might have been one seen on the stage,[2] or one of the many he had read about in the chronicles. Again there is no certain evidence for the date of *The Merchant of Venice*.

It has been argued that certain passages which speak of Shylock as a "stranger" in Venice are related to the anti-alien riots which flared up in London in 1588, 1593, and, most seriously, in 1595.[3] Contemporary literature alludes to these riots, and Shakespeare himself probably wrote the "Ill May Day" scene in *Sir Thomas More* which deals directly with the issues raised.[4] In this scene, More asks the rioters how they would like to be strangers among another nation who would "spurne you lyke dogges" (Fo. 9a, l. 135). The parallel to *The Merchant* is close when Shylock complains that the Christians "foot me as you spurn a stranger cur Over your threshold" (I. iii. 113–14), while Launcelot's badinage about raising the price of hogs by converting Jews to Christians (III. v. 19–33) echoes the fear of a dearth caused by the influx of refugee "strangers". The allusions seem clear enough, but they do not warrant the assumption that the play was directly prompted by the 1595 riots;[5] they are introduced incidentally and would have been of lively interest at any time in the last two decades of the sixteenth century.[6]

The most satisfactory allusion for dating *The Merchant* occurs in Act I Scene i:

1. See, for example, *1 H 6*, IV. i. 166; *3 H 6*, III. i. 78 and 94; and *2 H 4*, IV. iii. 70.

2. So Pooler; cf. the coronations in Greene's *James IV*, and *Alphonsus*.

3. Cf. A. Tretiak, *R.E.S.*, v (1929), 402–9.

4. Cf. A. W. Pollard and others, *Shakespeare's Hand in* Sir Thomas More (1923).

5. Cf. A. Tretiak, *op. cit.*, p. 402.

6. Cf. W. Cunningham, *Alien Immigrants to England* (1897), ch. iv.

> I should not see the sandy hour-glass run
> But I should think of shallows and of flats,
> And see my wealthy Andrew dock'd in sand
> Vailing her high top lower than her ribs
> To kiss her burial; ...[1] (ll. 25–9)

"Andrew" is in italic type in the quarto as if it were a proper name, and Dr Johnson's suggestion that it is the name of a ship has been generally accepted. But the passage remained puzzling because no contemporary parallel could be found for "Andrew". At last the passage was explained, and an earliest possible date for *The Merchant* was found, when Professor E. Kuhl saw that Shakespeare was referring to the Spanish vice-admiral, the St Andrew, which was captured at Cadiz in 1596.[2] A prize from the Cadiz expedition would be much talked of; the command had been shared by Essex and Howard, the Lord Admiral, and, when the spoil was found to be less than they expected, the rivalry between the commanders led to a crop of rival accounts of the expedition. It was appropriate to liken Antonio's "wealthy" argosy to a Spanish prize; the picture of his ships overpeering "the petty traffickers" (I. i. 9–14) had already recalled the difference in size between the Spanish and English ships which had fought each other in 1588. The Andrew and the Matthew (which was captured at the same time) became the largest ships at the Queen's command. They were both "well furnished"[3] when captured, and we know that the "Wines and ruske" which were found in them were worth some £5,000.[4]

Professor Kuhl thought this passage must have been written in the autumn of 1597, because fierce storms were encountered in the Islands Voyage of that year and the Andrew was among the ships damaged. But Shakespeare does not refer specifically to storms; running aground in sand is the imagined fate of Antonio's "Andrew". This would be particularly apposite immediately after the Cadiz expedition of 1596, for the Andrew had been captured while run aground in the harbour.[5] When she was brought to England, she nearly ran aground again among the sands and flats of the King's Channel off Chatham.[6] It follows that the allusion could have been written any time after the first news of the Cadiz action

1. Q reads "docks" for *dock'd*.
2. Cf. letter, *T.L.S.* (27 Dec. 1928).
3. Sir W. Raleigh, 'A Relation of Cadiz Action', *Works*, ed. T. Birch (1829), VIII. 674.
4. *H.M.C.*, *Hatfield House MSS.*, VI (1895), 389–90.
5. Cf. Boazio's engraved chart of Cadiz, reproduced in *The Naval Miscellany*, The Navy Records Society, I (1902), 68.
6. Cf. *Sir W. Monson's Naval Tracts*, ed. M. Oppenheim, The Navy Records Society, I (1902), 357.

reached the Court on 30 July 1596. It need not have been written immediately, for the Andrew was prominent in the Islands Voyage of the following year, and Essex had to ask for permission to anchor his returning fleet "under the Isle of Wight", reminding the Queen "how dangerous it will be for her great ships to go about the Sands this ill-time of the year, especially for the *St. Andrew*, . . ."[1] The Andrew was "wealthy", she was in the news, and she was repeatedly in danger of running aground; since there is no other explanation of the passage which can be supported,[2] the identification seems reasonably certain. *The Merchant of Venice* must have been written in its present form not earlier than August 1596.

Such an allusion might have been added after the rest of the play had been completed, but its date does agree with the impression gained by comparing the style of this play with that of others in the canon. Scholars who thought it must have been written in 1594 have had to postulate rewriting later in 1596, chiefly on grounds of style. In particular, Shylock's prose speeches have an immediacy unlike anything in the other early comedies mentioned by Francis Meres; they are closer to those of Falstaff, or Benedick and Beatrice. The grace and freedom of its versification also links the play with *Much Ado*, and with *As You Like It*, and *Twelfth Night*. So does its heroine, Portia, who is a worthy compeer of Beatrice, Rosalind, and Viola. Such comparisons cannot give a precise date for *The Merchant*,[3] but they do agree with the limits derived from the Stationers' Register, Meres' *Palladis Tamia*, and the allusion to the Andrew—limits which date the play after 30 July 1596 and before 22 July 1598.

3. THE SOURCES

Shakespeare's story of the bond for human flesh is of ancient origin,[4] and is found, in rudimentary form, in religious tales from Persia and India. In the West, the ancient Roman Laws of the

1. *Hatfield House MSS.*, VII (1899), 440.

2. Verity suggested an allusion to St Andrew, the fisherman and apostle, but quoted no parallel.

3. Minor supporting evidence is noted elsewhere in this edition; cf. the possible use of *The Orator* (p. xxxi) and the 1595 edition of *Gesta Romanorum* (p. xxxii), and the note on I. ii. 74. There are considerable parallels between III. ii and *Troil.*, III. ii; see *Mer.V.*, l. 8, note, ll. 111–14, 144, 175–7 and *Troil.* ll. 19, 23–7, 38–41, and 58.

4. Its genesis has been often studied, most usefully by T. Niemeyer, *Der Rechtsspruch gegen Shylock* (1912); J. L. Cardozo, *The Contemporary Jew in the Elizabethan Drama* (1925); B. V. Wenger, *Shakespeare Jahrbuch*, LXV (1929), 92–174; and Bullough, I (1957), 446–7.

Twelve Tables gave a legal basis for further tales and ballads.[1]
Here, the story was retold many times, the first known English version being found in the *Cursor Mundi*, which dates from the end of
the thirteenth century and has a Jew as creditor.[2] The next extant
version in English is found in fifteenth-century manuscript translations of the *Gesta Romanorum*, and by this time a story of wooing
had been added to that of the flesh-bond.[3]

But the version which is closest to *The Merchant of Venice* is the
first story of the fourth day in Ser Giovanni's *Il Pecorone*. This collection of tales was written in Italian at the end of the fourteenth
century and was printed at Milan in 1558. A translation is given as
Appendix I of this edition but a brief synopsis will help to show its
correspondence to Shakespeare's play:

Ansaldo, a rich merchant of Venice, borrows money from a Jew so
that his "godson" Giannetto can go to sea to seek his fortune.
A bond is made that if the money is not repaid by a certain day, the
Jew may take a pound of Ansaldo's flesh from whatever part of his
body pleases him. Unknown to his godfather, Giannetto goes as
suitor to the "Lady of Belmonte", and on this, his third attempt, he
wins her for his wife. Giannetto forgets the bond until it is too late
and then, hurrying to Venice, he finds that the Jew implacably
demands his pound of flesh. The Jew's designs are defeated by the
lady who, unknown to her husband, has come to Venice disguised
as a lawyer. She establishes that the bond does not entitle the Jew to
shed one drop of blood, nor to take more or less than an exact
pound; in anger, the Jew tears up the bond. The young lawyer
refuses payment, but begs a ring which had been given to Giannetto by his lady. Giannetto then travels with Ansaldo to Belmonte,
only to find that his lady, who has returned before him, is angry
because he has lost her ring. She asserts that he must have given it
to one of his mistresses in Venice. After many protestations, the
ring is restored, the stratagem disclosed, and the story ends happily.

The wooing of the lady is quite different from that in *The Merchant*
and no English translation of the tale is known, but *Il Pecorone* is the
only earlier version of the flesh-bond story which corresponds in so
many details. The details are more numerous than a synopsis can
show, and for others reference should be made to the translation.

1. According to the Twelve Tables, creditors could, under certain circumstances, divide the body of a debtor among themselves; there is no record that
this was ever enforced. H. J. Griston in *Shaking the Dust from Shakespeare* (1924)
put forward a theory that *The Merchant* was set in the second decade of the
fourth century A.D., under the law of the Twelve Tables.

2. Cf. L. Toulmin Smith, *New Shakespeare Soc. Trans.* (1875-6), 181-9.

3. Cf. *The Old English Versions of the Gesta Romanorum*, ed. Sir F. Madden,
Roxburghe Club (1838).

It is highly probable that Shakespeare based his play on the Italian
Il Pecorone, or on a lost English version, closer to its original than
any now known.[1]

Many scholars have thought that such an English version did at
one time exist, and that its author was responsible for changing the
manner in which the lady is won to the riddle of the caskets as
found in *The Merchant*. The evidence for this is Stephen Gosson's
The School of Abuse (1579) which describes a play called the *Jew*.[2]
Having castigated the players as corrupters of the commonwealth,
Gosson makes exception of a few plays that were "without rebuke",
among them:

> The *Iew* and *Ptolome*, showne at the Bull, the one representing the
> greedinesse of worldly chusers, and bloody mindes of Usurers: The
> other very liuely discrybing howe seditious estates, with their owne
> deuises, false friendes, with their own swoordes, and rebellious
> commons in their owne snares are ouerthrowne: neither with
> Amorous gesture wounding the eye: nor with slouenly talke hurting
> the eares of the chast hearers. (ed. Arber, p. 40)

The representation of "the greedinesse of worldly chusers" has
been equated with the casket scenes in *The Merchant*, and that of the
"bloody mindes of Usurers" with the Shylock ones; "chooser"
seems to be used for "lover" in *The Merry Wives*, IV. vi. 11,[3] and
Shylock's desires are called "bloody" in *The Merchant*, IV. i. 138. On
this interpretation, the author of the *Jew* was responsible for com-
bining the casket story with that of *Il Pecorone*, and his play was, in
all probability, the source (or some would say the first draft) of
Shakespeare's play.

But despite its general acceptance, this theory is most insecure.
Knight was the first to dissent, pointing out that the skill in combin-
ing two plots which was credited to the unknown author of the
Jew was beyond anything that might be expected from the "rude
dramatists of 1579". Professor T. M. Parrott has endorsed Knight's
opinion, and added that the suggested interpretation of the
"greedinesse of worldly chusers" stretched

the phrase beyond what it can reasonably bear. Neither Morocco
nor Arragon is really guilty of greediness in his choice; in a worldly
sense each is a suitable match for Portia.[4]

1. Shakespeare may have been able to read Italian; cf. F. P. Wilson, *Shake-speare Survey*, III (1950), 15.
2. Douce was the first to state this view; he has been followed by Furness, J. D. Wilson, Chambers, and many others. G. Bullough guessed that R. W[ilson], *Three Ladies of London* (1584) was a rival play to *The Jew* (cf. *Bullough*, I. 450–1).
3. So Cardozo, *op. cit.*, p. 307, n. 2.   4. *Shakespearean Comedy* (1949), pp. 137–8.

Recently, Mr Ernst Honigmann has argued[1] that since Gosson frequently amplifies his matter by parallel phrases (as, "neither with Amorous gesture . . . nor with slouenly talke, . . .") the two phrases "the greedinesse of worldly chusers" and "bloody mindes of Usurers" could describe a single theme; there is no evidence that the *Jew* had a double plot, nor that *Ptolome* had a treble one. Mr Honigmann glossed the first phrase as the "greediness of those who choose the worldly way of life",[2] and quoted a usurer in Munday's *Zelauto* (1580) to show that they were often called "worldly": "we are accoumpted couetous carles, worldly wretches, and such like" (Appendix III, p. 160). The epithet "bloody" was also commonly used of usurers, and does not necessarily imply a flesh-bond motive in the lost play.

If a plot for the *Jew* must be found, it is easier to accept Dr Janet Spens' suggestion that the third book of Munday's *Zelauto* (1580) represents a re-working of the lost play mentioned by Gosson a year earlier. The dialogue of this third book is more vigorous than that of the rest of the novel, and suggests a dramatic model.[3] To be sure, the usurer in *Zelauto* is a Christian, but this change may have been effected in adapting the story for the novel. It has already been noted that this usurer calls his kind "worldly", and the word is repeatedly used of Ruscelli, the miserly father who accepts the richest suitor for his daughter. The "bloody mindes of Usurers" are fully "represented" in a bond for the right eyes of two men and a legal judgement based on the inability to take the forfeit without shedding blood.[4]

Clearly there is insufficient evidence to claim that a lost *Jew* play was the direct source of *The Merchant of Venice*, and it remains at least a strong probability that Shakespeare himself adapted the story as found in *Il Pecorone*.[5] Shakespeare often used more than one source for a single play, and there is no reason why he should not have done so for *The Merchant*.

Several secondary sources for the flesh-bond story have been suggested, and the most likely of these are reprinted as Appendices to this edition. Appendix II reprints the ballad of *Gernutus*. This has

1. 'Shakespeare's "Lost Source-Plays" ', *M.L.R.*, XLIX (1954), 293–307.

2. Cf. *O.E.D.*, "Worldly", 4.

3. Cf. *An Essay on Shakespeare's Relation to Tradition* (1916), pp. 23–4.

4. Book III of *Zelauto*, which is probably a secondary source for *The Merchant* (*vide infra*), is quoted in epitome in Appendix III.

5. Two other lost plays have suggestive titles: "the Venesyon [i.e., Venetian] comodye" which was noted in Henslowe's Diary eleven or twelve times between 25 August 1594 and 8 May 1595 (ed. Greg, pp. 19–22) and Dekker's *The Jew of Venice* which is known only by an entry in the *S.R.* on 9 September 1653. Without further information speculation is fruitless.

not been dated certainly, but it claims to be from Italian sources and may well be earlier than *The Merchant*.[1] It might have supplied Shakespeare with the "merry ieast" (st. 13), and the "whetted blade" (st. 29). Book III of Munday's *Zelauto* (1580) is reprinted in epitome as Appendix III. This is especially close to *The Merchant* in the judge's plea for mercy (pp. 164–5), but there are numerous minor verbal echoes which are pointed out in footnotes. This story may also have given Shakespeare several hints for re-working his main theme: its usurer has a daughter and, like Shylock's, she is won in marriage; the young suitor, like Bassanio, has a close friend who at first is a "disdayner of looue"; two ladies are disguised as attornies in the trial; and the usurer's son-in-law becomes his heir.[2] Appendix IV reprints Declamation 95 from L. P[iot's] translation of Silvayn's *The Orator* (1596). This may have suggested some of Shylock's arguments in the trial scene—the "credit" of the state, the practice of keeping slaves and "A man may aske why I would not rather take siluer . . . then his flesh" are each used on the Jew's behalf.

In addition to versions of the flesh-bond story, Shakespeare was probably influenced by Marlowe's *The Jew of Malta*, first performed about 1589. Verbal parallels between the two plays are pointed out in annotations to the text,[3] but more important is the probability that Marlowe's successful portrait of the villain Barabas coloured Shakespeare's conception of a Jew. Abigail, the Jew's daughter who turns Christian, may also have played a part in suggesting Shylock's Jessica.

More intangible is the possible influence that real Jews, living in London in Shakespeare's time, may have had upon the creation of Shylock. Shylock is a figure of fiction, but the possibility of this additional source for touches of characterization has been hotly debated. Through the researches of Professor C. J. Sisson and Dr Cecil Roth,[4] it can now be definitely stated that Jews did live in London at this time, and that while they may have professed Christianity in accordance with the long-standing laws against the residence of Jews in England, they did retain certain elements of their ancient worship and way of life.

1. Cf. *The Pepys Ballads*, ed. H. E. Rollins (1929), I. 16–17. A "ballad called the vserers rewarde" was entered in the *S.R.*, 19 June 1594.
2. The relationship of *Zelauto* to *The Merchant* is discussed by F. Brie, *Shakespeare Jahrbuch*, XLIX (1913), 97–108 and Celeste Turner, *Anthony Mundy* (1928), pp. 32–4.
3. For the most part they were first noted by A. W. Ward, *Hist. Eng. Dram. Lit.* (1875), I. 188–92.
4. Cf. C. J. Sisson, *E. & S.*, XXIII (1937), 38–51, and C. Roth, *A History of the Jews in England* (1941), pp. 139–44.

The major change which Shakespeare probably made in the story found in *Il Pecorone* was the substitution of the choice of caskets for the original wooing test; in so doing, he would use a story of ancient origin, existing in many versions. A selection of stories from the *Gesta Romanorum* was printed in an English translation by Richard Robinson in 15[7]7 and again in 1595; the story of the flesh-bond was not included, but a version of the casket story was, and of the sixteenth-century versions now extant, this is the closest to that of *The Merchant of Venice*. Extracts from the revised edition of 1595 are reprinted as Appendix v; this text is close in date to *The Merchant* and a slight verbal connection with the casket scenes[1] suggests that, if Shakespeare did in fact consult this version of the story, this was the edition he used.

The story of Jessica and Lorenzo may well have arisen from the suggestions furnished by *Zelauto* and *The Jew of Malta*, but one other possible source should be mentioned. It is the fourteenth Novella of Masuccio di Salerno written towards the end of the fifteenth century. It tells how the daughter of a miser escapes with her father's jewels by the help of a slave, and so joins her lover. The father discovers all, and for the loss of his ducats "he felt no less grief" than for the loss of his daughter. [2]

Secondary sources such as these probably influenced Shakespeare in re-shaping the story as found in *Il Pecorone*, but how *The Merchant* was created—what other sources were used, what possibilities rejected—will never be fully known. However, something more may be learnt by comparing the play with its primary source, and trying to see how the changes which were made conformed with, or differed from, Elizabethan life and literary conventions. This will be attempted in the course of the Critical Introduction.

4. STAGE HISTORY

Before the first quarto was printed in 1600, *The Merchant of Venice* had been "diuers times acted by the Lord Chamberlaine his Seruants", but the first performance of which there is specific record was by the King's Men at Court on Shrove Sunday, 10 February 1605. The play must have pleased, for the King commanded a second performance on the following Tuesday. [3] No further performance is recorded until 1741.

1. Cf. p. 173, n. 1. G. Bullough, *Narrative and Dramatic Sources*, I (1957), 506-11, reprints another choice-story from *Confessio Amantis*.

2. Cf. J. Dunlop, *Hist. of Fiction* (3rd ed. 1845), p. 254, and Bullough, I. 454-7 and 497-505.

3. The evidence is quoted and discussed in *William Shakespeare*, II. 330-2.

In the meantime, *The Jew of Venice*, an adaptation by George Granville, later Lord Lansdowne, was often played. First performed in May 1701 at Lincoln's Inn Fields, it was designed to provide a large and noble part for Betterton as Bassanio, and to make the play acceptable to the taste of the time. To these ends, a masque of Peleus and Thetis was added, the number of incidents and characters curtailed, and much of the verse omitted or rewritten. The part of Shylock was considerably lightened: he drinks the health of his mistress "Money" at a banquet given by Bassanio, his rage at the flight of Jessica is toned down, and his forced conversion is omitted. The part was played by Doggett, a famous "low" comedian, who probably modelled his Jew on the disreputable sharpers of the Exchange of his own day.[1]

The Jew continued to be played until 14 February 1741, when Charles Macklin persuaded the management of Drury Lane to restore Shakespeare's play in a text which included both the Gobbos, Morocco, Arragon, and Tubal. Although Macklin was to play Iago in 1744, he was renowned as a comedian, and at this time played Osric, Touchstone, and Trinculo. His Shylock cannot have been "tragic", but all witnesses affirm that he gave full vent to the Jew's contrasted passions. *The Merchant of Venice* at once became popular, and before the end of the month it had been played eight times.[2] Mrs Clive played Portia in these early performances, and used the part as an opportunity to ape the mannerisms of well-known lawyers. It was not long before Arragon and Morocco were cut from the play. Lorenzo, and sometimes Jessica and Portia, were given songs, and occasionally dances were introduced. Mrs Woffington and Mrs Siddons were famous Portias, but there is every indication that *The Merchant* had become Shylock's play. More "serious" actors undertook the role; Henderson (his Jew was a "black Lear"), George Frederick Cooke, and John Philip Kemble were among the most noted.[3]

Edmund Kean chose the part for his first appearance in London on 26 January 1814. His interpretation was original; Raymond, the Manager of Drury Lane, tried to dissuade him from "innovation" but he persisted, and the "terrible energy" of his Jew "drew down a thunder of applause" from a half-filled theatre. He was a man stung into rage who, with a sardonic, contemptuous scorn, fought to the very last. Hazlitt was in the audience on the first night, and until then, he decided, he had

1. Cf. J. H. Wilson, *P.Q.*, XIII (1934), 1–15.

2. Cf. C. B. Hogan, *Shakespeare in the Theatre* (1952), p. 313.

3. Cf. J. R. Brown, 'The Realization of Shylock', *Early Shakespeare, Stratford-upon-Avon Studies*, iii (1961), for a detailed account of famous Shylocks on the stage.

formed an overstrained idea of the gloomy character of Shylock, probably more from seeing other players perform it than from the text of Shakespeare. Mr. Kean's manner is much nearer the mark ... his Jew is more than half a Christian. Certainly, our sympathies are much oftener with him than with his enemies. He is honest in his vices; they are hypocrites in their virtues.[1]

As early as 1709, Nicholas Rowe had protested against the comic Shylock:

tho' we have seen the Play Receiv'd and Acted as a Comedy, and the Part of the *Jew* perform'd by an excellent Comedian, yet I cannot but think that it was design'd Tragically by the Author. There appears in it such a deadly Spirit of Revenge, such a savage Fierceness and Fellness, and such a bloody designation of Cruelty and Mischief, as cannot agree either with the Stile or Characters of Comedy.[2]

But the first notion that Shylock was not wholly malignant has been found[3] in Richard Hole's 'Apology for the Character and Conduct of Shylock', in *Essays by a Society of Gentlemen at Exeter* (1796). Suppose the situation was reversed, Hole argued—what would be thought if Shylock had subjected Antonio to the same indignities?

After Kean, Shylock was played with special success by Macready, Charles Kean, and Edwin Booth. In accordance with nineteenth-century taste, the staging became more and more elaborate. Charles Kean's acting version locates the first scene in St Mark's Place, and directs

Various groups of Nobles, Citizens, Merchants, Foreigners, Water-Carriers, Flower Girls, &c., pass and repass. Procession of the Doge, in state, across the square

—and only then, does Antonio begin the play. Bridges, gondolas, and Venetian carnivals were often called for, and very beautiful effects were attempted. The Bancrofts, who presented the play at the Prince of Wales's Theatre in 1875, spent part of the preceding year in Venice selecting the views to be reproduced on the stage.

Sir Henry Irving's production of 1 November 1879 ran for 250 consecutive performances, and his Shylock was one of the main reasons for this unprecedented success. It was a personal triumph. "Shylock," he is reported to have said, "is a bloody-minded monster,—but you mustn't play him so, if you wish to succeed; you

1. *The Chronicle* (6 Apr. 1816); reprinted, *A View of the Eng. Stage* (1821), pp. 226-7. See also *Characters of Shakespeare's Plays* (1817); *Wks* (ed. 1930), IV. 320-4.
2. 'Life', *Wks of Shakespeare* (1709).
3. Cf. F. T. Wood, *Eng. Studies*, xv (1933), 209-18.

must get some sympathy with him."[1] Shylock became a vehicle for
Irving's noble style of acting; all his evil qualities appeared to be
due to the persecution of his race and the indignities inflicted upon
himself. He was not defeated in the trial scene, but kept "a firm
front to the last, and . . . [had] a fine curl of withering scorn upon
his lips for Gratiano, as he . . . [walked] away to die in silence and
alone."[2] His interpretation became harder and more merciless, but
its main lines seem to have remained unaltered. Details were frequently copied by other actors, in particular the interpolated
scene in which Shylock returned to his house after Jessica had
eloped with the revellers. Irving was content to knock at the door
and to stand silent as the curtain fell, but some of his imitators
rushed into the house to return with a letter, or crying "My
daughter! O my ducats! O my daughter! . . ." Richard Mansfield's
Shylock (1893) at Herrmann's Theatre, New York, went far beyond Irving's by giving himself a death wound with his knife before
leaving the stage on "I am not well" at the end of the trial scene.

Irving's production was also famous ior Ellen Terry's Portia.
The casket scene with Bassanio had been severely cut, but she enchanted almost all who saw her. Some complained that she had too
much of the "coming-on disposition",[3] and others believed that
she "hid the part", presenting herself rather than Portia.[4] But
Portia has often aroused conflicting opinions; for instance, one
report praised Violet Vanbrugh's (1905), for its "dignity" and
"greatness", and another blamed it for missing "all the lightness
and girlishness".[5]

In the main, *The Merchant* continued to be Shylock's play, the
part being notably performed by Tree, Benson, Forbes-Robertson,
and Maurice Moscovitch. But sometimes the emphasis was changed. When Arthur Bourchier played Shylock at the Garrick in 1905,
he engaged Mr Alan McKinnon as producer. Mr McKinnon
chose scenes from Veronese, introduced the customary Venetian
crowds, and made Shylock spit as he heard an organ play within a
church, but, more important, he acknowledged that the "friendship of Antonio and Bassanio, . . . is the main thread which runs
throughout,"[6] and he directed that the two men should hold the
stage at the last curtain. A more thorough attempt to present the
whole play had been made in 1898 by William Poel, who

1. Quoted W. Winter, *Shakespeare on the Stage* (1912), p. 175.

2. *Blackwood's Magazine* (Dec. 1879), p. 655.

3. *Op. cit.*, p. 653; see also *Scribner's Monthly Mag.* (Jan. 1881), quoted A. C.
Sprague, *Shakespeare and the Actors* (1944), p. 25.

4. So Sybil Thorndike, *Evening Standard* (20 Jan. 1930).

5. *Morning Post* and *Standard* (12 Oct. 1905).   6. *Souvenir*, pp. 4–5.

Revived [it] before the Members of the [Elizabethan Stage] Society and their guests, after the manner of the 16th Century, and with the music performed upon the original instruments of the time.[1]

In 1921, Max Reinhardt gave a unity to the play when he presented it at the Grosses Schauspielhaus, Berlin, as something approaching a farce. Venice was a blue and white cubist construction and Shylock walked with flat feet, talked loudly and laughed boisterously. No jarring note marred a "general atmosphere of laughter".[2]

In England, the public welcomed frequent productions, but critics began to grow weary of them. The day following a performance by the Old Vic Company at the Lyric, Hammersmith, on 17 October 1927, *The Times* complained:

Like a garment that one may admire without wishing to wear it too often, this is an ill-fitting play with brilliant embroideries. The worst of it is that even of the embroideries, ... one grows tired. The casket scene—alas, how prolix are Aragon and Morocco! Portia's pleading with the Jew—how rigid has its beauty become ... !

The romantic elements no longer found favour, and the same critic praised Lewis Casson for making Shylock "a man of middle stature —neither a giant in his hatred nor a cur in his humiliation." This Shylock did "much to give something of the balance of human reason to a strangely arbitrary play."

But *The Merchant of Venice* has continued to fill the theatres. In Germany it has been especially popular, Schröder, Devrient, Bassermann, Rudolph Schildkraut, and Werner Krauss being noted Shylocks. It has been frequently in the repertories of the Old Vic and Stratford-upon-Avon. Shylock has been played with particular success by George Arliss, Ernest Milton, Randle Ayrton, Sir John Gielgud, Donald Wolfit, Frederick Valk, and Paul Rogers. Sybil Thorndike, Mary Newcombe, Diana Wynyard, and Irene Worth have been admired Portias. The 1953 production at Stratford-upon-Avon emphasized the relationship of Antonio and Bassanio, being remarkable for the fine Merchant of Mr Harry Andrews as well as for Mr Redrave's Shylock and Miss Ashcroft's Portia. At the same theatre in 1960 Mr Peter O'Toole gave a Shylock whose flashing transitions of mood recalled accounts of Kean's and whose dignity those of Irving's; he was hailed as "magnificent" by the press.[3]

1. *Programme.*   2. *Observer* (20 Mar. 1921).
3. See detailed reviews by N. Dennis in *Encounter* (June 1960) and by J. R. Brown in *Shakespeare Survey*, xiv (1961).

5. CRITICAL INTRODUCTION

One quality of *The Merchant of Venice* is already clear: its characters are capable of many different interpretations. Their apparent reality encourages this, and so does the tendency to view them out of their dramatic context, in the light of partisan predispositions. They are complex creations and all critics have not seen the same aspects. At the risk of confusion, one must first try to see them whole, and then relate them to the play as an entity of its own.

*   *   *

Judging from the "wicked Jew" of *Il Pecorone*, Shylock is largely Shakespeare's creation. No one reading this source would question the Jew's intentions or motives, but in *The Merchant* attention is focused on them by dialogue and soliloquy. Some hint for the development of Shylock may have come from Silvayn's *The Orator*. In this account of the flesh-bond story, the acknowledged motive for the Jew pursuing vengeance is the "antient and cruell hate" which he bears towards Christians, and Shakespeare makes it clear that this is part of Shylock's motive too. In his first soliloquy, he is made to say explicitly, "I hate him for he is a Christian" (I. iii. 37).

When these words were spoken to an Elizabethan audience they evoked ideas and superstitions which were centuries old. Officially Jews had been expelled from England since the reign of Edward I, but if they conformed outwardly to Christianity, they could live peaceably in London and maintain some features of their ancient life and religion.[1] In the decade during which *The Merchant* was written, the only widespread and militant anti-Jewish feeling was occasioned by the trial and execution of Roderigo Lopez for alleged high treason. It was clearly a latent rather than an active feeling, and due to inherited suspicion rather than current religious or social thought.[2] In England at this time, the Jews were not a people to fear, but were rather a fabulous and monstrous bogey belonging to remote times and places. Legends, like that of St Hugh of Lincoln who was crucified as a child by the Jews, were widely known, and miracle plays had given a kind of actuality to some terrible fictions, like the "grotesque dance performed by the Jews, . . . round the cross on which Christ hangs."[3] In contemporary

1. See above, p. xxxi.

2. Cf. H. R. Walley, 'Shakespeare's Portrayal of Shylock', *Essays in Dram. Lit.* (1935), p. 222. J. W. Draper (*M.P.*, xxxiii (1935), 37, n. 2) quoted a sermon by John Foxe (1578) to the effect that although the Jews murdered Christ, they were a race not "altogether forsaken of God".

3. H. Michelson, *The Jew in Early Eng. Lit.* (1926), p. 60.

literature, the Jew was almost invariably an exotic figure who lived outside England, in Italy or Turkey, and plotted with cunning and malice against all Christians.[1] Famous examples are Zachary and Zadock, the Jews of Rome in Nashe's *The Unfortunate Traveller* (1594), and Barabas in Marlowe's *The Jew of Malta*; and it is in the light of such characters that Shylock's hatred of the Christian Antonio must be viewed.

Marlowe's play almost certainly influenced Shakespeare, and it may be instructive to compare their two Jews. There is a significant change of spirit, for Shylock has little of the exuberance of Barabas. He is given no chance to exult over fabulous riches, or talk of his argosies which venture across the seas. In Shakespeare's play, Antonio, not the Jew, is the Merchant Venturer. Shylock, by all accounts, is a niggard in his house, and has no time for masques and revelry; in contrast, Barabas boasts a cellar full of wines and claims "the governor feeds not as I do" (IV. vi. 64). Barabas speaks in Marlowe's ambitious, sensuous vein, and he is in the prime of life; Shylock is old, and can speak with the solemnity of an Old Testament prophet.

But there are similarities. Both have daughters who deceive their fathers and, if conversion is a sign of grace, both dramatists expected their audience to approve. In this they followed ancient precedent, for there were many medieval stories of a Christian youth and a fair Jewess, where the Christian enjoys his love, and, no matter how ignoble the circumstances, has the approval of the story-teller.[2] Shylock has something of Barabas' sense of humour too: they both sarcastic at the expense of the Christians and show a cynical disregard of consequences. Shylock's humour, unlike that of most of Shakespeare's characters, is hard and vicious; he turns a malapropism from jest to earnest, makes a pun on the damnation of his daughter, and jokes about eating Antonio's flesh.[3]

To the Christians in Marlowe's play, all Jews are "accursed in the sight of heaven" (II. ii. 64) and Barabas himself is "cast off from heaven" (II. iii. 159). He lives up to his reputation and is proud to boast:

> Now tell me, worldlings, underneath the sun
> If greater falsehood ever has bin done?
>
> (V. v. 49–50)

1. Cf. J. L. Cardozo, *The Contemporary Jew in the Elizabethan Drama* (1925), ch. ii.

2. Cf. B. D. Brown, *M.L.N.*, XLIV (1929), 227–32. See also J. L. Wilson, *S.A.B.*, XXIII (1948), 20–3.

3. Cf. II. v. 21, III. i. 29 and 47–8.

So in Shakespeare's play, the Christians are in no doubt that Shylock is a thorough villain; nine times he is called a devil and, as his
hatred leads him to kill like an animal,[1] they can find no answer to
"excuse the current" of his cruelty (IV. i. 64). Shylock declares his
malice openly; he refuses many times the sum which is owed him
and insists on taking Antonio's life. This was his settled resolve, for
Jessica heard him say so soon after the bond was sealed,[2] and in his
first soliloquy, he is already looking for an opportunity to "feed fat
the ancient grudge" he bears Antonio (I. iii. 42). Barabas is a
villain for his own aggrandisement and pleasure; Shylock is a villain because of the hate he bears Antonio, the Christian.

This was Shakespeare's emphasis in creating his Jew, but it does
not follow that his play is anti-Jewish. It has been pointed out that
Shylock and Tubal are not considered to be typical;[3] the devil himself would have to "turn Jew" before there was another one like
them (III. i. 70–1). There are only two slurs on Jews in general, one
by Launcelot the clown, "my master's a very Jew" (II. ii. 100),
and one by Antonio in the trial scene, though even here it is "*His*
Jewish heart" which is exclaimed against (IV. i. 80). Shylock is moti-
vated by his hate of a Christian, but, in spite of the latent prejudice
this must have aroused in Elizabethan minds, he is not condemned
out of hand; he is at least given a chance to show how he counted
his own deeds as righteousness.

Professor Charlton thought that Shakespeare planned *The Merchant of Venice* as a play "to let the Jew dog have it", but that when
he came to write, he had to "exhibit a Jew who is a man."[4] Whatever Shakespeare's intentions may have been, the "humanity" of
Shylock has been proved many times in the theatre. He is not
merely a monster to revile and curse; his viewpoint is fully given
and can, on occasion, command the whole sympathy of an audience. The first full opportunity for this is his sarcastic dialogue with
Antonio:

> Shall I bend low, and in a bondman's key
> With bated breath, and whisp'ring humbleness
> Say this:
> "Fair sir, you spet on me on Wednesday last,
> You spurn'd me such a day, another time
> You call'd me dog: and for these courtesies
> I'll lend you thus much moneys"?
>
> (I. iii. 118–24)

1. He is likened to a ravenous animal III. ii. 274–5 (see note), and to a wolf
IV. i. 73–4, and 133–8.
2. Cf. III. ii. 283–9.   3. Cf. N. Nathan, *S.A.B.*, XXIII (1948), 158 f.
4. *Shakespearian Comedy* (1938), pp. 127–32.

xl THE MERCHANT OF VENICE

The early contact with Antonio, who is already known as the generous and good Merchant, does not seem the most suitable place for Shakespeare to make Shylock bid for understanding, but Antonio gives a cold answer which reinforces Shylock's argument:

> I am as like to call thee so again,
> To spet on thee again, to spurn thee too. (ll. 125–6)

The next full opportunity for Shylock to state his case is the speech "Hath not a Jew eyes?..." in Act III, Scene i, and here he claims a hearing on the grounds that he suffers as other men, and will take revenge like them.

So powerful has Shylock's justification proved, that it is sometimes forgotten that a villain is speaking. It has to be pointed out that "what is commonly received as Shylock's plea for tolerance is in reality his justification of an inhuman purpose."[1] Shakespeare has created in Shylock an outcast who suffers and is driven to extremity in his suffering,[2] but no matter how harshly the Christians treat him, he remains the Jew who intends to kill his enemy,[3] a harsh, cynical, and ruthless villain. Whether his suffering forces him to be a villain, or whether his villainy causes him to suffer, Shakespeare is not concerned to say. But there is a judgement: at the end of the trial scene, Shylock's designs are defeated and he has to accept conversion to Christianity. This was a punishment from Shylock's point of view (as it was a threatened punishment for Marlowe's Barabas),[4] but from Antonio's point of view, it also gave to Shylock a chance of eternal joy.[5] The significance of this judgement must be reserved for fuller treatment later.

*   *   *

In the meantime there are other aspects of Shylock which must be considered. Besides being a Jew, he is also an old man[6] with a

1. J. Palmer, *Comic Characters of Shakespeare* (1946), p. 79.
2. In the Ill May Day scene of *Sir Thomas More*, Shakespeare was probably responsible for More's eloquent defence of "strangers" in the city of London; cf. p. xxv above for Shylock as a "stranger".
3. J. W. Lever (*S.Q.*, III (1952), 385–6) has argued that Shylock renounces his Jewish principles in the speech of justification (III. i)—he "will behave as in practice all human beings do". But he remains a Jew; in III. iii, he is still opposed to "Christian intercessors" (l. 16), and in the trial scene, he is repeatedly called a Jew, and swears by his "holy Sabbath" (IV. i. 36), remembers his "oath in heaven" (l. 224), and shows his scorn of all Christians (ll. 291–3).
4. Cf. *Jew of Malta*, I. ii. 73–4.
5. This has been eloquently argued by Nevill Coghill, *Shakespeare Quarterly*, I (London, 1948), 16.
6. Cf. II. v. 2, III. i. 32, and IV. i. 171.

young daughter who escapes from him to marry the man she loves. Many critics have believed that Shakespeare intended this part of the play to gain more sympathy for Shylock. In their view, Jessica is a minx who heartlessly runs away from her old father, steals his money and the ring given to him by his beloved wife, and shamelessly joins his detractors and enemies. It is thought that these wrongs cause Shylock to harden his heart against Antonio. [1]

But nowhere in the play does Shylock show any tenderness towards his daughter; in their one scene together, he merely enjoins her to lock up his possessions and not to watch the Christian revelry. It has already been noted that as a Jewess, loved by a Christian, Jessica stood in a fair way for the audience's sympathy; as the daughter of an old man who escapes from duress, she had another claim. Munday's *Zelauto*, which was probably one of Shakespeare's sources for *The Merchant*, tells of a young daughter acting against her father, and love, beauty, happiness, and goodness are all on her side. It is a romance theme which is constantly repeated. [2] In Masuccio's 14th Novella, which is a possible source for Jessica's escapade, the daughter makes off with her father's money, and yet all is condoned. In both these examples, the father is avaricious and this also tells against him. It ranks him with the miserly fathers in Elizabethan [3] and classical comedies, who are only fit to be the dupes of their children—"for the instinct inherent in human nature is to prefer the prodigal to the miser." [4]

Old Shylock is also a miser; Launcelot says he is "famish'd in his service" (II. ii. 101-2), Jessica that his "house is hell" (II. iii. 2), and Shylock himself says that money is the means whereby he lives. [5] In such a role, he is fair game for the young lovers; even his own child can rob him and retain the sympathy of the audience. [6] They will laugh with Salerio and Solanio at the old man's passionate outcry "My daughter! O my ducats! O my daughter!..." (II. viii. 15-

1. Cf., for example, *N.C.S.*, pp. xviii–xxi and xxviii. See also H. B. Charlton, *op. cit.*, pp. 156–8, and T. M. Parrott, *Shakespearean Comedy* (1949), p. 139.

2. Parallels have been noted by R. Pruvost, *Les Langues Modernes*, XLV (1951), 99–109.

3. E.g., *A Knack to Know an Honest Man* (1594), W. Haughton, *Englishmen for my Money* (pf. c. 1597–8), and *Wily Beguiled* (p.. c. 1601). A. B. Stonex (*P.M.L.A.*, XXXI (1916), 190–210) showed the prevalence of this theme in Elizabethan plays. J. R. Moore (*Boston Public Library Quarterly*, I (1949), 33–42) pointed out that Shylock had some of the characteristics of Pantaloon of the Italian *Commedia dell' Arte*: he is a widower, the head of a household, and avaricious, but he is not the ridiculous lover, nor a Magnifico of Venice (such as Antonio).

4. W. Poel, 'Shakespeare's Jew and Marlowe's Christians', *Westminster Review*, CLXXI (1909), 59.

5. Cf. IV. i. 371-3.

6. For this view see, for example, J. M. Murry, *Shakespeare* (1936), p. 194.

22) for it is a comic revelation that he loves money before all else. The same is true of Shylock's:

I would my daughter were dead at my foot, and the jewels in her ear: would she were hears'd at my foot, and the ducats in her coffin.
                                                                    (III. i. 80–2)

Professor Stoll has called this an example of the familiar dramatic trick of comical anti-climax, of

taking the audience in for a moment and . . . then clapping upon the seemingly pathetic sentiment a cynical, selfish, or simply incongruous one.

Another trick is used in making Shylock repeat, with alteration, Tubal's mention of a monkey; "I would not have given it for a wilderness of monkeys" (III. i. 112–13) is a kind of comic climax by repetition.[1]

Professor Stoll is among the critics who have seen Shylock as a wholly comic figure, but there is a duality about Shylock as an old curmudgeon as there is in his role as a Jew. Many of his speeches are so phrased that they can be said in the theatre without any humour, simply as cries of anguish. Such duality is found elsewhere in Shakespeare. For instance, in 2 Henry IV, the audience does not only laugh at Shallow and Silence, alternating between the death of old Double and the price of bullocks at Stamford fair.[2] The trick of comical anti-climax is used in these speeches, but there is also a moving picture of two old men with wandering minds, trying to make the good even with the bad, and trying to understand mortality. There is a somewhat similar alternation when Shylock hears of Antonio's losses.[3] The tone, of course, is very different; instead of an old man alternating meditatively between simple good and evil, Shylock is storm-tossed, viciously plunging from one side to another, from hope to despair. An audience may tend to laugh at the old miserly father foiled in his plans, but it is hard to laugh at the old man with his mind out of control, and his passion raging. The reaction of the audience is more complex still when he is seen to regain control and bend all his energies towards the object of his hate: "I will have the heart of him if he forfeit."

*   *   *

The picture of Shylock is not yet complete. A Jew says, "I will have the heart of him if he forfeit," but a usurer continues: "for were he out of Venice I can make what merchandise I will." In his

1. Cf. E. E. Stoll, *Shakespeare Studies* (1927), pp. 312–13.
2. III. ii. 36–58.   3. III. i. 89–120.

first soliloquy, he says he hates Antonio because he is a Christian:

> *But more*, for that in low simplicity
> He lends out money gratis, and brings down
> The rate of usance here with us in Venice. (I. iii. 38–40)

Antonio's active opposition to usury is said to be the chief reason for Shylock's hatred.[1]

In contrast to the "Jewish problem", the rights and wrongs of usury were a living issue to Elizabethans. There was general agreement that usury (the "lending for gaine, by compact, not adventuring the principall") was a great evil, but some said that it should be legalized and controlled. The Scriptures and the Fathers seemed to condemn it outright, but Calvin, Beza, and some other divines acknowledged that it had to be tolerated in a modern commonwealth. Bacon's essay "Of Usury" (1625) argued that it was "inevitable", and the laws of England, while calling usury a sin and aiming at its repression, permitted borrowing up to the rate of ten per cent. The evils of usury were widely known, for borrowing had become a necessity to many. Great Elizabethans, like Sidney, Essex, Leicester, and Southampton were each thousands of pounds in debt,[2] and Queen Elizabeth was forced to borrow very large sums from European bankers. Shakespeare's Company, the Chamberlain's Men, built the Theatre and the Globe on money taken up at a rate of interest which was a continual burden to them.[3] In spite of all the sermons preached against it, usury became increasingly common; the translator of Philip Caesar's *Discourse against Usurers* (1578) believed that if inquiry were made, "the stocke of many Churches would bee founde out at Vsurie" (Sig.** I). In 1595 he was "counted a shameles man" who made request "to borrow without offering vsurie."[4] But although usury at a limited rate was sometimes allowed in theory, and more and more people took advantage of it in practice, it seems to have been generally agreed that evil consequences followed its unbridled use. All classes of people would remonstrate with the rapacious and ruthless usurer, and would revile and mock him.

The literature of the time did so frequently.[5] In *Zelauto*, for instance, Munday made a usurer the villain of a flesh-bond story.

1. This point is made by J. W. Draper, *M.P.*, xxxiii (1935), 37–47. See also E. C. Pettet, *E. & S.*, xxxi (1946), 19–33.

2. Cf. R. H. Tawney, Introduction, Sir T. Wilson, *Discourse upon Usury* (ed. 1925), p. 36.

3. Cf. *William Shakespeare*, II. 65–6.

4. M. Mosse, *Arraignment of Usury*, C3ᵛ.

5. A. B. Stonex (*P.M.L.A.*, xxxi (1916), pp. 190–210) found 71 plays, written between 1553 and 1640, which contain attacks on usurers.

The ballad of Gernutus tells a similar story about a Jewish usurer, and the author brought home the moral of his strange tale by pointing out:

> That many a wretch as ill as he
> doth live now at this day,

and wishing them like sentence to the Jew's.

As a rapacious usurer who drew his victims to their ruin,[1] Shylock would be condemned by every member of an Elizabethan audience. In picturing him as such, and in giving a long argument on the rights and wrongs of usury, Shakespeare added to his source as found in *Il Pecorone*. Shylock's opening dialogue might have been studied from life: the astute man of business plays his own game, bides his time, and makes Bassanio do the talking. Bassanio is not practised at this, and his impatience soon betrays how much he needs the money; in return he receives a long disquisition on Antonio's hazards. When Antonio enters, Shylock maintains the lead in the conversation, ordering it to his own ends.[2] A usurer was cunning and deceitful by profession, and when Shylock proffers friendship to Antonio and proposes the "merry" bond, an Elizabethan audience might fear the worst: it was said that a "Vsurer lendeth like a friend but he couenanteth like an enemie."[3] Some critics have thought that Shylock's desire for friendship is genuine,[4] but in view of the usurer's reputation, it is more probably a gamble for the monstrous forfeiture. If Antonio's ships *did* come home, at the worst Shylock would only lose the interest his money might have gained at usury elsewhere; at the best, he could use one of the many tricks, familiarized in novels, plays, sermons, and treatises, by which a usurer could delay the payment beyond the named day. Such a trick is alluded to in *Zelauto*, where the usurer is away from home on the expiration of the bond. In *The Orator*, the merchant suspects that the Jew has caused his money to be delayed "by secret meanes."[5] Shylock is risking very little in proposing his "merry" bond, and even Bassanio sees the danger. Antonio's generosity must have been very great when he walked into the usurer's trap.

Even as a usurer, Shylock is given an opportunity to justify him-

1. Cf. III. iii. 22–3.
2. The annotations of this edition illustrate this scene from descriptions of Elizabethan usurers.
3. H. Smith, *Examination of Usury* (1591), B1. See also, I. iii. 134, note.
4. E.g., H. B. Charlton, *op. cit.*, and H. B. Walley, 'Shakespeare's Portrayal of Shylock', *Essays in Dram. Lit.* (1935), p. 235.
5. For further examples of a usurer's guile, cf. *Gernutus* (Appendix II), st. 17–20 and Lodge and Greene, *Looking Glass* (1594), B3^v–4.

self.[1] It seems as if Shakespeare was determined not to create a "stage villain", who would always evoke a simple, hostile response. Shylock is a most complex and dominating character; he appears in only five scenes and yet for many people he is the centre of the play's interest. As an old miserly father he is comic, as a Jew he is savage and ruthless, as a usurer he seeks to ensnare the needy and Antonio, their protector. Yet in all these roles he is also a man who suffers and triumphs, speaks at times with great nobility, and has a "kind of wild justice" in his cry for revenge.[2]

*   *   *

The Christians in the play are often judged by their relationships to Shylock. So Jessica is either "the unfilial daughter of a persecuted Jew", or she is entirely charming, "a princess held captive by an ogre."[3] Lorenzo, Launcelot, Salerio, Solanio, and Gratiano are all capable of provoking similarly opposed interpretations. Gratiano, for instance, is to some critics a heartless bully who beats a broken man, to others he is merely a little wild, rude, and bold of voice, parts which, on most occasions, become him happily enough.

In contrast, Antonio is drawn firmly. Although he spurns Shylock, he is the "good Antonio", the "royal merchant", and his good deeds are reported by Shylock himself.[4] Above all, he is the generous and brave friend of Bassanio. In *Il Pecorone*, the merchant is Giannetto's godfather, but Shakespeare has added a new theme by making them friends. Friendship, or "amity", was a high theme, and its virtues were often praised; for instance, in Lyly's *Euphues* (1578):

a friend is in prosperitie a pleasure, a solace in aduersitie, in griefe a comfort, in ioy a merrye companion, at all times an other I, in all places yᵉ expresse Image of mine owne person: insomuch that I cannot tell, whether the immortall Gods haue bestowed any gift vpon mortall men, either more noble, or more necessary, then friendship . . .[5]

Many of Shakespeare's sonnets express the nobility of friendship and, at the climax of *The Two Gentlemen of Verona*, Valentine gives to his friend his dearest possession—all that was his in Silvia—and it is this act of friendship which brings the story to a successful conclusion.

Antonio and Bassanio are two such friends. At the beginning of

1. He has convinced some critics; cf. I. iii. 72–85, note.
2. So P. Alexander, *Shakespeare's Life and Art* (1939), p. 113.
3. J. M. Murry, *Shakespeare* (1936), p. 194.
4. Cf. I. iii. 38–40, III. i. 43–4 and 117–18, and III. iii. 2.   5. *Wks*, I. 197.

the play Antonio is melancholy because Bassanio is about to leave him,[1] yet he puts his life into the power of a usurer so that his friend may have his wish. When Bassanio hears of Antonio's danger, he leaves his wife on their wedding day and goes to Venice where he would lose life, wife, and all the world to save his friend.[2] But nothing can be done, and Antonio, who "only loves the world" for his friend's sake (II. viii. 50), resolutely faces death. The theme is continued to the end of the play. In *Il Pecorone*, Giannetto gives his wife's ring away of his own accord, but Shakespeare has directed that Bassanio should do so only on the persuasion of his friend. The ring is restored, and the play ends happily, only after Antonio has given a new pledge, this time for his soul.[3]

The story does not allow Bassanio to show the same nobility in friendship as Antonio does; he is dependent on his friend and can only *say* that he would do brave things for his sake. Shakespeare has however protected him from the charge of thoughtlessness. In *Il Pecorone*, Giannetto completely forgets Ansaldo when he is at Belmonte and is reminded of his predicament only by an accident. In *The Merchant*, Antonio tells Bassanio that he can look after himself and that there is no need for him to worry about the bond:

> Let it not enter in your mind of love:
> Be merry, . . . (II. viii. 42–3)

With this assurance, Bassanio has good reason to stay at Belmont until news comes from Venice that Antonio is in danger.

*   *   *

Bassanio's chief part in the play is, of course, as the wooer of Portia, and here Shakespeare has presented a very different story from the one found in *Il Pecorone*. Whereas Giannetto succeeded merely because a maid servant gave away her mistress' secret, Bassanio wins his lady because he chooses the right casket. Bassanio is sometimes dismissed as a spendthrift who borrows three thousand ducats "to equip himself to go off and hunt an heiress in Belmont",[4] but the fact that he chooses rightly shows that he marries for the best of reasons: "If you do love me," says Portia, "you will find me out" (III. ii. 41).

1. Cf. I. i. 1, note. Sir E. K. Chambers suggested that this part of the play might be the "intrusion of a personal note"; judging from the *Sonnets*, Shakespeare "like Antonio, had lost a friend, and had lost him through a woman" (*Shakespeare: a Survey* (1925), p. 117).

2. Cf. IV. i. 112–13, and note, and 278–83.

3. Cf. v. i. 249–55. This point was made by M. C. Bradbrook, *Shakespeare and Elizabethan Poetry* (1951), p. 178.

4. *N.C.S.*, p. xxv.

When Bassanio tells Antonio about Portia, he mentions first her wealth—this is not surprising, for the dowry was frankly discussed in planning any Elizabethan marriage[1] and, in any case, Portia has all perfections; then he mentions her beauty—that also is expected; but he reserves her chief attraction to last:

> And she is fair, and (fairer than that word),
> Of wondrous virtues, . . . (1. i. 162–3)

Clearly he will choose the right casket; "many men desire" wealth and outward beauty, typified by the golden casket; a few would be ignorant enough to think that they deserved them; but only one who loved Portia for her virtues would accept her in a leaden casket, and be prepared to "give and hazard all he hath."

The reasons for Bassanio's choice are made explicit in his deliberation in Act III, Scene ii (ll. 73–107), and as Professor C. R. Baskervill has pointed out,[2] they represent Renaissance belief in an ideal love. Similar sentiments were implied in the familiar distinction between "fancy" and "true affection"[3] and were discussed at length in books of courtesy and amatory novels like Greene's *Mamillia* (c. 1583):

he which maketh choyce of bewty without vertue commits as much folly as *Critius* did, in choosing a golden boxe filled with rotten bones.[4]

The story of the caskets in the *Gesta Romanorum* was intended as a moral exemplum, and in some manuscript copies, and in Robinson's translation, a "Moral" is given; the gold casket is the choice of "worldly men, both mightie men & riche, which outwardly shine," the silver is the choice of "Justices & wise men of this world which shine in faire speach," and the lead is the choice of the "simple" and "poore" who "at the iudgement day . . . be espoused to our Lord Jesu Christ."[5]

Portia, like Bassanio, is ennobled by the substitution of the casket story for the wooing of *Il Pecorone*. The original lady of Belmonte was a widow who had ruined many gentlemen, but Portia, like the King's daughter in the *Gesta Romanorum*, is the heroine of a romance story; she is fair, noble, maiden, an only daughter who loves simply and unquestioningly. To Morocco, she is the pattern of perfection:

1. So H. Craig, *Shakespeare* (1935), p. 329, n. See also H. P. Pettigrew, *P.Q.*, XVI (1937), 296–306.

2. 'Bassanio as an Ideal Lover', *Manly Anniversary Studies* (1923), pp. 90–103.
3. Cf. III. ii. 63, note.   4. *Wks*, II. 114.
5. Appendix V, p. 174; see also, *The Old English Versions of the Gesta Romanorum*, ed. Sir F. Madden (1838), pp. 245–6.

> . . . all the world desires her.
> From the four corners of the earth they come
> To kiss this shrine, this mortal breathing saint.
>
> (II. vii. 38–40)

Bassanio's praise is no less ideal; she is rich, fair, and virtuous, fit to be ranked with noble Portia of Rome, courted by princes, and of such legendary wealth and beauty that heroes cross the seas in quest of her.[1]

So poets speak of Portia, and it is with this expectation that the audience must await her first appearance. They may expect to find her in a castle, attended by one faithful maid, very beautiful, and remote. So, perhaps, imagination saw her in the Elizabethan theatre, and the audience would await the procession of her suitors. But it is she who speaks:

> By my troth Nerissa, my little body is aweary of this great world.
>
> (I. ii. 1–2)

and at once the focus has altered. The words are written from her point of view. This first prose scene establishes the romance princess as a character, ardent and intelligent. But the magic is carefully kept—the lottery of the caskets will "no doubt" never be chosen rightly but by the right person—and the poetry of Morocco's two scenes re-establishes her fabulous perfections. Portia simply and easily fulfils the outline drawn ages ago in the Romances, but the picture has come alive; her beauty is matched with a spirit to give it motion.

This is especially true of the final casket scene. Portia does not merely wait for Bassanio to solve the riddle, for Shakespeare has kept her sentiments constantly before the audience. The speech with which she sends Bassanio to his hazard—"Away then! I am lock'd in one of them, . . ." (III. ii. 40–62)—is as complex as Portia herself, and as simple; it is poised and beautiful poetry, and yet expresses perfectly her hopes and fears. It gives associations—music, a swan, a new-crowned monarch, a wedding morning, Alcides, sacrifice, a contest. It shows Portia's humbleness and ardour: she thinks first of failure and finds beauty even there; but he may win,

> And what is music then? Then music is . . .

so the words hurry to her thoughts. Then she thinks of the event itself and of its strange reversals, the inequality of the contest:

---

1. Cf. I. i. 161–72.

go Hercules!
Live thou, I live—with much much more dismay,
I view the fight, than thou that mak'st the fray.

This scene prepares the audience for the wit, courage, control, and common sense of the trial scene, and for the gaiety, lightness, and underlying calm of the garden at Belmont when it is almost morning.

*   *   *

The discussion of individual characters and scenes is a preliminary to asking what sort of play *The Merchant of Venice* is. On a first examination, its many elements may seem to have no single theme. Half the play is set in Venice, full of gallants, masquers, and idle talkers. In this gay and trifling city, lives a Jewish usurer, cruel beyond reason, yet thriving and pulsing with life. For the sake of a friend, the Merchant of Venice gives a bond to the Jew for his own flesh, and when he is overwhelmed by an improbable catastrophe, the Jew insists on his rights. The other half of the play is set in Belmont, a palace which is reached across the sea. The owner is the greatest wonder of Belmont, a heroine who combines beauty, ardour, and intelligence. It is she, disguised as a young man, who finally defeats the villainous schemes of the Jewish usurer—by a verbal quibble which had not occurred to the wisest men in Venice. Surely Shakespeare is at his most irresponsible and it is irrelevant to ask for themes or meanings. Fantasy and wilfulness continue to the end. When the main conflict is over, the scene is set in a garden graced with moonlight and the gentle throb of music, and the talk is of heavenly harmony and ancient loves; into this garden walk the romantic leads and, in a moment, they fall to wrangling and talk of cuckoldry and unfaithfulness. The play ends with a bawdy joke about the chastity of a waiting-woman.

Shakespeare seems to have been quite unembarrassed about the improbabilities of his story. According to a sonnet prefixed to the first edition of *Il Pecorone*, it was written of fools, for fools, and by a fool, and yet *The Merchant* accentuates some of its improbabilities. Ansaldo's misfortunes depend on the loss of one vital ship; but Antonio's depend on the simultaneous loss of six. In *Il Pecorone*, the lady comes to Venice of her own accord, and has to contrive to get her legal judgement accepted; but Portia anticipates the Duke's request for her uncle's advice and has a full court waiting her arrival. This is almost in the spirit of an early version of the flesh-bond story in *Dolopathos*, where the lady is disguised by magic. Clearly Shakespeare was not concerned, at these points, to make his story credible in everyday terms. To Granville-Barker, the play was a "fairy tale", and he saw "no more reality in Shylock's bond and the Lord of Belmont's will than in Jack and the Beanstalk."[1]

There are some plays written only for entertainment, but despite its wilfulness, its fantasy, romance, and improbability, *The Merchant* is not generally considered to be such. It does entertain; the plot is exciting, the events colourful, the characters varied; the dialogue has strength, beauty, delicacy, raciness, humour; and the action develops with apparent artlessness. But it does more than entertain. The argument about usury (I. iii), the talk about friendship (III. iv), and the plea for mercy (IV. i) bring issues of great importance directly before the audience. And, more important, *The Merchant* is not merely a fairy tale in the colloquial sense of something strange, pretty, and remote; it is full of marvels, yet it is also full of human sentiment and passions. Shakespeare's dramatic skill has made all his strange creation real and lively in the theatre, and, while the play is on, the audience is implicated in Shylock's impassioned rhetoric and Portia's ardent advocacy.

In the words of Dr Johnson, "nothing can please many, and please long, but just representations of general nature", and, inevitably, critics have tried to explain what lies behind the delightful fantasy of *The Merchant of Venice*—why its fiction can be so absorbing, and its resolution so satisfying.

*   *   *

Mr Nevill Coghill saw *The Merchant* as a presentation, or "allegory", of "Justice and Mercy, of the Old Law and the New."[2] In this view, the trial scene, where Justice and Mercy are opposed, is the cardinal point of the play, and the suggestion that Shakespeare was here indebted to the medieval *Processus Belial*[3] is especially pertinent—this told how the Devil claimed mankind on the grounds of justice and the Blessed Virgin advocated and obtained mercy. The theme of justice in the trial scene is clear when Shylock demands his rights: "I stand for judgement,—answer, shall I have it?", "I stand here for law", and "My deeds upon my head! I crave the law" (IV. i. 103, 142, and 202).

But some critics see irony in Portia

singing the praises of mercy when she is about to insist that the Jew

---

1. *Prefaces*, 2nd series (1930), p. 67.

2. 'The Governing Idea', *Shakespeare Quarterly*, I (London, 1948), 9–17.

3. Cf. J. D. Rea, *P.Q.*, VIII (1929), 311–13. Shakespeare's use of medieval allegory is discussed in Sir Israel Gollancz, *Allegory and Mysticism in Shakespeare*, ed. A. W. Pollard (1931).

shall have the full rigours of justice according to the strict letter of
the law[1]

and in the eyes of modern law, Portia's conduct is very strange if not
reprehensible:

no sensible judge, who wishes to bring about a compromise, will
assure the party whom he wishes to persuade that he is certain of
success if he persists in his legal claim; and no fair judge could give
assurances of that kind knowing them to be false.[2]

From this point of view, *The Merchant of Venice* has been called the
"most ingenious satire on justice and courts of law in the literature
of the world."[3]

   But according to Mr Coghill, the trial must be viewed ideally or
allegorically; the plea for mercy is made absolutely and, when Shylock denies it, it is right that he who lived by the law should perish
by the law. The verbal trick is merely "a device to turn the tables
and to show justice in the posture of a suppliant before mercy."[4] It
is perhaps significant that Shakespeare has added a

third and quite new point to o'ertop the quibbles—that old
Venetian law condemns to death and confiscation of goods the
alien who plots against the life of a citizen of Venice.[5]

This is not found in any of the probable sources of the play and may
have been added to emphasize that Shylock is defeated on his own
grounds of law and justice. Finally, Shylock is compelled to become
a Christian—there is still the possibility of mercy for him, "even if
the way of mercy is a hard way." The last act crowns all; the scene
returns to Belmont

to find Lorenzo and Jessica, Jew and Christian, Old Law and New,
united in love; and their talk is of music, Shakespeare's recurrent
symbol of harmony.[6]

   Mr Coghill's interpretation gives significance to the opposition
of Shylock and Portia in the trial scene, but it is difficult to see how
it provides a "governing idea" for the whole play. Shylock as a
usurer demanding his rights, and as an old father curtailing the
freedom of his daughter are well enough, but the half-comic elements of his part in the trial[7] scene—tantalizing the Christians by ex-

   1. J. Palmer, *Comic Characters of Shakespeare* (1946), p. 87. See also H. B. Charlton, *op. cit.*, p. 159.
   2. Lord Normand, *Univ. of Edinburgh Journal*, x (1939), 44.
   3. H. Sinsheimer, *Shylock* (1947), p. 139.   4. N. Coghill, *op. cit.*, p. 15.
   5. T. M. Parrott, *op. cit.*, p. 139.   6. N. Coghill, *op. cit.*, pp. 16 and 17.
   7. These are pointed out by E. E. Stoll, *op. cit.*, p. 319, and J. Palmer, *op. cit.*,
p. 87.

plaining, yet not explaining, his motives, looking to see if a surgeon
is mentioned in the bond, encouraging the judge who is going to
condemn him, asking for his money back as soon as it is evident that
he cannot have the flesh, and incurring Gratiano's gibes—all this
may be in the tradition of the medieval half-comic Devil, but seems
to have little relevance to justice or the Old Law. Nor does the
story of Portia and Bassanio or the bawdy talk of the last act seem
to be apposite. Mercy may be a sufficient significance or "intend-
ment" for Portia in the trial scene, but it does not illuminate much
of the action at Belmont.

A different "governing idea" or theme is suggested by the casket
scenes—that of appearance and reality. It is treated directly in
Bassanio's deliberation on the caskets, "So may the outward shows
be least themselves" (III. ii. 73), and in the scrolls contained in the
caskets: "All that glisters is not gold" (II. vii. 65), "There be fools
alive . . . Silver'd o'er" (II. ix. 68–9), and "You that choose not by
the view" (III. ii. 131). Bassanio rightly loves because he loves more
than outward show. The story of the bond also illustrates this
theme; Shylock's justification of usury calls forth the comment,"O
what a goodly outside falsehood hath!" (I. iii. 97), and the bond
itself provokes "I like not fair terms, and a villain's mind" (I. iii.
175). The theme is repeated in many details. Jessica is a Jew, but in
her heart the true lover of a Christian: "though I am a daughter to
his blood I am not to his manners" (II. iii. 18–19). Launcelot's
proof that the fiend gives kinder counsel than his conscience, and
his father's recognition that he is his true son also bear indirectly on
the theme. The misunderstanding arising from the interchange of
rings is a comic statement too, for despite appearances Bassanio is
really true to Portia.[1] This theme was often in Shakespeare's mind
about the time that he wrote *The Merchant*; Prince Hal, for instance,
seems to be a wastrel, Hamlet probes the "seeming" of Claudius,
and Claudio is deceived by an appearance of guilt in Hero.[2] But in
The Merchant, as elsewhere, it is not the whole meaning of the play,
the explanation of the deep satisfaction which can derive from
watching a performance. The individual characters of Shylock and
Portia do not seem relevant to it,[3] nor does it greatly increase the
significance of the trial scene.

*   *   *

1. This point was made by C. B. Graham, *S.Q.*, IV (1953), 150.

2. Cf., for example, *2 H 4*, v. ii. 125–9; *Ham.*, III. ii. 89–92; and *Ado*, IV. i.
101–5.

3. Shylock's hypocrisy has been emphasized by P. N. Siegel (*Studies in Shakespeare* (Univ. of Miami, 1953), pp. 129–38).

Many critics have found a theme in the contrast between Venice and Belmont. Professor Parrott, for example, differentiated two attitudes to wealth:

To Shylock money is merely a means to breed more money . . . [but to Portia] money is simply a means to promote the good life, to keep open house with music and entertainment for her guests, to spend without hesitation or calculation in order to rescue "noble amity" from threatening danger.[1]

Professor C. S. Lewis had earlier seen a similar contrast between the values of Shylock and Bassanio. Commenting on Bassanio's admission "all the wealth I had Ran in my veins" (III. ii. 253–4) he emphasized the contrast

between the crimson and organic wealth in his veins, the medium of nobility and fecundity, and the cold, mineral wealth in Shylock's counting-house.[2]

Miss Bradbrook has distinguished two contracts:

The pledge and bond of matrimony—which is both a sacrament and a legal contract—is set against the bond of the Jew and Antonio's pledge of his flesh.[3]

The contrast can be stated in more general terms, as by Mr J. W. Lever: on the one hand there is love which "comprehends the generous give and take of emotion, the free spending of nature's bounty, and the increase of progeny through marriage" and on the other, usury, which is the "negation of friendship and community."[4] Sir E. K. Chambers has put it very simply and comprehensively as a conflict between the "opposing principles of Love and Hate": Shylock whetting his knife upon his soul stands for the principle of Hate, and Antonio and Portia between them embody Love.[5]

The contrast between Venice and Belmont can be seen in small details of action and dialogue as well as in the wider concepts. For example, the long argument about usury, which is not found in any of the probable sources, gains in significance because it is between Shylock, the usurer of Venice, and Antonio who, in his friendship for Bassanio, maintains the ideals of Belmont. To Sir Thomas Wilson, friendship and usury were clearly opposed:

1. *Op. cit.*, p. 143.
2. 'Hamlet: the Prince or the Poem', *Proceedings of the British Academy* (1942), p. 146. See also, Max Plowman, *Adelphi*, II (1931), 508–13.
3. *Op. cit.*, p. 177.   4. *S.Q.*, III (1952), 383.
5. *Shakespeare: a Survey* (1925), pp. 112–15.

God ordeyned lending for maintenaunce of amitye, and declaration of loue, betwixt man and man: whereas now lending is vsed
for pryuate benefit and oppression, & so no charitie is vsed at all.[1]

This contrast was commonly made and Shakespeare could relate
Shylock and Antonio in a few words:

> If thou wilt lend this money, lend it not
> As to thy friends, for when did friendship take
> A breed for barren metal of his friend?
> But lend it rather to thine enemy, ... (I. iii. 127–30)

Shylock and usury are also contrasted with Portia, the embodi-
ment of love. Henry Smith's *Examination of Usury* (1591) makes this
distinction:

Loue seeketh not her owne, but vsurie seeketh anothers which is not her
owne,   (Sig. A5)

and again:

Charitie reioyceth to communicate her goods to other [men], and
Vsurie reioyceth to gather other mens goods to her selfe.   (A7)

Or in R. Wilson's *Moral of the Three Lords* (1590), Pomp says to
Usury:

you haue done Lady *Lucre* good seruice you say, but it was against
God and *Conscience* you did it, neither euer in your life did ye anie
thing for *Loue*.   (H2ᵛ)

But although love and usury were so contrasted, there were also
similarities between them, and usury was used as a paradoxical
image of love. So when Antony leaves Cleopatra, he promises "my
full heart Remains in use with you,"[2] and Spenser in *Epithalamion*
(1595) promises the bride:

> the wished day is come at last,
> That shall, for all the paynes and sorrowes past,
> Pay to her usury of long delight. (ll. 31–3)

Shakespeare used this comparison on several occasions,[3] but most
explicitly in the *Sonnets*. In *Sonnet* IV he asks:

> Profitless usurer, why dost thou use
> So great a sum of sums, yet canst not live?
> For having traffic with thyself alone,
> Thou of thyself thy sweet self dost deceive.

1. *Discourse*, N7.   2. *Ant.*,I. iii. 43–4.
3. Cf. *John*,III. iii. 21–2; *Rom.*,III. iii. 122–5; *Meas.*,III. ii. 6–11; *All's W.*,I. i.
139–45 and 160–3; and *Tim.*,II. ii. 61–2 and 103–8.

and in *Sonnet* VI:

> That use is not forbidden usury
> Which happies those that pay the willing loan.

Love was often spoken of in commercial terms,[1] and in these sonnets, Shakespeare sees it as a usury, where those who give and those
who receive are happy and free agents, and where the multiplica-
tion of happiness is a natural interest.

So there is a usury in Belmont. "In Belmont is a lady richly left"
(I. i. 161) are the first words spoken of Portia, and

> her sunny locks
> Hang on her temples like a golden fleece. (I. i. 169-70)

The golden fleece was a symbol of the fortunes for which merchants
ventured; in Lyly's *Euphues and his England* (1580), Callimachus,
left without money by his rich father, determined:

to seeke aduentures in straunge lands, and either to fetch the
golden fleece by trauaile, or susteine the force of Fortune[2]

and Sir Francis Drake returning from his voyage round the world
was said to have brought back with him "his goulden fleece".[3]
That the phrase was used of merchants' ventures, gives point to
Gratiano's boast:

> what's the news from Venice?
> How doth that royal merchant good Antonio?
> I know he will be glad of our success,
> We are the Jasons, we have won the fleece.
>   (III. ii. 237-40)

The laws which govern the usury of Belmont are explained in the
mottoes on the caskets. It is not enough merely to "desire" it, nor
can one stand upon one's rights to "get as much as [one] deserves"
—as Shylock does in the trial scene. To win in this venture, one
must "give and hazard". To the ordinary man, this is nonsense:
"men that hazard all Do it in hope of fair advantages" (II. vii. 18-
19)—the remark is especially pertinent, for in Venice "advantage"
denotes usury:

> Me thoughts you said, you neither lend nor borrow
> Upon advantage. (I. iii. 64-5)

The commercial terminology of Venice is often used in Belmont,

---

1. Cf., for example, *Rom.*, II. ii. 84, and III. ii. 26-7.   2. *Wks*, II. 21.
3. G. Whitney, *Emblems* (1586), C2. Steevens quoted a similar reference to
Frobisher (1577).

and it accentuates the parallel and the contrast between the two usuries. In Venice, Antonio says:

> Shylock, albeit I neither lend nor borrow
> By taking nor by giving of *excess*, . . .   (I. iii. 56–7)

and when Bassanio has chosen rightly, Portia exclaims:

> O love be moderate, allay thy extasy,
> In measure rain thy joy, scant this *excess*!
> I feel too much thy blessing, make it less
> For fear I surfeit. (III. ii. 111–14)

So love is prodigal in its natural interest or usury of blessing.

Consciously or unconsciously, the contrast was constantly in Shakespeare's mind when he wrote the speeches which bring the two lovers together. They do not talk in terms of the stars, but in terms of commerce. From the beginning Bassanio has had a mind presaging "thrift" (I. i. 175), and when he chooses rightly, and the scroll instructs him to claim his lady, he says:

> A gentle scroll: fair lady, by your leave,
> I come by note to give, and to receive. (III. ii. 139–40)

To "come by note" meant to present one's bill, or I.O.U.: he has "ventured" all and can now claim his "fortune". But he is to give as well; in the commerce of Belmont, every bill implies both giving *and* receiving. He stands half disbelieving his good fortune:

> As doubtful whether what I see be true,
> Until confirm'd, sign'd, ratified by you (ll. 147–8)

—that is, until the transaction has been formally completed. Portia answers in similar terms. For Bassanio's sake, she wishes to be:

> A thousand times more fair, ten thousand times more
>   rich,
> That only to stand high in your *account*,
> I might in virtues, beauties, livings, friends
> *Exceed account:* (ll. 154–7)

The commercial terms are found throughout Portia's speech: "the full sum of me" (l. 157), "to term in gross" (l. 158), and finally,

> Myself, and what is mine, to you and yours
> Is now *converted*. (ll. 166–7)

Her possessions and herself are "converted" to her lord's possession, and the "bargain of [their] faith" (l. 193) is ratified with the pledge of a ring.

So the transactions of Belmont and Venice are compared and contrasted, and the main theme of the play is stated. When Portia and Shylock face each other in the trial scene, they are representatives not only of justice and mercy, but also of possessiveness and generosity, of those who get as much as they deserve and those who, for love, will give and hazard all they have. Described in these terms, the play may sound rigorously formal, and the outcome of the trial scene appear undramatically inevitable. But Shakespeare has not contrived a simple opposition of black and white. The conflict cannot be watched dispassionately and the villain consigned to punishment without compunction. An audience is made to feel with Shylock, as well as against him; it is made to realize the cost of victory as well as its joys.

The recognition of the contrast between the wealth, or usury, of Belmont and Venice illuminates many details in the play. For instance, Portia's assertion "Since you are dear bought, I will love you dear" (III. ii. 312), which Pope relegated to the foot of the page as unworthy of Shakespeare, is no longer a cold calculation, but a joyful acknowledgement of the pleasures of giving for love. And it becomes natural for Portia to exceed "customary bounty" (III. iv. 9), and for her mind to be no "more mercenary" than to be satisfied with doing deeds of mercy (IV. i. 414). When Antonio says "I once did lend my body for his wealth" (V. i. 249), he seems to allude not only to "health and wealth", but to all the wealth of Belmont. Jessica and her "unthrift love" (V. i. 16) amply earn their part in the story, squandering in a night the Venetian wealth they have stolen, and finding peace and harmony at Belmont. Launcelot, too, Shylock's "unthrifty knave" (I. iii. 172), finds a new master to receive his father's gift of doves, and counts it a fine preferment to leave

> a rich Jew's service, to become
> The follower of so poor a gentleman. (II. ii. 140–1)

There is wisdom in his "parting" of the old proverb: Bassanio has the "grace of God", and Shylock has "enough" (II. ii. 143–4).

The harmony of the last act obviously has its rightful place after the struggle of the trial scene. But the interchange of rings and the bawdy talk are also significant, for the transaction of Belmont is not complete until the very end of the play. The story of Bassanio and Portia has been left with Portia committing her spirit and possessions to Bassanio:

> to be directed,
> As from her lord, her governor, her king. (III. ii. 164–5)

The contract of love is not so simple as that. The game of the rings is needed to remind Bassanio (and the audience) that Portia freed his friend. Bassanio is still indebted and will always be indebted, and Portia has still more to give. Love is not like merchandise; it is not simply a question of possessor and possessed. And the talk of unfaithfulness and cuckoldry which arises from the misunderstandings is a light-hearted reminder that, in one sense, the usury of love has to be possessed and guarded, even though it is free and belongs exclusively to neither one of those who made the contract. Like all venturers, those who deal in love have to be watchful; so Gratiano finishes the play:

> Well, while I live, I'll fear no other thing
> So sore, as keeping safe Nerissa's ring. (v. i. 306–7)

Portia and Bassanio are not left on the "beautiful mountain" in a castle of romance; they are going to live together, like Gratiano and Nerissa, like any two lovers.

So *The Merchant of Venice* dances to its conclusion, its many elements mingling together joyfully. Perhaps when the dance is in progress, it is undesirable to look too closely for a pattern. But the dance does satisfy, and it is worth while trying to find out why. Shall we say it is a play about give and take?—about conundrums such as the more you give, the more you get, or, to him that hath shall be given, and from him that hath not, shall be taken away even that which he hath? The two parts of the play are linked by these problems: Portia is the golden fleece, the merchants venture and hazard as any lover, the caskets deal all in value, the bond and the rings are pledges of possession. In the scramble of give and take, when appearance and reality are hard to distinguish, one thing seems certain: that giving is the most important part—giving prodigally, without thought for the taking.[1]

---

1. For a further discussion of how this idea informed Shakespeare's writing, both in this comedy and in other plays, see J. R. Brown, *Shakespeare and his Comedies* (1957), chapters 3, 6, and 7.

THE MERCHANT
OF VENICE

DRAMATIS PERSONÆ

THE DUKE OF VENICE.
THE PRINCE OF MOROCCO, } *suitors to Portia.*
THE PRINCE OF ARRAGON, }
ANTONIO, *a Merchant of Venice.*
BASSANIO, *his friend, and suitor to Portia.*
GRATIANO, }
SALERIO, } *friends to Antonio and Bassanio.*
SOLANIO, }
LORENZO, *in love with Jessica.*
SHYLOCK, *a Jew.*
TUBAL, *a Jew, his friend.*
LAUNCELOT GOBBO, *a clown, servant to Shylock.*
OLD GOBBO, *father to Launcelot.*
LEONARDO, *servant to Bassanio.*
BALTHAZAR, } *servants to Portia.*
STEPHANO, }

PORTIA, *an heiress, of Belmont.*
NERISSA, *her waiting-woman.*
JESSICA, *daughter to Shylock.*

Magnificoes of Venice, Officers of the Court of Justice, a Gaoler, Servants and other Attendants.

SCENE: *Venice, and Portia's house at Belmont.*

DRAMATIS PERSONÆ] first listed in Q3.

SALERIO, . . . SOLANIO] Early editors who thought that Q2 was the first edition (cf. Introduction, p. xviii), listed three characters, Salanio, Salarino, and Salerio. Prof. J. D. Wilson, basing his text on Q1, was the first to suggest the arrangement adopted here (*N.C.S.*, pp. 100–4). *Solanio* is regular in Q1, except for the entries at I. i and II. iv, and a speech prefix at I. i. 15, where "Salanio" (an easy misreading) is found. *Salerio* is authenticated in the verse dialogue and stage direction of III. ii, and in the speech prefixes of IV. i. 15 and 107. *Salerio* in III. ii is a "messenger from Venice" and the knowledge he shows of Antonio's affairs suggests that he is identical with "Salarino" or "Salerino" of earlier stage directions and "Salari" and "Saleri" of some speech prefixes. Possibly the compositors (or a scribe, as Prof. Wilson thought) expanded Shakespeare's "Salario" or "Salerio" mistaking the dot of an *i* for a mark of abbreviation. Or, perhaps, Shakespeare modified the name when he had occasion to use it in verse. In either

2

case it is simplest to regularize as *Salerio*.

A minor confusion of Salerio and Solanio is discussed in a note on the entry direction for III. iii.

SHYLOCK] The origin of the name is obscure: (1) M. A. Lower (*N. & Q.*, i (1850), 184) suggested that it might be a form of *Shilôh* of *Genesis*, xlix. 10, which R. F. H[errey]'s *Two . . . Concordances* (1578) glossed as "dissoluing, or . . . mocked or deceiuing" (quoted E. N. Alder, *Jewish Forum*, xvi (1933), 25–32); (2) Sir Israel Gollancz (*A Book of Homage* (1916), pp. 171–2) thought it might have been culled from Joseph ben Gorion's *History . . . of the Jews' Commonwealth* (tr. 1558) where "Schiloch" is the name of a Babylonian; (3) Sir Israel also thought there might be an incorrect association with "Shallach", Hebrew for cormorant, which was often used of usurers (see, for example, Introduction, p. xxiv and Appendix III, p. 160); (4) J. L. Cardozo (*The Contemporary Jew in Elizabethan Drama* (1925), p. 219) suggested *Shylock* was a form of *Shelaḥ* (*Genesis*, x. 24), the father of Eber (i.e., Hebrew); and (5) N. Nathan (*S.A.B.*, xxiii (1948), 152) quoted *O.E.D.*, "Shullock": "*Obs.* exc. *dial* . . . [Of obscure origin: cf. dial. *shallock*, *shollock* vb., to idle about, to slouch.] Used as a term of contempt."

M. A. Lower (*op. cit.*) found "Richard Shylok" as a proper name at Hoo, Sussex, in 1435.

News from Rome (1606) contains "certaine prophecies of a Iew . . . called Caleb Shilocke, prognosticating many strange accidents, which shall happen the following yeere, 1607." Farmer originally drew attention to a ballad based on this book (Pepys, 1. 38): Halliwell showed that it was probably printed "many years" before 1606 and then re-issued, and M. A. Shaaber (*N. & Q.*, cxcv (1950), 236) quoted a reference in Nashe's *Have with You to Saffron-Walden* (1596) to "the newes of the Iewes rising vp in armes to take in the Land of promise" (*Wks*, iii. 74) which may well allude to an earlier version of *News from Rome*.

J. L. Cardozo (*op. cit.*, pp. 223–4) thought Shylock should be pronounced with a short *i*, to make a pun of Launcelot's "when I shun Scylla (your father), . . ." (III. v. 14–15).

TUBAL] taken with Chus (III. ii. 284), from *Genesis*, x. 2 and 6; R. F. H. (see previous note) glossed "borne worldly or confusion or slaunder."

GOBBO] In Q and F, this form occurs only in a stage direction and speech prefixes for Old Gobbo; in the dialogue, the form "Iobbe" is used (II. ii. 3 ff.) which is either a misreading of Gobbo, or an Italianized form of Job (cf. Introduction, p. xxii).

JESSICA] probably from *Genesis*, xi. 29 (cf. note on *Tubal* above); in some early Bibles the form was Iesca. The Hebrew signifies spy or looker-out (so Elze, *Essays*, tr. 1874, p. 282).

THE MERCHANT OF VENICE

[ACT I]

[SCENE I.—*Venice.*]

Enter ANTONIO, SALERIO, *and* SOLANIO.

Ant. In sooth I know not why I am so sad,
    It wearies me, you say it wearies you;
    But how I caught it, found it, or came by it,
    What stuff 'tis made of, whereof it is born,
    I am to learn: 5
    And such a want-wit sadness makes of me,
    That I have much ado to know myself.
Sal. Your mind is tossing on the ocean,

ACT I

Scene I

Act I] *om. Q;* Actus primus *F.*   Scene I] *Rowe; om. Q, F.*   *Venice*] *om. Q, F;
a Street in Venice Theobald.*   Salerio] *N.C.S.;* Salaryno *Q, F;* Solarino *F3;*
Salerino *Capell.*   Solanio] *Capell;* Salanio *Q, F.*   5–6. I . . . me] *as Q3; one
line Q, F.*   8. Sal.] *F; Salarino. Q.*

1. *In . . . sad*] Schücking thought this
"unexplained" melancholy was a relic
of an earlier version of the play (*Character Problems* (1922), p. 171) but,
since Antonio knows about Portia (cf.
ll. 119–21) the imminent parting with
Bassanio, his friend, is ample motive
for it. "Amity", or friendship, is an
important theme in the play (cf. Introduction, pp. xlv–xlvi). Shakespeare
may have used this oblique beginning
for the theme in order to arouse interest and speculation in the audience;
the motive for the melancholy becomes clear as soon as Antonio and
Bassanio are left alone (l. 119).

It was usual to be unaware of the
cause of one's melancholy (cf. *Cym.*, I.

vi. 61–3), or at least to be secretive
about it (cf. L. Babb, *The Elizabethan
Malady* (1951), pp. 137 and 159).
K. B. Danks (*N. & Q.*, n.s., I (1954),
111) related Antonio's melancholy to
other instances of dramatic foreboding
in Shakespeare.

5. *I . . . learn*] i.e., I am ignorant (cf.
3 H 6, IV. iv. 2). *N.C.S.* thought the
short line was a sign of revision in the
playhouse, but it may imply a pause in
delivery, indicative of Antonio's embarrassment in speaking of his melancholy. In any case an irregular short
line is readily explained as due to foul-
paper copy (cf. Intro., pp. xiv–xviii).

7. *know myself*] Cf. Ascham, *Toxophilus* (1545), *Eng. Wks* (1904), p. 111:

There where your argosies with portly sail
Like signiors and rich burghers on the flood,   10
Or as it were the pageants of the sea,
Do overpeer the petty traffickers
That cur'sy to them (do them reverence)
As they fly by them with their woven wings.

Sol. Believe me sir, had I such venture forth,   15
The better part of my affections would
Be with my hopes abroad. I should be still
Plucking the grass to know where sits the wind,
Piring in maps for ports, and piers and roads:
And every object that might make me fear   20
Misfortune to my ventures, out of doubt
Would make me sad.

---

10. on] *Q, F;* of *Capell conj., Var. '93.*   13. cur'sy] *Q;* curtsie *F;* courtesy *Hudson.*   15. *Sol.*] *Salanio. Q; Salar. F; Sola. F3.*   venture] *Q, F;* ventures *Hanmer.*   19. Piring] *Q;* Piering *Q2;* Peering *F;* Prying *Q3.*

"that wise prouerbe of Apollo, *Knowe thy selfe*: that is to saye, learne to knowe what thou arte able, fitte, and apte vnto, and folowe that." It is common in Shakespeare, e.g., *Ant.,* II. ii. 89–91.

9. *argosies*] merchant ships from Ragusa or Venice; an adaptation from It. (cf. *O.E.D.*).

portly sail] *portly* in its modern sense of corpulent or swollen would fit the context (cf. *MND.,* II. i. 128–9), but Shakespeare used it so only of Falstaff (*Wiv.,* I. iii. 69, and *1 H 4,* II. iv. 464). The older sense of stately, majestic is probably required (cf. I. i. 124, and III. ii. 280). If *sail* means either a group of ships (cf. *Per.,* I. iv. 61) or the act of sailing (cf. *Oth.,* v. ii. 268), the phrase completes the comparison of l. 13; Antonio's ships sail majestically past lesser vessels.

11. *pageants*] an allusion to the large machines shaped like castles, ships, giants, etc., that were drawn about the streets in ancient shows or pageants (so Douce, i. 250). The shows sometimes took place on the Thames at London (cf. *Elizabethan Stage,* I. 138–9).

12. *overpeer*] look down upon. Pooler compared Greene's description of the Armada: "seeing our ships like little Pinasses, and their huge barkes built like Castles, overpeering ours" (*Wks,* v. 280). There may be a pun on peer of the realm, suggested by *signiors* and *burghers.*

13. *cur'sy*] a common variant of curtsy; both forms derive from courtesy (so *O.E.D.*). The simile is probably suggested by the rocking of the *petty traffickers* caused by the wake of the passing argosies (so Furness).

15. *venture*] a commercial enterprise involving risk; cf. I. iii. 18–23.

17. *still*] continually.

18. *Plucking*] Johnson quoted Ascham, *Toxophilus* (1545), *Eng. Wks* (1904), p. 114: "I toke a fether or a lytle lyght grasse and so well as I coulde, learned how the wynd stoode."

19. *Piring*] related to verbs pry and peer, the latter unrecorded before 1590 (so *O.E.D.*); it was listed in A. E. Baker, *Glossary of Northamptonshire Words and Phrases* (1854). Q's spelling avoids the jingle with *piers.*

roads] anchorages, or "open harbour[s]" (Cotgrave, *rade*).

Sal.   My wind cooling my broth,
Would blow me to an ague when I thought
What harm a wind too great might do at sea.
I should not see the sandy hour-glass run   25
But I should think of shallows and of flats,
And see my wealthy Andrew dock'd in sand
Vailing her high top lower than her ribs
To kiss her burial; should I go to church
And see the holy edifice of stone   30
And not bethink me straight of dangerous rocks,
Which touching but my gentle vessel's side
Would scatter all her spices on the stream,
Enrobe the roaring waters with my silks,
And in a word, but even now worth this,   35
And now worth nothing? Shall I have the thought
To think on this, and shall I lack the thought
That such a thing bechanc'd would make me sad?
But tell not me, I know Antonio
Is sad to think upon his merchandise.   40
Ant. Believe me no, I thank my fortune for it—
My ventures are not in one bottom trusted,
Nor to one place; nor is my whole estate
Upon the fortune of this present year:
Therefore my merchandise makes me not sad.   45

22. *Sal.*] *F; Salar. Q*.   27. see] *Q, F;* see ! *Keightley conj.*   27. Andrew] *italic Q, F;* Andrew's *Collier conj.*   dock'd] *Rowe;* docks *Q, F;* decks *Collier conj., Delius;* dock *Keightley.*   28. high top] *Q, F; hyphened Var. '93.*   36. nothing?] *Q2;* nothing. *Q, F.*

26. *flats*] shoals, level tracts of sand covered by shallow water; cf. III. i. 5.

27. *Andrew*] the name of a Spanish galleon captured at Cadiz in 1596; cf. Introduction, pp. xxv–xxvii.

28–9. *Vailing . . . burial*] Steevens quoted Bullokar, *English Expositor* (1616): "to vail" is to "putte off the hatt, to strike saile, to giue signe of submission." There also seems to be an allusion to the phrase "to kiss the ground" in token of homage, as in *Mac.*, v. viii. 28; *burial*, or place of burial (cf. *Ham.*, v. i. 28), is substituted for "ground". The nautical

phrase is thus used in an extravagantly exaggerated form.

33–4. *spices . . . silks*] So Barabas' argosy from Alexandria was "Loaden with spice and silks" (*Jew of Malta*, I. i. 45, quoted Pooler).

35–6. *but . . . nothing*] at this moment worth all this concern, at the next, worth nothing. Or possibly *this* refers to the value of the cargo.

42–5. *My . . . sad*] "Antonio speaks more freely to Bassanio in private" (Pooler; cf. ll. 177–9).

42. *bottom*] hold, ship. For proverb, "Venture not all in one bottom" (Tilley, A209), see *1 H 6*, IV. vi. 32–3.

Sol. Why then you are in love.
Ant.   Fie, fie!
Sol. Not in love neither: then let us say you are sad
    Because you are not merry; and 'twere as easy
    For you to laugh and leap, and say you are merry
    Because you are not sad. Now by two-headed Janus,   50
    Nature hath fram'd strange fellows in her time:
    Some that will evermore peep through their eyes,
    And laugh like parrots at a bagpiper:
    And other of such vinegar aspect,
    That they'll not show their teeth in way of smile   55
    Though Nestor swear the jest be laughable.

    Enter BASSANIO, LORENZO, *and* GRATIANO.

    Here comes Bassanio your most noble kinsman,
    Gratiano, and Lorenzo. Fare ye well,
    We leave you now with better company.
Sal. I would have stay'd till I had made you merry,   60

46. *Sol.*] Sola. *Q*, *F*; *Salar. Q2*.   fie!] fie. *Q*, *F*.   47. *Sol.*] Sola. *Q*, *F*; *Salar, Q2*.   neither:] *Q*, *F*; neither? *Q2*.   let us] *Q*, *F*; let's *Pope*.   you are] *Q*, *F*; you're *Pope*.   48. and] *Q*, *F*; om. *Pope*.   49. you are] *Q*, *F*; you're *Pope*.   50. Because you are] *Q*, *F*; 'Cause you're *Hanmer*.   53. bagpiper:] bagpyper. *Q*, *F*.   54. other] *Q*, *F*; others *Pope*.   56. S.D.] *as Q*, *F*; *after l. 64 Dyce.*   57. Here] *N.C.S.*; *Sola.* Here *Q*, *F*; *Salan.* Here *Q2*.   Here . . . kinsman] *as Q*; . . . Bassanio, / Your . . . *F*.   58. Fare ye well] *Q3*; Faryewell *Q*, *F*; Fare you well *Capell*.   60. *Sal.*] Sala. *Q*, *F*; *Salar. Q2*; *Sola. F3*.

46. *Fie, fie*] *N.C.S.* thought the copy might have read "Anth. o no" which was read by the compositor as "Anthonio". But the hesitation suggested by the incomplete decasyllabic and the ambiguous nature of Antonio's answer (it is an exclamation of reproach rather than a clear negative) might indicate that Solanio has got close to the real cause of the melancholy; cf. l. 1, note, and IV. i. 273, note.

47–8. *sad . . . merry*] proverbial; cf. *Gent.*, IV. ii. 26–9 and Tilley, S14.

50. *Janus*] an appropriate god to swear by; one of his faces was smiling, the other frowning.

52. *peep*] as "in laughing, when the eyes appear half shut" (Warburton).

53. *laugh . . . bagpiper*] The parrot was proverbially foolish (cf. III. v. 42–3,

and *Oth.*, II. iii. 281) and the bagpipe gave a melancholy sound (cf. *1 H 4*, I. ii. 86–7); the contrast is between those who foolishly laugh at what is melancholy and those who will not smile even when gravity, personified by Nestor, recommends the joke.

54. *other*] an old plural, as in *2 H 6*, II. i. 176.

aspect] usually accented on the second syllable; cf. II. i. 8.

57. *kinsman*] The relationship is not mentioned elsewhere; in *Il Pecorone* (Appendix I) Ansaldo is several times referred to as Giannetto's *nonno*.

60. *I . . . merry*] Antonio's friends are not talking idly or frivolously, they are trying to talk him out of his melancholy; according to Burton (*Anatomy*, ed. Shilleto, ii. 132) no cure is so effec-

    If worthier friends had not prevented me.

Ant. Your worth is very dear in my regard.

    I take it your own business calls on you,

    And you embrace th'occasion to depart.

Sal. Good morrow my good lords.   65

Bass. Good signiors both when shall we laugh? say, when?

    You grow exceeding strange: must it be so?

Sal. We'll make our leisures to attend on yours.

              Exeunt Salerio, and Solanio.

Lor. My Lord Bassanio, since you have found Antonio

    We two will leave you, but at dinner-time   70

    I pray you have in mind where we must meet.

Bass. I will not fail you.

Gra. You look not well Signior Antonio,

    You have too much respect upon the world:

    They lose it that do buy it with much care,—   75

    Believe me you are marvellously chang'd.

Ant. I hold the world but as the world Gratiano,

    A stage, where every man must play a part,

    And mine a sad one.

65. *Sal.*] *Q, F; Salar. Q2.*   **68.** *Sal.*] *Q, F; Salar. Q2.*   S.D.] *as Q, F; after you (l. 72) Rowe.*   *Salerio*] *N.C.S.; Salarino Q, F; Solarino F4.*   *Solanio*] *Q, F; Salanio Q2.*   69. *Lor.*] *Q, F; Sola. Rowe.*   you have] *Q, F;* you've *Pope.*   72.] S.D., *Exit (at end of line) Q2.*   75. lose] loose *Q, F.*   79. mine] *Q, F;* mine's *Hanmer.*

tive as "a cup of strong drink, mirth, musick, and merry company."

61. *prevented*] forestalled.

66. *laugh*] i.e., have a merry meeting (so Verity).

67. *strange*] distant, unfriendly; cf. *Sonn.*, xlix. 5. In the context it may be a polite exaggeration; Pooler compared Greene, *Mamillia (c.* 1583), *Wks,* ii. 217: "*Pharicles* seeing them in earnest talke . . . began to withdraw himselfe out of the garden. . . What Master *Pharicles*, quoth he, is it the fashion in Padua to be so strange with your frendes . . . ?"

70. *We . . . you*] A hint thrown away on Gratiano (so Pooler); every one except Gratiano seems aware that it is tactful to leave Antonio and Bassanio together.

74. *You . . . upon*] You pay too much regard to; for *upon*, cf. Abbott, ¶191.

75. *They...care*] Cf. *Matthew,* xvi. 25. *lose*] Q's "loose" was a variant spelling.

77. *I . . . world*] Gratiano has made substantially the same charge as Salerio and Solanio; Antonio answers that he gives no more thought to the affairs of the world than its transitoriness warrants. Or possibly, he means I only hold the affairs of the world as all the world holds them; cf. iv. i. 17. He gives a quite different impression to Solanio (cf. ii. viii. 50).

78. *A stage*] a commonplace (cf. Tilley, W882); the *locus classicus* is *AYL.,* ii. vii. 139–66.

79. *sad*] Furness glossed this as "grave", but Antonio's earlier use

Gra.   Let me play the fool,
          With mirth and laughter let old wrinkles come,   80
          And let my liver rather heat with wine
          Than my heart cool with mortifying groans.
          Why should a man whose blood is warm within,
          Sit like his grandsire, cut in alablaster?
          Sleep when he wakes? and creep into the jaundice   85
          By being peevish? I tell thee what Antonio,
          (I love thee, and 'tis my love that speaks):
          There are a sort of men whose visages
          Do cream and mantle like a standing pond,
          And do a wilful stillness entertain,   90
          With purpose to be dress'd in an opinion
          Of wisdom, gravity, profound conceit,
          As who should say, "I am Sir Oracle,

84. alablaster] *Q, F;* Alabaster *Pope.*   87. 'tis] *Q;* it is *F.*   93. Sir] *Pope;*
Sir *Q;* sir an *F.*

(I. i. 1–11) suggests that "melancholy" is the more appropriate meaning.

play the fool] simply "act foolishly", but here it punningly continues Antonio's comparison, hence "play the fool's part". Gratiano was the traditional name for the comic doctor in the Italian *Commedia dell'Arte.*

80. *With . . . come*] i.e., let mirth and laughter pucker the face and so bring about the wrinkles normally associated with old age; cf. the "wrinkle of a smile" (*Troil.,* I. i. 38). For *old* meaning characteristic of old age, Pooler compared *Tp.,* I. ii. 369, but it is just possible that the colloquial sense of plentiful, abundant is required, as in IV. ii. 15.

81–2. *let . . . groans*] Sighs and groans were thought to drain blood from the heart; Clarendon compared *MND.,* III. ii. 96–7: "pale of cheer,/With sighs of love, that costs the fresh blood dear."

84. *alablaster*] a common form of alabaster. The reference is to alabaster effigies in churches. The earliest known sitting effigy in England is dated 1605 (cf. Esdaile, *English Church Monuments* (1946), p. 54), so *sit* is prob-

ably used in the sense "to continue or remain, in a certain state" (*O.E.D.,* 7).

85. *wakes*] perhaps, stays awake for watching or revelry as in *Ham.,* I. iv. 8.

88. *sort*] considerable number, band; cf. *R 2,* IV. i. 246. Or, possibly, "kind"; cf. *Oth.,* III. iii. 416.

89. *cream and mantle*] gravity covers the face with a mask both pale and sour; cf. *Mac.,* v. iii. 11: "cream-faced loon", and *Lr.,* III. iv. 139: "the green mantle of the standing pool."

90. *do*] *a sort of men* is the subject of this verb.
wilful stillness] i.e., "obstinate silence" (Malone).
entertain] keep up, maintain.

91. *opinion*] reputation; cf. *1 H 4,* v. iv. 48.

92. *conceit*] understanding; cf. *AYL.,* v. ii. 48.

93. *As . . . say*] as much as to say; *O.E.D.* compared Fr. *comme qui dirait* (Should, 20e).
Sir Oracle] Cf. "Sir Prudence" (*Tp.,* II. i. 286), "Sir Smile" (*Wint.,* I. ii. 196), etc.

And when I ope my lips, let no dog bark."
O my Antonio, I do know of these   95
That therefore only are reputed wise
For saying nothing; when I am very sure
If they should speak, would almost damn those ears
Which (hearing them) would call their brothers fools,—
I'll tell thee more of this another time.   100
But fish not with this melancholy bait
For this fool gudgeon, this opinion:—
Come good Lorenzo,—fare ye well a while,
I'll end my exhortation after dinner.

Lor. Well, we will leave you then till dinner-time.   105
I must be one of these same dumb wise men,
For Gratiano never lets me speak.

Gra. Well keep me company but two years moe
Thou shalt not know the sound of thine own tongue.

Ant. Fare you well, I'll grow a talker for this gear. 110

---

95. Antonio,] *Q2, F;* Anthonio *Q.*   these] *Q, F;* those *Q2.*   97. when] *Q, F;* who *Rowe.*   I am] *Q, F;* I'm *Pope.*   98. would] *Q, F;* 'twould *Collier (ii).*
102. fool gudgeon] *Q, F;* fool's gudgeon *Pope;* fool-gudgeon *Malone.*   103. fare ye well] *Q3;* faryewell *Q, F;* farwell *Q2.*   108. moe] *Q, F;* more *Rowe.*
110. Fare you well] *Q, F;* Farwell *Q2.*

94. *let . . . bark*] It was proverbial that dogs barked at a person in disgrace or at a disadvantage; cf. *R 3,* I. i. 23, and *Lr.,* III. vi. 66.

96–7. *only . . . nothing*] Cf. *Proverbs,* xvii. 28: "Even a fool, when he holdeth his peace, is counted wise: and he that shutteth his lips is esteemed a man of understanding."

97. *when*] Rowe read "who" in order to provide a subject for *would* (l. 98), but no change is needed; the subject is understood, and the loose syntax is characteristic of Gratiano's garrulity.

98–9. *If . . . fools*] They are "such stupid Praters, that their Hearers cannot help calling them *Fools,* and so incur the Judgment denounc'd in the *Gospel*" (Theobald); cf. *Matthew,* v. 22.

101–2. *But . . . opinion*] *fool* is probably adjectival (so Schmidt), as in "fool multitude" (II. ix. 26). A *gudgeon*

is a very small fish used as bait; the word was used for a credulous fool, as in Lodge, *Wit's Misery* (1596), B2ᵛ: "his smooth tongue [is] a fit bait to catch Gudgeons; . . . [who feed] on the vanity of his tongue with the foolish credulity of their eares." So Gratiano says that melancholy should not be used as a bait to gain a reputation, which is founded on foolish credulity. "To swallow a gudgeon" meant to believe a false tale; this suggests an alternative reading, "don't use melancholy in order to create a reputation, which would only be a false tale for others to swallow."

104. *I'll . . . dinner*] an allusion to the practice of Puritan preachers (so Warburton).

108. *moe*] more in number (from O.E. *ma*).

110. *gear*] "a colloquial expression perhaps of no very determinate im-

Gra. Thanks i'faith, for silence is only commendable
In a neat's tongue dried, and a maid not vendible.
                                    Exeunt [Gratiano and Lorenzo].
Ant. It is that anything now.
Bass. Gratiano speaks an infinite deal of nothing (more
than any man in all Venice), his reasons are as two   115
grains of wheat hid in two bushels of chaff: you
shall seek all day ere you find them, and when you
have them, they are not worth the search.
Ant. Well, tell me now what lady is the same
To whom you swore a secret pilgrimage—   120

112. tongue] *Q2, F;* togue *Q.*   *Exeunt] Q; Exit F.*   *Gratiano and Lorenzo]*
Theobald subs.; om. Q, F.   113. It is] *Q, F, Collier;* Is *Rowe;* Ay! is *Lettsom*
conj.   that] *Q, F;* that:— *Collier.*   anything] *Staunton;* any thing *Q, F.*
now.] *Q, F, Collier;* now? *Rowe;* new? *Johnson conj.*   114. nothing] *Q;*
nothing, *Q2, F.*   115. as] *Q; om. F.*

port" (Steevens). *N.C.S.* glossed "purpose, business", which is acceptable at
II. ii. 158, but here it may imply "mere
talk" (cf. *O.E.D.,* 11a).

111–12. *commendable ... vendible*] the
jingle probably justifies the arrangement as verse. Abbott attempted
scansion with stress on *comméndable*
(¶490).

112. *neat's ... dried*] i.e., a tongue
ready for eating. A neat's tongue was a
delicacy but because "it is moyst, [it]
is not very holsome" and it was therefore stopped with cloves "whereby the
moystenes is dyminisshed." (Salerno,
Regimen Sanitatis (tr. 1557), O1ᵛ).
There is a bawdy allusion, as in N.
Field, *A Woman is a Weathercock* (1612),
I. ii: "But did that little old dried
neat's tongue, that eel-skin, [be]get
him?": cf. also *Wint.,* I. ii. 123.

maid not vendible] old maid; cf. *All's
W.,* I. i. 168.

113. *It ... now*] Collier's punctuation would mean that Antonio says *It
is that* in agreement with Gratiano and
then, a moment later, adds *anything
now* as if he was weary of talk. Lettsom's conjecture implies that the compositor misread "I" (a spelling of
"Ay") as "It". Rowe's emendation

has, however, general approval; the
compositor may have read "Is" as "It"
and then, consulting his copy again,
added the correct reading without a
capital. Thus emended the passage
means, "Does what he has just said
amount to anything or mean anything?" (so Steevens).

However, Q may stand, for *anything*
can be used adverbially, meaning
in any measure, to any extent, as in
Spenser, *Virgil's Gnat* (1591), l. 439:
". . . that anie thing could please /
Fell Cerberus." Shakespeare frequently used "something" adverbially (as in l. 124 below), and *anything*
is so used in *Ven.,* 1078: "What canst
thou boast / Of things long since, or
any thing ensuing?" So here, Antonio may imply that there is no limit
to the extent that Gratiano's silence
would be commendable to him at that
moment. This is not an easy reading,
but it avoids emendation and is in
keeping with Antonio's feeling at this
moment (cf. l. 1, note).

117. *shall*] must (cf. Abbott, ¶315).
119. *is the same*] i.e., is she; an absolute use.
120. *pilgrimage*] Cf. II. vii. 40, and
note.

That you to-day promis'd to tell me of?

Bass. 'Tis not unknown to you Antonio
How much I have disabled mine estate,
By something showing a more swelling port
Than my faint means would grant continuance: 125
Nor do I now make moan to be abridg'd
From such a noble rate, but my chief care
Is to come fairly off from the great debts
Wherein my time (something too prodigal)
Hath left me gag'd: to you Antonio   130
I owe the most in money and in love,
And from your love I have a warranty
To unburthen all my plots and purposes
How to get clear of all the debts I owe.

Ant. I pray you good Bassanio let me know it,   135
And if it stand as you yourself still do,
Within the eye of honour, be assur'd
My purse, my person, my extremest means
Lie all unlock'd to your occasions.

Bass. In my school-days, when I had lost one shaft,   140
I shot his fellow of the self-same flight
The self-same way, with more advised watch

121. of?] *F;* of. *Q.*   133. To unburthen] *Q, F;* T'unburthen *Pope.*   141, 142. self-same] *hyphened Q 2;* selfsame *F.*

121. *That*] Furness pointed out that this could refer to *lady* or *pilgrimage.*

124. *something*] to some extent; an adverbial use as in l. 129 below.

port] state, style of living.

126. *to be abridg'd*] about being abridged (cf. Abbott, ¶356).

127. *rate*] manner, style.

128. *fairly*] "properly, fitly" (*O.E.D.,* 4), "honourably" (*N.C.S.*), or (a more usual 16th-c. sense) completely, fully (cf. *Rom.,* II. iv. 48).

129. *time*] life-time, or, perhaps, youth; cf. *Cym.,* I. i. 43, and *Zelauto,* O4: "wasted out theyr web of youthfull time."

130. *gag'd*] bound, pledged.

133. *unburthen*] a common form of unburden.

136–7. *stand . . . honour*] For *eye*= sight, presence of, Pooler compared Fletcher, *Loyal Subject* (pf. 1618), I. v: "would ye do nobly / And in the eye of honour truly triumph." Antonio says "if your proposal is honourable as you continually are..."

139. *occasions*] needs, requirements.

140–4. *In . . . both*] Collier quoted [Armin], *Quips upon Questions* (1600), D1: "Another shaft they shoote that direct way / As whilome they the first shot, . . ./ . . . [So] The former Arrow may be found againe."

Arrows of the same *flight* should have the same power of flight and are of equal size and weight (so *O.E.D.*).

142. *advised*] careful, judicious.

To find the other forth, and by adventuring both,
I oft found both: I urge this childhood proof
Because what follows is pure innocence.   145
I owe you much, and (like a wilful youth)
That which I owe is lost, but if you please
To shoot another arrow that self way
Which you did shoot the first, I do not doubt,
(As I will watch the aim) or to find both,   150
Or bring your latter hazard back again,
And thankfully rest debtor for the first.
Ant. You know me well, and herein spend but time
To wind about my love with circumstance,
And out of doubt you do me now more wrong   155
In making question of my uttermost
Than if you had made waste of all I have:
Then do but say to me what I should do
That in your knowledge may by me be done,
And I am prest unto it: therefore speak.   160
Bass. In Belmont is a lady richly left,
And she is fair, and (fairer than that word),

143. and by] *Q,F;* by *Pope;* and, *Dyce (ii) conj.*   adventuring] *Q,F;* aduen-
tring *Q2;* ventring *Pope;* venturing *Dyce (ii) conj.*   155. me now] *Q; om. F.*

143. *To . . . both*] Attempts have
been made to regularize the metre,
but the irregularity may enforce the
difficulty and embarrassment with
which Bassanio speaks.

forth] out; Staunton compared
Gent., II. iv. 186: "I shall inquire you
forth."

144. *childhood proof*] "childish test or
experiment" (Clarendon), "experi-
ence of my youth" (Pooler, who compared *Tw.N.,* III. i. 135), or, possibly,
wise saying from childhood (cf. *Wiv.,*
IV. ii. 104).

145. *innocence*] Furness and Wilson
glossed "foolishness", but there are
other possible meanings; (1) freedom
from moral fault or cunning (so Johnson), and (2) childlike friendship and
affection (cf. *MND.,* III. ii. 202: "O, is
it all forgot? / All school-days' friendship, childhood innocence?" and
Wint., I. ii. 69). Bassanio may allude to

his proposal to borrow money, or to
the mutual affection which permits
him to do so; the meaning is suitably
imprecise.

146. *wilful*] i.e., self-willed.

148. *self*] same.

150–1. *or . . . Or*] either . . . or.

151. *hazard*] that which is risked or
staked, as in *I H 4,* I. iii. 128: "I make a
hazard of my head."

154. *To . . . circumstance*] To use a
devious course of argument; Halliwell
compared *Greene's Tu Quoque* (1614),
Dodsley, xi. 283: "You put us to a
needless labour, sir, / To run and wind
about for circumstance; / When the
plain word, "I thank you," would
have serv'd."

156. *In . . . uttermost*] "i.e., in doubting that I would do my utmost for
you" (Pooler).

160. *prest*] prepared, willing.

162. *fairer . . . word*] i.e., "what is

Of wondrous virtues,—sometimes from her eyes
I did receive fair speechless messages:
Her name is Portia, nothing undervalu'd   165
To Cato's daughter, Brutus' Portia,
Nor is the wide world ignorant of her worth,
For the four winds blow in from every coast
Renowned suitors, and her sunny locks
Hang on her temples like a golden fleece,   170
Which makes her seat of Belmont Colchos' strond,
And many Jasons come in quest of her.
O my Antonio, had I but the means
To hold a rival place with one of them,
I have a mind presages me such thrift   175
That I should questionless be fortunate.

Ant. Thou know'st that all my fortunes are at sea,
Neither have I money, nor commodity
To raise a present sum, therefore go forth
Try what my credit can in Venice do,—   180
That shall be rack'd even to the uttermost
To furnish thee to Belmont to fair Portia.
Go presently inquire (and so will I)
Where money is, and I no question make
To have it of my trust, or for my sake.   *Exeunt.* 185

---

163. sometimes] *Q*,*F;* sometime *Theobald.*   171. strond] *Q*, *F;* strand *Johnson.*

better still" (*N.C.S.*), or possibly, without parenthesis, she is more beautiful than the conventional epithet implies (so Eccles).

163. *sometimes*] formerly, as in *Ham.*, I. i. 49.

166. *Cato's . . . Portia*] Cf. *Cæs.*, II. i. 296-7, "Think you I am no stronger than my sex, / Being so father'd and so husbanded?"

170. *golden fleece*] Portia is a golden prize; cf. Introduction, p. lv.

171. *strond*] a form of strand; found also *1 H 4*, I. i. 4, and *2 H 4*, I. i. 62.

175. *thrift* (1) (mercenary) profit, as in I. iii. 45 and 85, and (2) success, luck (cf. Drayton, *Heroical Epistles* (1597), King John, l. 91: "Now all good Fortune give me happy Thrift"). The word is a link between the affairs

of Venice and Belmont; cf. Introduction, pp. lv-lvii.

176. *questionless*] Presumably Bassanio does not know about the caskets; he had visited Belmont while Portia's father was still alive (cf. I. ii. 108-10) and the "lottery" of the caskets was not devised until the time of his death (cf. I. ii. 27-9).

178. *commodity*] merchandise (cf. *Shr.*, II. i. 330) or, perhaps, opportunity.

179. *present sum*] i.e., ready money; cf. "present money" (III. ii. 272).

181. *rack'd*] strained, stretched; cf. "rack-rent".

183. *presently*] at once.

185. *of my trust . . . sake*] "i.e., on my credit or for friendship sake" (*N.C.S.*).

[SCENE II.—*Belmont.*]

Enter PORTIA *with her waiting-woman* NERISSA.

Por. By my troth Nerissa, my little body is aweary of this
great world.

Ner. You would be (sweet madam), if your miseries were
in the same abundance as your good fortunes are:
and yet for aught I see, they are as sick that surfeit   5
with too much, as they that starve with nothing; it is
no mean happiness therefore to be seated in the
mean,—superfluity comes sooner by white hairs, but
competency lives longer.

Por. Good sentences, and well pronounc'd.   10

Ner. They would be better if well followed.

Por. If to do were as easy as to know what were good to do,
chapels had been churches, and poor men's cottages
princes' palaces,—it is a good divine that follows his
own instructions,—I can easier teach twenty what   15
were good to be done, than be one of the twenty to
follow mine own teaching: the brain may devise laws
for the blood, but a hot temper leaps o'er a cold

Scene II

Scene II] *Rowe; om. Q, F.*   Belmont] *om. Q, F; Belmont. Three Caskets are set out,
one of Gold, another of Silver, and another of Lead Rowe; Belmont. A Room in Portia's
House Capell.*   4. abundance] *Q2, F;* abundance *Q.*   7. mean] *Q;* smal *F.*
16. than] *F;* then *to Q.*

7. *mean*] F's "small" gives the sense
but loses the pun (so Clarendon).

8. *superfluity . . . hairs*] Pooler compared, *The Cold Year* (1614), A3ᵛ: "Oh
Sir! riotts, . . . surfets ouernights, and
early potting it next morning, sticke
white haires vpon Young-mens
chinnes, when sparing dyets holds
colour."

10. *sentences*] maxims, *sententiae.*

pronounc'd] spoken, delivered. There
is possibly a pun on passing judgement
or sentence; cf., for example, *LLL.*,
I. i. 302. Portia uses several legal
phrases in her next speech: "*laws . . .
decree . . . good counsel . . . will*" (ll. 17–
24).

16. *than be*] The compositor may
have caught "to" (Q) from the preceding phrase.

18. *blood*] "The supposed seat of
emotion, passion" (*O.E.D.*, 5); ana-
logous to *temper* (l. 20) as in *2 H 4*,
IV. iv. 36–41. It sometimes refers specifically to sensual appetite, as in III.
i. 31–2.

hot temper] The disposition of a man
was thought to depend upon the mix-
ture or *temper* of the four humours; a
hot temper would have an excess of
choler (hot and dry) or of blood (hot
and wet). Blood was particularly associated with youth, high spirits, and
quick action.

decree,—such a hare is madness the youth, to skip
o'er the meshes of good counsel the cripple; but this   20
reasoning is not in the fashion to choose me a husband,—O me the word "choose"! I may neither
choose who I would, nor refuse who I dislike, so is the
will of a living daughter curb'd by the will of a dead
father: is it not hard Nerissa, that I cannot choose   25
one, nor refuse none?

Ner. Your father was ever virtuous, and holy men at their
death have good inspirations,—therefore the lott'ry
that he hath devised in these three chests of gold,
silver, and lead, whereof who chooses his meaning   30
chooses you, will no doubt never be chosen by any
rightly, but one who you shall rightly love. But what
warmth is there in your affection towards any of
these princely suitors that are already come?

Por. I pray thee over-name them, and as thou namest   35
them, I will describe them, and according to my
description level at my affection.

---

21. reasoning] *Q;* reason *F.*   the] *Q;* om. *F.*   22. "choose"!] choose, *Q, F.*
23. who . . . who] *Q;* whom . . . whom *F.*   25. is it] *Q;* it is *F.*   26. none?]
none. *Q, F.*   28. lott'ry] *Q;* lotterie *F.*   31. will no doubt] *Q, F;* no doubt
you wil *Q2.*   32. who] *Q, F;* whom *Pope.*   you] *Q, F;* om. *Q2.*   love.
But] loue: But *Q.*

19–20. *skip . . . cripple*] In winter
hares were hunted on foot with nets;
Pooler quoted Topsell, *History of Four-
footed Beasts* (1607), T4ᵛ: if the hare
"avoide the net, he [the hunter] must
follow her by the foot unto her next
lodging place."

21. *reasoning . . . fashion*] Like
Nerissa, Portia has pronounced sentences—and added her own comments. For the currency of the maxims
she uses, see Tilley, P537a, and Y43;
for *a good divine* (l. 14) Verity compared *Ham.*, I. iii. 47–51. Unlike Antonio, Portia tells the cause of her more
light-hearted discontent (cf. ll. 1–2
above)—no amount of talking will
find a husband for her.

23. *who . . . who*] i.e., whom, as frequently (cf. Abbott, ¶274).

24. *will . . . will*] punningly used.

27–8. *holy . . . inspirations*] It was
proverbial that men spoke true at
death; cf. Shakespeare's John of
Gaunt (*R 2*, II. i. 5–8 and 31).

31–2. *will . . . love*] Furness preferred
Q2, thinking it important that the
suitor should love rightly (cf. III. ii. 41:
"If you do love me, you will find me
out"). But the present context is concerned with Portia's affection and inability to choose; Nerissa's next question follows from this (so Rolfe). The
idea recurs ll. 60–2.

32. *who*] whom; see l. 23, note
above.

35. *over-name*] i.e., from one end of
the list to the other; cf. "o'er-read"
(*2 H 4*, III. i. 2, etc.). Shakespeare
seems to be reworking a passage from
Gent., I. ii. 4–33.

37. *level*] guess; cf. *Ant.*, v. ii. 339.

Ner. First there is the Neapolitan prince.

Por. Ay that's a colt indeed, for he doth nothing but talk
of his horse, and he makes it a great appropriation to   40
his own good parts that he can shoe him himself: I
am much afeard my lady his mother played false
with a smith.

Ner. Then is there the County Palatine.

Por. He doth nothing but frown (as who should say, "and   45
you will not have me, choose"), he hears merry tales
and smiles not, (I fear he will prove the weeping
philosopher when he grows old, being so full of unmannerly sadness in his youth), I had rather be married to a death's-head with a bone in his mouth, than   50
to either of these: God defend me from these two.

Ner. How say you by the French lord, Monsieur Le Bon?

Por. God made him, and therefore let him pass for a man,
—in truth I know it is a sin to be a mocker, but he!
why he hath a horse better than the Neapolitan's, a   55
better bad habit of frowning than the Count Palatine, he is every man in no man, if a throstle sing, he

42. afeard] *Q;* afraid *F.*   44. Then] *Q2;* Than *Q, F.*   is there] *Q, F;*
there is *Q2.*   Palatine] *Q2;* Palentine *Q, F.*   45. (as] *Q, F.*   49. youth),]
youth,) *Q.*   rather] *Q;* rather to *F.*   52. Bon] *Capell;* Boune *Q, F.*
54. he!] hee, *Q, F.*   56–7. Palatine] *Q2;* Palentine *Q, F.*   57. throstle]
Pope; Trassell *Q, F;* Tassell *F3.*

39. *colt*] i.e., a young and foolish
person.

44. *County Palatine*] *County* is a form
of Count which apparently retains the
final syllable of Fr. and It. Steevens
suspected a joke here and compared
Alchemist, II. iii. 331: he shall be "A
Count, nay, a *Count-palatine.*"

45. *as ... say*] as much as to say.
and] if; cf. common phrase "and it
please . . .".

46. *choose*] have it your own way, do
as you please (so Pooler who quoted
Three Ladies of London (1584), CI^v:
"And thou wilt do it do it, and thou
wilt not choose, . . .").

47–8. *weeping philosopher*] Heraclitus
of Ephesus; cf. *Batman upon Bartholome*
(1582), ¶3^v: "a Philosopher, which
always wept when he behelde the

People, considering how busie they
wer to gather treasure, and how negli-
gent in the well bringing vppe of their
children: his workes, of purpose, were
obscure, . . ."

48–9. *unmannerly*] possibly a quibble
on *youth.*

50. *death's-head . . . mouth*] a varia-
tion of a common phrase; cf. Tilley,
B517, and S. Harsnet, *Declaration*
(1603), PI^v: "stands like a mute . . .
with a bone in his mouth, and dares
not speake one word." Pooler suspected an allusion to the skull and
cross-bones cut on old tombstones.

52. *by*] concerning (cf. Abbott,
¶145).

57–8. *if . . . cap'ring*] i.e., he will
dance whoever calls the tune.

57. *throstle*] thrush. "Trassell" (Q

falls straight a-cap'ring, he will fence with his own
shadow. If I should marry him, I should marry
twenty husbands: if he would despise me, I would   60
forgive him, for if he love me to madness, I shall
never requite him.

Ner. What say you then to Falconbridge, the young baron
of England?

Por. You know I say nothing to him, for he understands   65
not me, nor I him: he hath neither Latin, French,
nor Italian, and you will come into the court and
swear that I have a poor pennyworth in the English:
he is a proper man's picture, but alas! who can con-
verse with a dumb-show? How oddly he is suited! I   70
think he bought his doublet in Italy, his round hose
in France, his bonnet in Germany, and his behaviour
everywhere.

Ner. What think you of the Scottish lord his neighbour?

Por. That he hath a neighbourly charity in him, for he   75

61. shall] *Q;* should *F.*   69. alas!] alas *Q, F.*   70. How] how *Q, F.*
suited!] suted, *Q, F.*   74. Scottish] *Q;* other *F.*

and F) is possibly a dialect or phonetic
form, but "a" and "o" are confused
elsewhere in this text (e.g., I. iii. 17 and
II. ii. 94) and the form is unknown to
O.E.D.; "thrassel", its closest form, is
not recorded before 1661.

59. *should . . . should*] the second
should may be compulsive (cf. Abbott,
¶322).

63. *Falconbridge*] for similarity with
other persons of this name in Shakespeare, cf. E. Honigmann, Introduction, *King John* (Arden edn., 1954),
p. xxiv.

67–8. *come . . . swear*] i.e., "bear me
witness" (Clarendon).

68. *pennyworth*] a double meaning;
(1) small quantity (as in *1 H 4*, II. iv.
26), (2) bargain (as in *Wint.*, IV. iv.
649.)

69. *he . . . picture*] i.e., he looks fine.
For *picture* = mere appearance, cf.
Ham., IV. v. 86.

70. *dumb-show*] a device, or part of a
play, in which no words were spoken.
    suited] dressed, with, possibly, a pun

on dressed in a suitable way (cf. *All's
W.*, I. i. 170–1).

71–3. *bought . . . everywhere*] Such was
the Englishman's reputation; cf.
Nashe, *Unfortunate Traveller* (1594),
Wks, ii. 281: "I, being a youth of the
English cut, . . . imitated foure or fiue
sundry nations in my attire at once."
In *Ado*, III. ii. 31–9, it is a sign of love to
be "in the shape of two countries at
once" (so Pooler).

74. *Scottish*] F's correction is Jacobean; cf. Introduction, p. xx. There
was an outbreak of disorder on the
Scottish border when *The Merchant*
was probably written; a proclamation
issued on 20 Aug. 1596 commanded
"all persons vpon the Borders of England, to keepe peace towards Scot-
land" and another followed on 13
Aug. 1597, by which time James VI
had "caused order to be taken . . . for
deliuery of Pledges," in accordance
with the recommendations of a commission on compensation for Scottish
raids.

borrowed a box of the ear of the Englishman, and
swore he would pay him again when he was able: I
think the Frenchman became his surety, and seal'd
under for another.

Ner. How like you the young German, the Duke of   80
Saxony's nephew?

Por. Very vildly in the morning when he is sober, and
most vildly in the afternoon when he is drunk: when
he is best, he is a little worse than a man, and when he
is worst he is little better than a beast,—and the   85
worst fall that ever fell, I hope I shall make shift to go
without him.

Ner. If he should offer to choose, and choose the right casket, you should refuse to perform your father's will,
if you should refuse to accept him.   90

Por. Therefore for fear of the worst, I pray thee set a deep
glass of Rhenish wine on the contrary casket, for if
the devil be within, and that temptation without, I
know he will choose it. I will do anything Nerissa
ere I will be married to a sponge.   95

Ner. You need not fear lady the having any of these lords,
they have acquainted me with their determinations,
which is indeed to return to their home, and to
trouble you with no more suit, unless you may be
won by some other sort than your father's imposition,   100
depending on the caskets.

97. determinations] *Q, F;* Determination *Rowe.*   99. suit] *Q, F;* Suits *Rowe.*

78–9. *Frenchman . . . another*] "Alluding to the constant assistance, or rather
constant promises of assistance, that
the *French* gave the *Scots* in their quarrels with the *English*" (Warburton).
The Scot has "sealed" a bond for a box
on the ear and his surety has *seal'd
under* for another (so Clarendon).

82. *vildly*] a variant form of vilely.

84–5. *best . . . beast*] a pun; Kökeritz
compared *MND.,* v. i. 231–2. The
idea was proverbial; cf. "hees a beast
and he be drunke" (Porter, *Two Angry
Women* (1599), M.S.R., l. 989.)

88–9. *should . . . should*] Cf. l. 59,
note, above.

92. *Rhenish*] Cf. iii. i. 36, note.
contrary] unfavourable, wrong. Since
both gold and silver caskets are *contrary,* it has been suggested that there
were "only two caskets in the original
form of the play" (Pooler); but Portia
is not speaking precisely, or perhaps
the detail has survived from Shakespeare's foul papers. Cf. l. 117, note,
below.

100. *sort*] manner; cf. *by the manner*
(l. 103). Elsewhere Shakespeare used
a construction with "in", e.g. "in
a moved sort" (*Tp.,* iv. i. 146), so here,
perhaps, *sort* = "casting or drawing of
lots" which *O.E.D.* last recorded in

Por. If I live to be as old as Sibylla, I will die as chaste as
    Diana, unless I be obtained by the manner of my
    father's will: I am glad this parcel of wooers are so
    reasonable, for there is not one among them but I   105
    dote on his very absence: and I pray God grant them
    a fair departure.

Ner. Do you not remember lady in your father's time, a
    Venetian (a scholar and a soldier) that came hither
    in company of the Marquis of Montferrat?   110

Por. Yes, yes, it was Bassanio, as I think so was he call'd.

Ner. True madam, he of all the men that ever my foolish
    eyes look'd upon, was the best deserving a fair lady.

Por. I remember him well, and I remember him worthy
    of thy praise.   115

Enter a Servingman.

How now, what news?

Serv. The four strangers seek for you madam to take their

106. pray . . . grant] *Q;* wish *F.*   111. think] *Q;* thinke, *F.*   so . . . he] *Q, F;*
he was so *Q2;* so he was *Var.* '78.   115. S.D.] *as Staunton; after l. 116 Q.*
116. How . . . news] *Q; om. F.*   117. for] *Q; om. F.*

1525. Shakespeare used *sort* = lot,
choice, in *Troil.*, I. iii. 376 (so Clarendon).

imposition] command, charge.

102. *Sibylla*] The Latin simply
means prophetess (as in *Oth.*, III. iv.
70), but it was often used as a proper
name for Deiphobe of Cumae (cf. *Shr.*,
I. ii. 70: "As old as Sibyl"); Apollo
promised that her years should be as
numerous as the grains of sand she was
holding in her hand (cf. Ovid, *Met.*,
xiv).

104. *parcel*] company, lot, set. The
word can have a contemptuous ring
(so *N.C.S.*) as, perhaps, in *Tit.*, II. iii.
49, but here the implication may be
that the *parcel* is only a portion of a
larger company, as in *LLL.*, v. ii. 160.

106. *pray God*] F's reading is a Jacobean revision; cf. Introduction, p. xx.

109. *scholar . . . soldier*] complemen-
tary graces in a renaissance courtier;
see, for example, *Ham.*, III. i. 159.
Henry V could "reason in divinity"

(*H 5*, I. i. 38). W. Thomas, *History of
Italy* (1549), noted that Italian stu-
dents "studie more for knowlage and
pleasure, than for curiositee or luker,"
and "the greatest dooers" of tilting
and feats of arms are "scholers" (Sig.
A3).

111. *as I think*] "Portia fears she has
spoken too eagerly" (Pooler).

116. *How . . . news*] Some editors
have adopted F's reading on the
grounds that these words are not de-
corous enough for Portia, but the
abruptness of her speech may show an
eagerness to change the subject; the
repetition in the previous sentence indicates the same mood. Pooler pointed
out that Portia "speaks familiarly to a
servant" again (II. ix. 85).

117. *four*] Perhaps the "number
originally [i.e., in a pre-Shakespearian
play] was only four, and . . . the two
added on a revisal were the English
and Scottish lords, the better to please
an English audience" (Hunter, i. 323);

leave: and there is a forerunner come from a fifth,
the Prince of Morocco, who brings word the prince
his master will be here to-night.   120
Por. If I could bid the fifth welcome with so good heart as
I can bid the other four farewell, I should be glad of
his approach: if he have the condition of a saint, and
the complexion of a devil, I had rather he should
shrive me than wive me.   125
Come Nerissa, sirrah go before:
Whiles we shut the gate upon one wooer, another
knocks at the door.   *Exeunt.*

[SCENE III.—*Venice.*]

Enter BASSANIO *with* SHYLOCK *the Jew.*

Shy. Three thousand ducats, well.

121. good] *Q,F; good a Q2.*   126–7. Come . . . door] *as Knight; prose Q,F.*

Scene III

Scene III] *Rowe; om. Q,F.*   Venice] *Rowe; om. Q,F; a publick Place in Venice Theobald.*   1. ducats,] *Q, F;* Ducats? *Rowe (iii).*   well.] *Q, F;* well? *Hudson conj., Pooler.*

the use of Shakespeare's papers for copy would account for the discrepancy without postulating an earlier play (cf. Introduction, pp. xiv–xviii).

123. *condition*] character, disposition; cf. *Shr.*, v. ii. 167–8: "our soft conditions and our hearts / Should well agree with our external parts."

124. *complexion . . . devil*] Cf. *John*, IV. iii. 121–2; and *Lust's Dominion* (pf. *c.* 1600), Dodsley, xiv. 122, speaking of a Moor: "truth to tell, / Seeing your face, we thought of hell."

126–7. *Come . . . door*] Except in *Err.* and *Shr.*, Shakespeare usually restricts doggerel to 'low' characters, but Gratiano uses it elsewhere in *Mer. V.* (I. i. 111–12). Wilson (*N.C.S.*, p. 113) suspected that this couplet was a relic from an earlier play, but a single doggerel couplet is used at the end of a prose speech in *Err.*, III. ii. 150–1 and at the close of a scene in *1 H 4*, IV. ii. 85-6.

Scene III

1–9.] Q's lining is peculiar. Compositors sometimes set short lines in order to fill out a page after the excision of an error, but, of these three instances, only the first (l. 4) affects the number of lines on the page; an easier way of filling out would be to increase the space between the end of Sc. ii and the beginning of Sc. iii. It follows that the lining of this passage probably reproduces that of the copy. The passage may have been added in the margin of the MS. where the space only permitted short lines. Such marginal additions might be found in either a revised prompt-book or the author's foul papers. It is just possible that Shakespeare intended the short lines to indicate the correct phrasing and timing for delivery.

1. *ducats*] In Italy there was both a golden and a silver ducat, and the word was also used for a sum of money

Bass. Ay sir, for three months.

Shy. For three months, well.

Bass. For the which as I told you, Antonio shall be bound.

Shy. Antonio shall become bound, well.   5

Bass. May you stead me? Will you pleasure me? Shall I
    know your answer?

Shy. Three thousand ducats for three months, and An-
    tonio bound.

Bass. Your answer to that.   10

Shy. Antonio is a good man.

Bass. Have you heard any imputation to the contrary?

Shy. Ho no, no, no, no: my meaning in saying he is a good
    man, is to have you understand me that he is suffic-
    ient,—yet his means are in supposition: he hath an   15
    argosy bound to Tripolis, another to the Indies, I
    understand moreover upon the Rialto, he hath a
    third at Mexico, a fourth for England, and other
    ventures he hath squand'red abroad,—but ships are
    but boards, sailors but men, there be land-rats, and   20

3. months,] *Q, F; Months? Rowe (iii).*   well.] *Q, F; well? Hudson conj., Pooler.*
4. For . . . bound] *as Pope; . . . you, / Anthonio . . . Q, F.*   5. bound,] *Q, F;*
bound? *Rowe (iii).*   well.] *Q, F;* well? *Hudson conj., Pooler.*   6–7. May . . .
answer] *as Pope; . . . me? / Shall . . . Q, F.*   7. answer?] *Q2;* aunswere. *Q, F.*
8–9. Three . . . bound] *as Pope; . . . months, / and . . . Q, F; . . . months, / And
. . . Rowe.*   9. bound.] *Q, F;* bound? *Rowe (iii).*   12. contrary?] *Q2;* contrary. *Q, F.*   17. Rialto] *F2;* Ryalta *Q, F.*   19. hath] *Q, F;* hath,
Theobald.

(cf. Coryat, i. 423). Here a ducat is a
golden coin; cf. II. vi. 49 and I. iii. 170.
Coryat, who visited Venice in 1608,
said that a ducat was worth 4s. 8d.; at
this rate Bassanio asks for £700, a sum
which was considered a splendid endowment for Anne Page (*Wiv.*, I. i. 51–
3).

    well.] Q's punctuation may stand:
Shylock is "understanding" Bassanio's proposal point by point. Bassanio needs no encouragement to
speak, for his impatience is evident
(cf. ll. 6–7 and 10).

    6. *stead*] assist, help (cf. *Oth.*, I. iii.
344), or supply.

    11. *good*] commercially sound (cf.
ll. 13–15); "good" and "sufficiency"
have become synonymous for Shylock

(so Pettet, *E. & S.*, XXXI (1946), 25).
It may be an ironic pun.

    14–15. *sufficient*] i.e., as a surety; a
technical use of the word. It also had a
more general sense of substantial, well-
to-do, as in *Meas.*, II. i. 286.

    17. *Rialto*] Staunton quoted Coryat,
i. 312: "The Rialto . . . is a most
stately building, being the Exchange
of Venice, where the Venetian Gentlemen and the Merchants doe meete
twice a day."

    19. *squand'red*] This has been glossed
"scattered", but Shakespeare's only
other use of the word seems to be in
apposition to "wise": "The wise man's
folly is anatomized / Even by the
squandering glances of the fool"
(*AYL.*, II. vii. 56–7).

water-rats, water-thieves, and land-thieves, (I mean
pirates), and then there is the peril of waters, winds,
and rocks: the man is notwithstanding sufficient,—
three thousand ducats,—I think I may take his bond.

Bass. Be assur'd you may.   25

Shy. I will be assur'd I may: and that I may be assured, I
will bethink me,—may I speak with Antonio?

Bass. If it please you to dine with us.

Shy, Yes, to smell pork, to eat of the habitation which your
prophet the Nazarite conjured the devil into: I will   30
buy with you, sell with you, talk with you, walk with
you, and so following: but I will not eat with you,
drink with you, nor pray with you. What news on the
Rialto? who is he comes here?

Enter ANTONIO.

Bass. This is Signior Antonio.   35
Shy. [*Aside.*] How like a fawning publican he looks!

21. water-thieves, and land-thieves] *Q, F;* land-thieves and water-thieves *Johnson.*   22. pirates] Pyrats *Q, F.*   24. ducats,] *Q, F;* Ducats? *Rowe* (*iii*).
25. assur'd] *Q;* assured *Q2, F.*   26. *Shy.*] *Q2;* assur'd] *Q;*
assured *Q2, F.*   29. *Shy.*] *Q2; Iew. Q, F.*   29–33. Yes . . . pray with you]
marked as aside N.C.S.   34. Rialto?] Ryalto, *Q, F.*   36. *Shy.*] *Q2; Iew. Q, F.*
S.D.] *Rowe; om. Q, F.*   looks!] lookes. *Q, F.*

21. *water-thieves, and land-thieves*]
There is no need to suspect transposi-
tion; cf. III. i. 56–7 (so Furness).

22. *pirates*] This may be a "bad"
pun: pir-*rats*.

25–6. *assur'd . . . assured*] at first,
satisfied, told for certain (cf. *Ado*, IV. ii.
27), but its final use implies a more
commercial sense of guaranteed, having security (cf. *Shr.*, II. i. 345).

29–33. *Yes, . . . with you*] Possibly an
aside; "It would be unlike the Jew to
reveal his hate openly at this stage"
(*N.C.S.*).

30. *Nazarite*] Most Bibles before the
A.V. (1611), read *Nazarite* and not
Nazarene, *Matthew,* ii. 23 (so Fur-
ness).

32. *I . . . eat with you*] He does so
later, *in hate* (II. v. 14).

36. *fawning publican*] an odd com-

bination, for the *publicani* or farmers of
Roman taxes were likely to treat Jews
with insolence rather than servility (so
Clarendon). This has been explained:
(1) Shylock, who later cries "My deeds
upon my head" (IV. i. 202), scorns the
publican in *Luke,* xviii. 10–14 who
fawned on God (so K. Elze, *Shakespeare Jahrbuch,* xi (1876), 276), (2)
publican was a vague, cant term of
abuse—for this Pooler quoted Nashe,
Wks, I. 302: "this indigested Chaos of
Doctourship, and greedy pothunter
after applause, is an apparant Publican and sinner, . . ." However, the
primary sense of publican may be correct, for Antonio would beg a favour as
one unused to it. It was appropriate
for Shylock to call Antonio a *publican,*
i.e., a servant of Gentile oppressors
who robbed the Jews of lawful gains

I hate him for he is a Christian:
But more, for that in low simplicity
He lends out money gratis, and brings down
The rate of usance here with us in Venice.   40
If I can catch him once upon the hip,
I will feed fat the ancient grudge I bear him.
He hates our sacred nation, and he rails
(Even there where merchants most do congregate)
On me, my bargains, and my well-won thrift,   45
Which he calls interest: cursed be my tribe
If I forgive him!
Bass.   Shylock, do you hear?
Shy. I am debating of my present store,
And by the near guess of my memory
I cannot instantly raise up the gross   50
Of full three thousand ducats: what of that?
Tubal (a wealthy Hebrew of my tribe)
Will furnish me; but soft! how many months
Do you desire? [*To Antonio.*] Rest you fair good signior,
Your worship was the last man in our mouths.   55
Ant. Shylock, albeit I neither lend nor borrow

45. well-won] *Q;* well-worne *F.*   47. him!] him. *Q,F.*   hear?] heare. *Q,F.*   51. that?] *Q2,F;* that, *Q.*   53. soft!] soft, *Q,F.*   54. S.D.] *after* signior *Rowe; om. Q,F.*

(so F. T. Wood, *N. & Q.,* clxxxix (1945), 252–3).

R. G. Moulton suggested that l. 36 would be more appropriate if spoken by Antonio of Shylock (*Shakespeare as a Dramatic Artist* (1885), pp. 61–2, n. 1); it is true that Antonio does not "fawn" when he speaks (l. 56) but Shylock is probably being sarcastic; and Q's reading may stand.

38. *low simplicity*] humble foolishness. Perhaps *low* also has the sense of base, mean, as in *2 H 4,* II. ii. 194 and *Lr.,* II. ii. 149. Shylock may still be sarcastic; cf. Barabas in *Jew of Malta,* I. ii. 161–2: "Ay, policy! that's their profession, / And not simplicity, as they suggest."

40. *usance*] "a more clenly name" for usury (*Discourse,* E8ᵛ; quoted Reed); cf. ll. 45–6, note.

41. *upon the hip*] at a disadvantage; a proverbial phrase derived from wrestling (cf. Tilley, H474)—it was a hold preceding the throw. There may be an allusion to Jacob's wrestling with the angel; cf. *Genesis,* xxxii.

45–6. *thrift . . . interest*] Cf. *Death of Usury* (1594), F3ᵛ: "*Vsurers* are ashamed at this day of their title, . . . they are ashamed of the name and word of *vsurie.*" "Interest" was a better name than "usury", but by no means as fair sounding as *thrift,* the pursuit of which was a virtue in the eyes of citizens. Cf. l. 85 and note, below, and earlier use of *thrift* at I. i. 175.

48–53. *I . . . me*] Cf. T. Bell, *Speculation of Usury* (1596), B3ᵛ: the usurer "protesteth that hee hath no money at all, but that himselfe seeketh where to finde an vsurer . . ."; he pretends to find someone else to lend the money.

50. *gross*] full sum.

By taking nor by giving of excess,
Yet to supply the ripe wants of my friend,
I'll break a custom: [*To Bassanio.*] is he yet possess'd
How much ye would?

Shy.   Ay, ay, three thousand ducats.   60

Ant. And for three months.

Shy. I had forgot,—three months,—[*To Bassanio.*] you told
    me so.
Well then, your bond: and let me see,—but hear you,
Me thoughts you said, you neither lend nor borrow
Upon advantage.

Ant.   I do never use it.   65

Shy. When Jacob graz'd his uncle Laban's sheep,—
This Jacob from our holy Abram was
(As his wise mother wrought in his behalf)
The third possessor: ay, he was the third.

Ant. And what of him? did he take interest?   70

Shy. No, not take interest, not as you would say
Directly int'rest,—mark what Jacob did,—

---

59. S.D.] *after* would (*l. 60*) *Staunton; om. Q,F.*   is . . . possess'd] *Q,F, Theobald, Dyce* (*ii*); are you resolu'd, *Q2*; Are you yet possess'd, *Delius, Collier* (*ii*) *conj.*   60. ye] *Q*; he *Q2, F, Delius*; you *Theobald*; we *Walker conj., Dyce* (*ii*). would] *Q,F*; would haue *Q2.*   61. *Ant.*] *Q, F; Bass. Furnivall conj.*   62. S.D.] *om. Q,F.*   you] *Q,F;* he *Hanmer.*   64. Me thoughts] *Q,F;* Me-thought *Q2.*   68. (As . . . behalf)] *Q,F.*   69. third] *Q,F;* third,— *Dyce.*   70. him?] him, *Q,F.*   71. interest] *Q,F;* int'rest *Pope.*   72. int'rest] *Q;* interest *Q2, F.*

57. *excess*] Cf. P. Cæsar, *Discourse* (tr. 1578), D1ᵛ: "Vsurie, or as the woorde of God doeth call it, excesse, . . ."

58. *ripe*] i.e., they "can have no longer delay" (Johnson): cf. II. viii. 40.

59. *possess'd*] informed; cf. IV. i. 35.

60. *Ay, . . . ducats*] Shylock is trying to control the conversation and answers for Bassanio.

61. *And . . . months*] The short line may indicate a pause before Shylock replies; he must not seem too eager.

64. *Me thoughts*] a common form, as in *R 3*, I. iv. 9 (so Pooler).

65. *advantage*] another circumlocution for usury or interest; cf. ll. 40, 45–6, and 57, notes. It is so used in *John*, III. iii. 22.

66–85. *When Jacob . . .*] Cf. *Genesis*, xxx. 31–43.

67–9. *This . . . third*] Cf. *Genesis*, xxvii. This digression makes Antonio reveal his impatience, but it is also a matter of pride and satisfaction to Shylock, a descendant of Jacob. Cf. *Jew of Malta*, I. i. 103–4: "These are blessings promis'd to the Jews, / And herein was old Abraham's happiness: . . ."

72. *Directly*] Cf. *Death of Usury* (1594), D3: "If a man takes aboue 10. pound in the 100. directly, he is conuicted. . . . If a man takes aboue 10. pound in the 100. indirectly, he is in great daunger"; the anonymous author details some ways of taking "indirect interest, such as receiving a

When Laban and himself were compromis'd
That all the eanlings which were streak'd and pied
Should fall as Jacob's hire, the ewes being rank   75
In end of autumn turned to the rams,
And when the work of generation was
Between these woolly breeders in the act,
The skilful shepherd pill'd me certain wands,
And in the doing of the deed of kind   80
He stuck them up before the fulsome ewes,
Who then conceiving, did in eaning time
Fall parti-colour'd lambs, and those were Jacob's.
This was a way to thrive, and he was blest:
And thrift is blessing if men steal it not.   85
Ant. This was a venture sir that Jacob serv'd for,
A thing not in his power to bring to pass,

76. end] *Q, F;* th'end *Q2.*   79. pill'd] *Knight;* pyld *Q,* pil'd *F;* peel'd *Pope.*

gift in addition to the 10 per cent.
    72–85. *mark what Jacob did* . . .] Shy-lock argues that as Jacob "thrived" (i.e., increased his hire) by his skill in breeding sheep, so *thrift* (i.e., increase) of money is likewise a blessing; in other words, money can be made to breed. The Laban story has not been found in any 16th-c. book on usury. The argument has been variously interpreted; (1) it is "Shylock's bid for mutual understanding" and "under-mines the differentiation between "natural" and "unnatural" kinds of money-making by showing that profit is always "controlled by the exercise of human skill and ingenuity" (H. B. Charlton, *Shakespearian Comedy* (1938), pp. 141–2; but cf. ll. 87–8, note, below); (2) it is a "sophistical and specious defense of what to an Eliza-bethan was manifestly wrong" (H. R. Walley, *Essays in Dramatic Lit.,* ed. H. Craig (1935), p. 237); (3) it "indi-cates Shylock's preoccupation with the problem of . . . how he may match the cunning of his ancestor, . . . and collect interest without taking inter-est" (L. W. Wilkins, *M.L.N.,* lxii (1947), 28–30); and (4) it shows that Shylock expects a miracle—". . . as

God gave the flesh of cattle to Jacob [cf. ll. 87–8, note], so will He give Antonio's flesh to Shylock"—he thanks God when he hears of Antonio's losses (III. i. 93) and calls Portia "Daniel", i.e., "God is my judge" (IV. i. 219) (*S.Q.,* I (1950), 256–7). A. Williams, *Common Expositor* (1948), pp. 170–2, quotes Biblical commen-tators who justify Jacob's action (so F. Kermode, privately).
    73. *were compromis'd*] had come to terms.
    74. *eanlings*] new-born lambs.
    79. *pill'd*] stripped; a collateral form of peeled (so *O.E.D.*), which is found in many Bibles before the A.V.
    85. *steal*] But usury was equated with theft; cf. *Discourse,* D4: "what is vsury, otherwise then a fraudulent & crafty stealing of an other mans goodes, . . . " and P. Cæsar, *Dis-course* (tr. 1578), *4ᵛ: "Vsurie is thee-uerie."
    86. *serv'd*] was a servant.
    87–8. *A thing . . . heaven*] Cf. the mar-ginal comments in early Bibles; e.g., the Bishops' Bible (1568): "It is not lawfull by fraude to seke recompence of iniurie: therfore Moyses sheweth afterwarde that God thus instructed

But sway'd and fashion'd by the hand of heaven.
Was this inserted to make interest good?
Or is your gold and silver ewes and rams?   90

Shy. I cannot tell, I make it breed as fast,—
But note me signior.

Ant.   Mark you this Bassanio,
The devil can cite Scripture for his purpose,—
An evil soul producing holy witness
Is like a villain with a smiling cheek,   95
A goodly apple rotten at the heart.
O what a goodly outside falsehood hath!

Shy. Three thousand ducats, 'tis a good round sum.
Three months from twelve, then let me see the rate.

Ant. Well Shylock, shall we be beholding to you?   100

Shy. Signior Antonio, many a time and oft
In the Rialto you have rated me
About my moneys and my usances:
Still have I borne it with a patient shrug,

---

92. signior.] *Q, F;* signior. . . . *Keightley.*   Bassanio,] *Q, F;* Bassanio? *Pope.*
97. goodly] *Q, F;* godly *Rowe.*   hath!] hath. *Q, F.*   97.] S.D., *Aside to Bass.*
(at end of line) Keightley.   99. then. . . . rate.] *Q, F;* then, . . . see; the rate—
Lloyd conj., Cambridge.   100. beholding] *Q, F;* beholden *Pope.*   102. In] *Q,*
F; On *Capell conj., Collier (ii).*

Jacob" (i.e., in *Genesis*, xxxi. 9; quoted
C. D. Ginsbury, *Athenaeum* (28 Apr.
1883), p. 541).

89. *inserted*] i.e., in Scripture (so
Clarendon), or introduced into the
conversation (so Verity).

90. *Or . . . rams*] i.e., can *barren metal*
(l. 129 below) breed like animals. Cf.
Bacon, 'Of Usury', *Essays* (1625):
"They say . . . it is against Nature, for
Money to beget *Money*"; the saying was
constantly repeated and was derived
from Aristotle, *De Repub.*, lib. I.

93. *The . . . purpose*] Cf. *Matthew*, iv.
6, and *Jew of Malta*, I. ii. 111: "What,
bring you Scripture to confirm your
wrongs?" (Barabas to a Knight of
Malta).

95. *villain . . . cheek*] Antonio forgets
this precept later (l. 176); it is frequent
in Shakespeare, e.g., *3 H 6*, III. ii. 182,
and *Ham.*, I. v. 106–8.

97. *goodly*] Rowe's emendation is

attractive; "good" and "god" are
easily confused (Walker cited examples, I. 303) and *goodly* might have
been caught from the line above (so
Dyce).

100. *beholding*] beholden, a common
form.

102. *In the Rialto*] Shakespeare used
in, on, and *upon*; there is probably some
confusion between the Rialto as a public place and as a building similar to
the Royal Exchange, London (cf. l. 17,
note).

rated] reproved, reviled.

103. *moneys*] a common plural form,
properly meaning sums of money, but
often indistinguishable from sing.
money (so *O.E.D.*); cf. *Tim.*, II. i. 16.

104. *shrug*] Malone quoted *Jew of
Malta*, II. iii. 23–4: "I learn'd in
Florence how to kiss my hand, / Heave
up my shoulders when they call me
dog."

(For suff'rance is the badge of all our tribe)   105
You call me misbeliever, cut-throat dog,
And spet upon my Jewish gaberdine,
And all for use of that which is mine own.
Well then, it now appears you need my help:
Go to then, you come to me, and you say,   110
"Shylock, we would have moneys," you say so:
You that did void your rheum upon my beard,
And foot me as you spurn a stranger cur
Over your threshold, moneys is your suit.
What should I say to you? Should I not say   115
"Hath a dog money? is it possible
A cur can lend three thousand ducats?" or
Shall I bend low, and in a bondman's key
With bated breath, and whisp'ring humbleness
Say this: 120
"Fair sir, you spet on me on Wednesday last,
You spurn'd me such a day, another time
You call'd me dog: and for these courtesies
I'll lend you thus much moneys"?
Ant. I am as like to call thee so again,   125
To spet on thee again, to spurn thee too.

---

105. (For ... tribe)] *Q, F.*   106. call] *Q, F;* call'd *Rann.*   cut-throat] *Q, F;*
cut-throat, *Hudson.*   107. spet] *Q, F;* spit *F3;* spat *Rann.*   114. moneys] *Q,*
F; money *Q2.*   116. money] *Q, F;* monies *Keightley.*   117. can] *Q;* should
F.   120–1. Say ... last] *as Var. '93; one line Q, F.*   121. spet] *Q, F;* spat
Rowe (iii); spit *Pope.*   122. day, ... time] day ... time, *Q;* day; ... time *F.*
124. moneys"?] moneyes. *Q, F.*   126. spet] *Q, F;* spit *Rowe.*

---

105. *suff'rance*] endurance, suffering;
Marlowe's Barabas enjoins it upon
Abigail: "Be silent, daughter; suf-
ferance breeds ease" (*Jew of Malta*,
I. ii. 239).

badge] distinguishing mark; cf. *Tit.*,
I. i. 119: "Sweet mercy is nobility's
true badge." No actual sign or emblem
is implied.

107. *spet*] a common form for the
present or past tense of vb. to spit.

gaberdine] a loose upper garment (cf.
Trinculo's, *Tp.*, II. ii. 40); no particularly Jewish gaberdine is known. From
1412, all Moors and Jews in Spain had
to wear long robes over their clothes as

low as their feet, and, according to
some travellers, such robes were volun-
tarily worn in other countries (cf.
M. C. Linthicum, *P.M.L.A.*, xliii
(1928), 757–66). In Elizabethan
theatres, there was probably a standard, recognizable Jew's costume (so
G. F. Reynolds, *Staging* (1940), p. 175).

108. *use*] (1) the simple sense of employment, and (2) the specialized one
connected with usury, as in *Ado*, II. i.
288: "He lent it me awhile; and I gave
him use for it, ..."

mine own] Cf. *Matthew*, xx. 15: "Is it
not lawful for me to do what I will with
mine own?" (cf. Tilley, O99).

If thou wilt lend this money, lend it not
As to thy friends, for when did friendship take
A breed for barren metal of his friend?
But lend it rather to thine enemy,   130
Who if he break, thou may'st with better face
Exact the penalty.

Shy. Why look you how you storm!
I would be friends with you, and have your love,
Forget the shames that you have stain'd me with,   135
Supply your present wants, and take no doit
Of usance for my moneys, and you'll not hear me,—
This is kind I offer.

Bass. This were kindness.

Shy.   This kindness will I show,
Go with me to a notary, seal me there   140
Your single bond, and (in a merry sport)
If you repay me not on such a day

---

128. friends] *Q, F;* friend *F2.*   129. for] *Q;* of *F.*   131. Who] *Q, F;* Then
Eccles conj.   132. penalty] *Q;* penalties *F.*   133. storm!] storme, *Q, F.*   137-8.
Of . . . offer] *as Q, F;* . . . moneys, / And . . . *Collier.*   139. Bass.] *Q, F; Ant. Q3.*

127-9. *lend . . . friend*] Cf. *Discourse,*
N7: "God ordeyned lending for maintenaunce of amitye, and declaration of
loue, betwixt man and man: wheras
now lending is vsed for pryuate benefit
and oppression, & so no charitie is vsed
at all, . . ."
  129. *A . . . metal*] breed is here used
for interest; cf. l. 90 and note, above.
  131. *Who*] a mere link between
clauses (cf. *O.E.D.,* 12), as in *H 5,* III.
vi. 157.
  break] i.e., his day; cf. l. 159.
  134. *I . . . love*] The mention of the
penalty (l. 132) seems to have changed
Shylock's approach; cf. T. Bell, *Speculation of Usury* (1596), B3ᵛ: ". . . so
soone as the silly poore man maketh
mention of vsurie, . . . [the usurer]
abateth his sowre countenance, and
beginneth to smile; . . . and calleth him
neighbour and friend."
  136. *doit*] i.e., a trifling sum (originally a small Dutch coin).
  138. *kind*] used in a double sense;

(1) benevolent, generous, as in *1 H 4,*
v. ii. 2: "The liberal and kind offer
. . .", and (2), the primary sense of
natural, as in *H 5,* II. Prol. 19: "Were
all thy children kind and natural". In
the second sense, Shylock is answering
Antonio's objections to usury (cf. ll. 90
and 129). The pun may also be found
in *AYL.,* Epil. 24. The short line and
Bassanio's interjection suggest that
Antonio hesitates—so Shylock pro-
ceeds.
  141. *single bond*] Rushton (*Shakespeare's Testamentary Language* (1869),
p. 51) distinguished between a *single
bond* and one with a condition; it has
been suggested that Shylock used the
term craftily, to make his condition
seem a mere nothing or *merry sport.* An
alternative meaning is "a bond with
your own signature alone attached to
it, without the names of sureties"
(Clarendon). Schmidt compared *Tp.,*
I. ii. 432 for a non-legal sense of mere,
simple.

In such a place, such sum or sums as are
Express'd in the condition, let the forfeit
Be nominated for an equal pound   145
Of your fair flesh, to be cut off and taken
In what part of your body pleaseth me.

Ant. Content in faith, I'll seal to such a bond,
And say there is much kindness in the Jew.

Bass. You shall not seal to such a bond for me,   150
I'll rather dwell in my necessity.

Ant. Why fear not man, I will not forfeit it,—
Within these two months, that's a month before
This bond expires, I do expect return
Of thrice three times the value of this bond.   155

Shy. O father Abram, what these Christians are,
Whose own hard dealings teaches them suspect
The thoughts of others! Pray you tell me this,—
If he should break his day what should I gain
By the exaction of the forfeiture?   160
A pound of man's flesh taken from a man,
Is not so estimable, profitable neither
As flesh of muttons, beefs, or goats,—I say
To buy his favour, I extend this friendship,—
If he will take it, so,—if not, adieu,   165
And for my love I pray you wrong me not.

Ant. Yes Shylock, I will seal unto this bond.

Shy. Then meet me forthwith at the notary's,
Give him direction for this merry bond—

---

147. body] *Q;* bodie it *F.*   155. this] *Q, F;* the *Capel.*   157. dealings] *Q, F;*
dealing *F2.*   158. others!] others: *Q, F.*   165. not,] not *Q, F.*

145. *nominated for*] i.e., named as.

equal] in sense of L. *aequus*, fair, just,
impartial; cf. *just pound* (IV. i. 323 and
title-page of Q).

146. *fair flesh*] "This suggests Shylock's darker, Oriental hue" (Furness); cf. III. i. 34–6.

151. *dwell*] remain.

157. *dealings teaches*] Abbott (¶333)
defended Q, treating *teaches* as a nor-
thern plural. *N.C.S.* accepted F2's
dealing because the "harshness" of Q
probably "belonged to the compositor

and not to Shakespeare." Confusion of
final "s" is a common error, but cf.
thoughts (l. 158) to which *dealings* seems
to be in opposition.

163. *muttons, beefs*] common Elizabethan plural forms.

166. *for my love*] i.e., for my love's
sake (so Clarendon), or, simply, please
(so Pooler). Perhaps *love* = instance of
affection, act of kindness (cf. *O.E.D.*,
IC, which exemplified it with *John*, IV.
i. 49: "What good love may I perform
for you?").

And I will go and purse the ducats straight,   170
See to my house left in the fearful guard
Of an unthrifty knave: and presently
I'll be with you.   *Exit.*
Ant.   Hie thee gentle Jew.
    The Hebrew will turn Christian, he grows kind.
Bass. I like not fair terms, and a villain's mind.   175
Ant. Come on, in this there can be no dismay,
    My ships come home a month before the day.   *Exeunt.*

---

173. I'll] *Q*, *F*; I will *Theobald* (*ii*).   S.D.] *as Q*, *F*; *after* Jew *Capell.*   173-
4. Hie . . . kind] *as Q 3*; . . . turne / Christian . . . *Q*, *F*.   174. The] *Q*; This *F*.
175. terms] *Q*; teames *F*.

171. *fearful*] Adjectives in *-ful* often
had active or passive sense (cf.
Abbott, ¶3), so "not to be trusted, but
gives cause of fear" (Johnson), or
timid (cf. *3 H 6*, II. ii. 30).

172. *unthrifty*] Cf. Introduction, p.
lvii.

   knave] This could mean servant;
cf. *Oth.*, I. i. 45 and 49.

175. *I . . . mind*] Cf. ll. 95-7 above;
Tilley (F3) quoted many parallels in
Shakespeare and traced the proverb
back to Lyly, *Campaspe*, II. ii. 57: "faire
faces, but false heartes." The idea is
often repeated in *Mer. V.*, cf. Introduction, p. lii.

[ACT II]

[SCENE I.—*Belmont.*]

[Flourish Cornets.] Enter [the Prince of] MOROCCO (*a tawny Moor all in white*), *and three or four followers accordingly, with* PORTIA, NERISSA, *and their train.*

Mor. Mislike me not for my complexion,
    The shadowed livery of the burnish'd sun,
    To whom I am a neighbour, and near bred.
    Bring me the fairest creature northward born,
    Where Phœbus' fire scarce thaws the icicles,   5
    And let us make incision for your love,
    To prove whose blood is reddest, his or mine.

ACT II

Scene I

Act II] *om. Q;* Actus Secundus *F.*   Scene I] *Rowe; om. Q, F.*   Belmont] *Rowe; om. Q, F; Belmont. A Room in Portia's House Capell.*   Flourish Cornets] *om. Q; Flo. Cornets (after train) F; Flourish of Cornets Malone.*   the Prince of Morocco] *Capell subs.;* Morochus *Q, F.*   their] *Q, F; her F4.*   2. burnish'd] *Q, F;* burning *Collier (ii) conj.*

S.D. tawny Moor] possibly, in contrast to a "black" Moor; in *Tit.*, Aaron's "coal-black" child is called "tawny" when its father considers that it is "half me and half thy [white-skinned] dam" (v. i. 27).

S.D. white] Morocco who claims he is as good as anyone else (cf. l. 7), dresses in the colour of sanctity (cf. *Wint.*, III.iii. 22–3).

S.D. accordingly] i.e., complexioned and dressed as Morocco.

2. *shadowed*] shaded, umbrated (a heraldic term of blazonry). Cf. *Song of Solomon*, i. 6: "I am black, because the sun hath looked upon me."

livery] badge or cognizance; for "heraldry" in the face, cf. *Lucr.*, 57–70.

See also, Jonson, *Sejanus* (1605), v. 712: "superstitious *Moores* salute . . . [the sun's] light."

6. *incision*] perhaps an allusion to a "swaggering humour": see, for example, Jonson, *Cynthia's Revels* (1601), IV. i. 200–9: "I would see how *Loue* . . . could worke . . . by letting this gallant expresse himselfe . . . with stabbing himselfe, and drinking healths, or writing languishing letters in his bloud." *Lr.*, II. i. 35–7 alludes to this custom.

7. *reddest*] red blood is a "traditionary sign of courage" (Johnson). Cf. Webster, *White Devil* (1612), v. vi. 228–9, where Zanche the Moor says, "I have blood / As red as either of theirs."

I tell thee lady this aspect of mine
Hath fear'd the valiant,—by my love I swear,
The best-regarded virgins of our clime   10
Have lov'd it too: I would not change this hue,
Except to steal your thoughts my gentle queen.

Por. In terms of choice I am not solely led
By nice direction of a maiden's eyes:
Besides, the lott'ry of my destiny   15
Bars me the right of voluntary choosing:
But if my father had not scanted me,
And hedg'd me by his wit to yield myself
His wife, who wins me by that means I told you,
Your self (renowned prince) then stood as fair   20
As any comer I have look'd on yet
For my affection.

Mor.   Even for that I thank you,
Therefore I pray you lead me to the caskets
To try my fortune: by this scimitar
That slew the Sophy, and a Persian prince   25
That won three fields of Sultan Solyman,
I would o'erstare the sternest eyes that look:
Outbrave the heart most daring on the earth:
Pluck the young sucking cubs from the she-bear,

9. by . . . swear,] (by . . . swear) *Q*, *F.*   10. best-regarded] *hyphened Malone.*
18. wit] *Q*, *F*; will *Hanmer.*   20. (renowned prince)] *Q*, *F.*   then] *F2*; than
Q, *F.*   25. prince] *Q*, *F*; Prince, *Q2.*   27. o'erstare] *Q*, *F*; out-stare *Q2.*

9. *fear'd*] terrified; cf. *H 5*, I. ii. 155.
12. *steal*] take possession of.
13. *terms*] respect; the plural adds
little to the sense (cf. *Ham.*, v. ii. 257).
14. *direction*] guidance, instruction.
17. *scanted*] restricted, limited.
18. *wit*] "will" might be preferred
on the analogy of I. ii. 24, 89, and
104; but *wit* (= wisdom) makes good
sense. Possibly *wit* also means "will",
or "testament" (cf. *Neophil.*, xli (1957),
47).
20. *fair*] a quibbling allusion to
Morocco's complexion.
25. *Sophy*] i.e., King of Persia; the
name was used, like Prester John or
Grand Cham, as a type of magnifi-

cence and power (cf. *Tw.N.*, III. iv.
306).
25–6. *Persian . . . Solyman*] Q2's
punctuation would mean that Morocco had fought on both sides in the
Persian/Turkish wars. Pooler compared Kyd, *Soliman and Perseda* (entered *S.R.*, 20 Nov. 1592), I. iii. 51–4:
"Against the Sophy in three pitched
fields, / Vnder the conduct of great
Soliman, / Haue I been chiefe com-
maunder of an hoast, / And put the
flint heart Perseans to the sword."
27. *o'erstare*] The word is found only
here in Shakespeare, but cf. "o'er-
shine" (e.g., *2 H 4*, IV. iii. 57). For
Q2's "out-stare", cf. *Ant.*, III. xiii. 195.

Yea, mock the lion when a roars for prey   30
To win thee lady. But alas the while!
If Hercules and Lichas play at dice
Which is the better man, the greater throw
May turn by fortune from the weaker hand:
So is Alcides beaten by his rage,   35
And so may I, blind Fortune leading me,
Miss that which one unworthier may attain,
And die with grieving.

Por.   You must take your chance,
And either not attempt to choose at all,
Or swear before you choose, if you choose wrong   40
Never to speak to lady afterward
In way of marriage,—therefore be advis'd.

Mor. Nor will not,—come bring me unto my chance.

30. a] *Q; he Q2, F.*   31. thee] *Rowe (iii); the Q, F.*   alas . . . while!] alas,
. . . while *Q, F.*   35. rage] *Q, F; page Pope (ii); wag N.C.S.; rogue Sisson;*
rag *Galloway.*   36. me,] *Q2; me Q, F.*

30. *lion*] Cf. *Batman upon Bartholome*
(1582), Rrr4ᵛ: when a lion "seeth his
pray, he roareth full lowde, & at the
voyce of him other beasts . . . stand
astonyed and afeard, as it were abiding
yᵉ hest . . . of theyr King." Morocco's
dialogue is full of superlatives; cf.
John, II. i. 457–60: "Here's a large
mouth, indeed, / That spits forth death
and mountains, rocks and seas, / Talks
as familiarly of roaring lions / As maids
of thirteen do of puppy-dogs!"

31. *thee*] Morocco uses *the lady* frequently in II. vii, but here emendation
seems necessary because he is address-
ing Portia, as in l. 8 above.

32. *Lichas*] the attendant who
brought Hercules the poisoned shirt of
Nessus (see Ovid, *Met.*, IX); no story
of a game at dice is known.

33. *Which . . . man*] a title for which it
was usual to fight; cf. *Troil.*, I. iii.
377.

throw] a quibble; Hercules threw
Lichas into the sea for bringing the
shirt. It was also a term in wrestling
(see previous note).

35. *rage*] rash jest, wild folly. *O.E.D.*
illustrates the noun *rage* = "extrava-

gant, riotous jesting" until *c.* 1425; the
verb = "to behave wantonly, or
riotously" is illustrated until 1645.
Shakespeare associated *rage* with
wildness in *2 H 4*, IV. iv. 62–3, and *R2*,
II. i. 70, and *1 H 4*, III. i. 183 (so H.
Hulme, *Neophil.*, xli (1957), 48–9).
Used of Alcides, *rage* alludes to the
well-known phrase "Hercules *furens*".
The various emendations were
prompted by the fact that Lichas was
Hercules' servant. *N.C.S.* claimed that
Pope's *page* was "impossible palaeographically" and read "wag", which a
compositor might have misread as
"rag", an old-fashioned spelling of
"rage". However, "wag" is associated
with mischief and good fellowship and
is not fully appropriate here. Other
emendations are palaeographically
acceptable: for example, "rogue"
presuming the copy read "roge", a
possible 16th-c. spelling, or "rag",
meaning a "base, beggarly person", as
in *R 3*, v. iii. 328 (so D. Galloway,
N. & Q. (1956), pp. 330–1).

42. *advis'd*] careful; cf. I. i. 142.

43. *Nor will not*] i.e., speak to lady
afterward, . . . (so Pooler).

Por. First forward to the temple, after dinner
   Your hazard shall be made.
Mor.   Good fortune then,   45
   To make me blest or cursed'st among men!
                              [*Cornets.*] *Exeunt.*

[SCENE II.—*Venice.*]

Enter [LAUNCELOT GOBBO] (*the clown*) *alone.*

Laun. Certainly, my conscience will serve me to run from
   this Jew my master: the fiend is at mine elbow, and
   tempts me, saying to me, "Gobbo, Launcelot Gobbo,
   good Launcelot," or "good Gobbo," or "good
   Launcelot Gobbo, use your legs, take the start, run   5
   away." My conscience says "No; take heed honest
   Launcelot, take heed honest Gobbo," or as aforesaid

46. men!] men. *Q*, *F*.   *Cornets*] as *Dyce*; *om. Q*; *after l. 45 F*.

Scene II

Scene II] *Rowe*; *om. Q*, *F*.   *Venice*] *Rowe*; *om. Q*, *F*; *Venice. A Street Capell*.
Launcelot Gobbo] *Capell*; *om. Q*, *F*; Launcelot *Rowe*.   1. *Laun.*] *Rowe*;
Clowne. Q, *F*.   will] *Q*, *F*; will not *Halliwell*.   3, 4, 5. Gobbo] *Q2*; Iobbe *Q*,
F; Job *F3*.   6. away.] away, *Q*.   7, 8. Gobbo] *Q2*; Iobbe *Q*, *F*; Job *F3*.

44. *to the temple*] i.e. to take the oath (so Eccles); on his next appearance (II. vii) Morocco is ready for the hazard. For *temple* = church, cf. *Ado*, III. iii. 171.

46. *blest*] blessedest is perhaps implied from the following superlative (cf. Abbott, ¶398).

Scene II

S.D. clown] probably in two senses; (1) the part was played by the clown of the company, and (2) Launcelot is from the country, a rustic. For the double meaning cf. *AYL.*, II. iv. 66–7.

1. *serve*] allow; cf. IV. i. 440. Halliwell emended because conscience clearly advises *against* running away, but it is dangerous to try confusions

with Launcelot. He may well mean that although conscience speaks against it, he will show good reason why he should go—so his conscience must allow it (cf. ll. 26–8 below: "in my conscience, . . .")

2 ff. *the fiend . . . tempts me, . . .*] Launcelot imagines himself the central character of a morality play (cf. J. Isaacs, *Shakespeare and the Theatre* (1927), p. 94). Such arguments were common in Elizabethan literature; for example, E. Hutchins, *David's Sling* (1581) which contains "A battel betweene the Diuel and the Conscience: . . . made in forme of a Dialogue" (K5).

3–5. *Gobbo . . . Gobbo*] Launcelot affects legal precision.

"honest Launcelot Gobbo, do not run, scorn running
with thy heels." Well, the most courageous fiend
bids me pack, "Fia!" says the fiend, "away!" says   10
the fiend, "for the heavens rouse up a brave mind"
says the fiend, "and run." Well, my conscience
hanging about the neck of my heart, says very wisely
to me: "My honest friend Launcelot"—being an
honest man's son, or rather an honest woman's son,   15
for indeed my father did something smack, something grow to; he had a kind of taste;—well, my conscience says "Launcelot budge not!"—"Budge!"
says the fiend,—"Budge not!" says my conscience.
"Conscience" say I, "you counsel well,—Fiend" say   20
I, "you counsel well,"—to be rul'd by my conscience,
I should stay with the Jew my master, who (God

9. heels.] *Q 2;* heeles; *Q, F.*   10. Fia!] fia (*italic*) *Q, F;* Via *Rowe.*   away!]
away *Q, F.*   11. for] *Q, F;* 'fore *Collier (ii).*   12. run.] *Q 2;* runne; *Q, F.*
18. not!] not, *Q, F.*   Budge!] bouge *Q, F.*   19. not!] not *Q, F.*   conscience.] *Q 2;* conscience, *Q, F.*   20–1. I, . . . I,] I . . . I *Q, F.*   20. well] *Q,
F;* ill *Theobald.*   21. well] *Q, F;* ill *Q 2.*   22. who (God] *Q 2;* (who God *Q, F.*

8–9. *scorn . . . heels*] Cf. *Ado*, III. iv.
50–1: "O illegitimate construction! I
scorn that with my heels."
    10. *pack*] be gone.
    Fia!] It. *via;* "an aduerbe of en-
couraging, much vsed by riders to their
horses, and by commanders" (Florio,
World of Words (1598), quoted Dyce).
Elsewhere in Shakespeare the more
usual form *via* is found; here the spelling may be influenced by *fiend* following, or may represent a dialect (south-
ern) form (ctf. Kökeriz, p. 323).
    11. *for the heavens*] 'fore heaven, by
heaven; a petty oath (cf. Jonson, *The
Case is Altered* (1609), I. v. 42–3: "for
the heauens you mad *Capriccio*, hold
hooke and line"). The wit lies in
making the fiend use it (so Capell).
    11–12. *brave . . . run*] For a similar
absurdity, see *1 H 4*, II. iv. 51–4:
"darest thou be so valiant as to play
the coward with thy indenture, and
show it a fair pair of heels and run from
it?" (so Pooler).
    13. *hanging . . . heart*] i.e., like the
timid wife or mistress—a variant of

Hamlet's "conscience doth make
cowards of us all" (so *N.C.S.*).
    15. *honest*] For *honest* = chaste,
faithful, cf. *Lr.*, I. ii. 9.
    16. *something*] adv., to some degree,
a little.
    smack] have a flavour; for figurative
use cf. *John*, I. i. 208–9.
    17. *grow to*] "A household phrase
applied to milk when burnt to the bottom of the saucepan, and thence ac-
quiring an unpleasant taste" (Clarendon). But there is probably a bawdy
implication; cf. *Ven.*, 540 and Webster, *Devil's Law Case* (1623), I. ii. 278:
"how they grow together". *taste*] Cf.
Lucr., 699: "His taste delicious, . . ."
    20–1. *well . . . well*] Q 2's other "cor-
rections" in this scene (especially at
l. 35 below) show a lack of humour;
there is no reason to believe that *ill* is
authoritative.
    22–3. *God . . . mark*] Probably origi-
nating as a formula to avert an evil
omen (so *O.E.D.*), the phrase was used
as an apology before a profane or in-
decent remark; cf. *Gent.*, IV. iv. 21.

bless the mark) is a kind of devil; and to run away
from the Jew I should be ruled by the fiend, who
(saving your reverence) is the devil himself: certainly   25
the Jew is the very devil incarnation, and in my conscience, my conscience is but a kind of hard conscience, to offer to counsel me to stay with the Jew;
the fiend gives the more friendly counsel: I will run
fiend, my heels are at your commandment, I will run.   30

Enter Old GOBBO *with a basket.*

Gob. Master young man, you I pray you, which is the way
    to Master Jew's?
Laun. [*Aside.*] O heavens! this is my true-begotten father,
    who being more than sand-blind, high gravel-blind,
    knows me not,—I will try confusions with him.   35
Gob. Master young gentleman, I pray you which is the
    way to Master Jew's?
Laun. Turn up on your right hand at the next turning,
    but at the next turning of all on your left; marry at
    the very next turning turn of no hand, but turn down   40
    indirectly to the Jew's house.
Gob. Be God's sonties 'twill be a hard way to hit,—can

23. mark)] *Q, F.*   26. incarnation] *Q, F;* incarnall *Q2.*   27. but] *Q; om. F.*
31. young man] *Q2; hyphened Q, F.*   33. S.D.] *Johnson; om. Q, F.*   heavens!]
heauens, *Q, F.*   35. confusions] *Q, F;* conclusions *Q2.*   37. Jew's?] *Q2;*
Iewes. *Q, F.*   38. up on] *Q;* vpon *F.*   42. Be] *Q, F;* By *F4.*

25. *saving your reverence*] an apology
for an indelicate remark; cf. Harring-
ton, *Metamorphosis of Ajax* (1596), ed.
1814, pp. vii–viii: "old Tarlton was
wont to say, this same excellent word
save-reverence, makes it all mannerly."

26. *incarnation*] Cf. Mistress Quickly's blunder, *H 5,* II. iii. 35 (so *N.C.S.*).

31. *you*] Old Gobbo changes to the
more familiar "thou" when he accepts
Launcelot as his son (l. 87) (so Furness).

31–2. *the . . . Jew's*] The question is
ludicrous, for 5,000 Jews could live in
the Ghetto at Venice (cf. C. Roth,
R.E.S., IX (1933), 150–2).

34. *sand-blind*] purblind; "a vulgar

phrase for it, as *stone-blind* is for those
who are quite so: Launcelot finds a
blind between these, which he calls—
'*gravel-blind*'" (Capell).

high] an intensive; cf. "high good
turn" (*Tit.,* I. i. 397).

35. *confusions*] Cf. "try conclusions"
(*Ham.,* III. iv. 195).

38–41. *Turn . . . house*] Warburton
compared an "indirection" in Ter-
ence, *Adelphi,* IV. ii: "ubi eas præter-
ieris, / Ad sinistram hac recta platea:
ubi ad Dianæ veneris / Ito ad dextram.
prius quam ad portam venias, . . ."

42. *Be God's sonties*] By God's saints;
probably from L. *sanctus, -i,* or old
forms of saint such as sont, sant, sante.
Be is a dialect form.

you tell me whether one Launcelot that dwells with him, dwell with him or no?

Laun. Talk you of young Master Launcelot? [*Aside.*] 45
Mark me now, now will I raise the waters;—talk you of young Master Launcelot?

Gob. No "master" sir, but a poor man's son,—his father (though I say't) is an honest exceeding poor man, and (God be thanked) well to live. 50

Laun. Well, let his father be what a will, we talk of young Master Launcelot.

Gob. Your worship's friend and Launcelot sir.

Laun. But I pray you ergo old man, ergo I beseech you, talk you of young Master Launcelot. 55

Gob. Of Launcelot an't please your mastership.

Laun. Ergo Master Launcelot,—talk not of Master Launcelot father, for the young gentleman (according to fates and destinies, and such odd sayings, the Sisters Three, and such branches of learning), is in- 60
deed deceased, or as you would say in plain terms, gone to heaven.

Gob. Marry God forbid! the boy was the very staff of my age, my very prop.

44. no?] *Q2;* no. *Q, F.*   45. Launcelot?] *Q2;* Launcelet, *Q, F.*   S.D.] *after* now, *(l. 46) Johnson;* om. *Q, F.*   47. Launcelot?] *Q2, F;* Launcelet. *Q.*   53. sir] *Q;* om. *F.*   55. Launcelot.] *Q, F;* Launcelet? *Q 3.*   63. forbid!] forbid, *Q, F.*

45. *Master*] Carter, a rich yeoman, declines the title in *Witch of Edmonton* (pf. 1621), I. ii: "No Gentleman, I, Mr. *Thorney*; spare the Mastership, call me by my name, *John Carter*; Master is a title my Father, nor his before him, were acquainted with."

46. *waters*] i.e., tears.

50. *well to live*] well to do; cf. *Wint.*, III. iii. 125. Perhaps old Gobbo thought it meant "with every prospect of a long life" (Furness' paraphrase).

53. *Your . . . Launcelot*] Steevens compared *LLL.*, v. ii. 574: "Your servant, and Costard," where Costard seems to deprecate the title of Pompey the great.

54. *ergo*] therefore (from L.). The word was ludicrously overworked; according to Nashe, Harvey was "accustomed to make it the Faburden [or refrain] to anie thing hee spake . . . he was cald nothing but *Gabriell Ergo* vp and downe the Colledge" (*Wks*, III. 66–7). Clowns frequently used it on the stage; cf. *All's W.*, I. iii. 53, and *Err.*, IV. iii. 57.

58. *father*] a common form of address to an old man; cf. *Lr.*, IV. vi. 72.

60. *Sisters Three*] the Fates. The humour lies partly in the tautology of these "odd sayings", and partly in the incongruous elevation of style; cf. the heroics of Thisbe (*MND.*, v. i. 343), and Pistol (*2 H 4*, II. iv. 213).

Laun. [*Aside.*] Do I look like a cudgel or a hovel-post, a   65
   staff, or a prop?—Do you know me father?

Gob. Alack the day! I know you not young gentleman,
   but I pray you tell me, is my boy (God rest his soul)
   alive or dead?

Laun. Do you not know me father?   70

Gob. Alack sir I am sand-blind, I know you not.

Laun. Nay, indeed if you had your eyes you might fail of
   the knowing me: it is a wise father that knows his
   own child. Well, old man, I will tell you news of your
   son,—[*Kneels.*] give me your blessing,—truth will   75
   come to light, murder cannot be hid long, a man's
   son may, but in the end truth will out.

Gob. Pray you sir stand up, I am sure you are not Launcelot my boy.

Laun. Pray you let's have no more fooling about it, but   80
   give me your blessing: I am Launcelot your boy that
   was, your son that is, your child that shall be.

Gob. I cannot think you are my son.

Laun. I know not what I shall think of that: but I am
   Launcelot the Jew's man, and I am sure Margery   85
   your wife is my mother.

Gob. Her name is Margery indeed,—I'll be sworn if thou
   be Launcelot, thou art mine own flesh and blood:

65. S.D.] *Collier; om. Q, F.*   66. prop?] prop: *Q, F.*   you] *Q, F;* you not
Dyce (ii).   father?] Father. *Q, F.*   67. day!] day, *Q, F.*   68. God] *F;*
GOD *Q, Q2.*   69. dead?] dead. *Q, F.*   70. father?] *Q2;* Father. *Q, F.*
75. S.D.] *Collier; om. Q, F.*   76. murder] *F;* muder *Q;* Murther *Q2.*   80.
fooling] *Q2, F;* fooling, *Q.*

73–4. *it . . . child*] proverbial, but usually transposed (cf. Tilley, 309).

75. *give . . . blessing*] Henley (Var. '78) saw allusions to the deception practised on the blindness of Isaac; cf. the recognition by feeling Launcelot's hair.

75–6. *truth . . . long*] two proverbs (cf. Tilley, M1315 and T591). They are combined in Kyd, *Spanish Tragedy* (1594), II. vi. 58–60: "The heauens are iust, murder cannot be hid: / Time is the author both of truth and right, /

And time will bring this trecherie to light."

80. *fooling*] Q's comma might indicate that *about it* should be spoken *sotto voce*, in parenthesis; Launcelot allows himself the freedom of fooling about everything else.

82. *child . . . be*] Launcelot probably jokes on the idea of "second childhood" in old age, or else he means that his duty to his father shall, for the future, shew him to be his child (so Steevens).

Lord worshipp'd might he be, what a beard hast thou
got! thou hast got more hair on thy chin, than Dob-   90
bin my fill-horse has on his tail.

Laun. It should seem then that Dobbin's tail grows backward. I am sure he had more hair of his tail than I
have of my face when I last saw him.

Gob. Lord how art thou chang'd! How dost thou and thy   95
master agree? I have brought him a present; how
'gree you now?

Laun. Well, well, but for mine own part, as I have set up
my rest to run away, so I will not rest till I have run
some ground; my master's a very Jew,—give him a   100
present? give him a halter!—I am famish'd in his
service. You may tell every finger I have with my
ribs: father I am glad you are come, give me your
present to one Master Bassanio, who indeed gives
rare new liveries,—if I serve not him, I will run as   105
far as God has any ground. O rare fortune! here

90. got!] got; *Q, F.*   91. fill-horse] *Pope (ii)*; philhorse *Q, F;* Thill-horse
Theobald.   93. of his] *Q, F;* on his *Rowe.*   94. have] *Q, F;* had *Johnson.*
of my] *Q, F;* on my *F3.*   last] *Q2;* lost *Q, F.*   95. chang'd!] changd: *Q, F.*
96. agree?] *Q2;* agree, *Q, F.*   101. present? ... halter!] present, ... halter,
Q, F.   106. fortune!] fortune, *Q, F.*

89. *Lord . . . be*] *Lord* is an exclamation, and *worshipp'd might he be* a phrase
used to avoid irreverence (so Pooler).

what a beard] Stage tradition makes
Old Gobbo feel the back of his son's
head, and mistake the long hair for a
beard (so Staunton).

91. *fill-horse*] a horse which draws in
the "fills", or shafts; cf. *Troil.,* III. ii. 48.
Another form was "thills".

92–3. *backward*] i.e., shorter, with a
possible reference to the position of
Launcelot's "beard" (cf. l. 89, note;
so Pooler).

98–9. *set . . . rest*] determined; the
phrase originated in a card game
called Primero, where it means to venture one's final stake or reserve (so
O.E.D.). This is illustrated in *Err.,* IV.
iii. 27. The pun on *rest,* which Launcelot makes explicit, is reinforced by

another use of the phrase, unconnect-
ed with gaming, in the sense of take up
one's abode; so Lodge, *Rosalynde*
(1590), ed. W. W. Greg (1907), p. 51:
"Aliena resolved there to set up her
rest, . . . and so became mistress of the
farm." See also *Rom.,* v. iii. 110, and
Lr., I. i. 125 where both senses may be
implied.

100. *very*] in the fullest sense.

102. *service.*] "The Q. period denotes stage-business; probably the
traditional action by which La[u]nce-
lot seizes his father's hand and brings
it into contact with the fingers of his
own left hand which are extended rib-
like over his chest" (*N.C.S.*).

103. *me*] ethic dative.

105–6. *as far . . . ground*] proverbial;
Pooler compared *R 2,* I. iii. 251–2: "I
will ride, / As far as land will let me."

comes the man, to him father, for I am a Jew if I
serve the Jew any longer.

Enter BASSANIO *with* [LEONARDO *and*]
a follower or two.

Bass. You may do so, but let it be so hasted that supper be
   ready at the farthest by five of the clock: see these 110
   letters delivered, put the liveries to making, and
   desire Gratiano to come anon to my lodging.
                              [*Exit one of his men.*]
Laun. To him father.
Gob. God bless your worship.
Bass. Gramercy, wouldst thou aught with me?   115
Gob. Here's my son sir, a poor boy.
Laun. Not a poor boy sir, but the rich Jew's man that
   would sir as my father shall specify.
Gob. He hath a great infection sir, (as one would say) to
   serve.   120
Laun. Indeed the short and the long is, I serve the Jew,
   and have a desire as my father shall specify.
Gob. His master and he (saving your worship's reverence)
   are scarce cater-cousins,—
Laun. To be brief, the very truth is, that the Jew having 125
   done me wrong, doth cause me as my father (being I
   hope an old man) shall frutify unto you.

108. Leonardo *and*] *Theobald subs.; om.* Q, F.   112. S.D.] *Q2; om.* Q, F.
115. me?] *Q2;* me. Q, F.   116. boy.] Q, F; boy,— *Theobald.*   118. specify.]
Q, F; specifie,— *Theobald (ii).*   120. serve.] Q, F; serve.— *Johnson.*   122.
specify.] Q, F; specifie,— *Theobald (ii).*   123. (saving . . . reverence)] Q, F.
124. cater-cousins,] Q; catercosins. Q2, F.   127. you.] Q, F; you,—
Theobald (ii).

107. *a Jew*] a type of heartlessness;
cf. *Gent.,* II. iii. 12: "a Jew would have
wept. . ."

116–17. *poor . . . poor*] unfortunate
. . . needy.

119. *infection*] for affection (= inclination, desire, as in *Cor.,* I. i. 181).

124. *scarce*] possibly a quibble; (1)
scarcely, and (2) stingy, parsimonious
(cf. *O.E.D.,* 2).

cater-cousins] close friends; possibly
derived from cater, vb. to supply food,
and hence "fellow bread-eater"
(*O.E.D.*). No blood relationship is
implied.

127. *frutify*] for certify (so Clarendon), or notify; there is probably a
confusion with "fructify", which Sir
Nathaniel uses of his learning (*LLL.,*
IV. ii. 30).

Gob. I have here a dish of doves that I would bestow upon
    your worship, and my suit is—

Laun. In very brief, the suit is impertinent to myself, as 130
    your worship shall know by this honest old man, and
    though I say it, though old man, yet (poor man) my
    father.

Bass. One speak for both, what would you?

Laun. Serve you sir.   135

Gob. That is the very defect of the matter sir.

Bass. I know thee well, thou hast obtain'd thy suit,—
    Shylock thy master spoke with me this day,
    And hath preferr'd thee, if it be preferment
    To leave a rich Jew's service, to become   140
    The follower of so poor a gentleman.

Laun. The old proverb is very well parted between my
    master Shylock and you sir, you have "the grace of
    God" sir, and he hath "enough".

Bass. Thou speak'st it well; go father with thy son—   145
    Take leave of thy old master, and inquire
    My lodging out,—[*To his followers.*] give him
    a livery
    More guarded than his fellows': see it done.

Laun. Father in,—I cannot get a service, no! I have ne'er

129. is—] *Q2*; is. *Q,F.*   142. *Laun.*] *Q2; Clowne. Q,F.*   147. S.D.] *at end of*
line Johnson; om. Q,F.   149. *Laun.*] *Q2; Clowne. Q,F.*   no!] no, *Q,F.*

128. *dish of doves*] "A present thus given, and in our days too, and of doves, is not uncommon in Italy" (C. A. Brown, *Shakespeare's Autobiographical Poems* (1838), p. 110).

132. *though . . . it*] a common phrase; cf. Jonson, *Every Man Out* (1600), II. i. 46–7: "though I say it— / That should not say it."

139. *preferr'd*] recommended for advancement; cf. *Gent.*, II. iv. 157.

142. *proverb*] i.e., "The Grace of God is gear enough" (so Staunton); Tilley (G393) quoted *2 Corinthians*, xii. 9: "My grace is sufficient for thee."

148. *guarded*] braided; a common means of ornamenting clothing, but there is probably a special allusion to

the fool's "long motley coat guarded with yellow" (*H 8*, Prol. 16). L. Hotson (*Shakespeare's Motley* (1952), pp. 57–62) listed many references to a fool's guarded coat, e.g. Chapman, *Monsieur D'Olive* (1606), IV. ii. 50–1: "Well, I perceive Nature has suited your wits, and I'll suit you in guarded coats, answerable to your wits; . . ." From a mere rustic serving man (or clown), Launcelot may be promoted to fool in Bassanio's retinue. There are other signs of this new status: (1) his trial joke (ll. 142–4), (2) S.D. of II. v (see note), (3) he is called ".ool" (II. v. 43, III. v. 40 and 60), (4) II. v. 45 (see note), (5) the licence of his speech in III. v. (see note, l. 5), and (6) III. v. 61–4.

a tongue in my head: well, if any man in Italy have a   150
fairer table which doth offer to swear upon a book,
I shall have good fortune; go to, here's a simple line
of life, here's a small trifle of wives,—alas! fifteen
wives is nothing, aleven widows and nine maids is a
simple coming-in for one man, and then to scape   155
drowning thrice, and to be in peril of my life with the
edge of a feather-bed, here are simple scapes: well, if
Fortune be a woman she's a good wench for this gear:
father come, I'll take my leave of the Jew in the
twinkling.   *Exit [with old Gobbo].* 160
Bass. I pray thee good Leonardo think on this,—

150. head:] head, *Q, F.*   well,] *Q2;* wel: *Q, F.*   150.] S.D., *Looking on his
own hand. (after* well) *Hanmer.*   151. book,] *Q, F;* book.— *Johnson;* book
Knight; book! *Pooler.*   152. have] *Q, F;* have no *Malone conj.*   153. alas!]
alas, *Q, F.*   154. aleven] *Halliwell;* a leuen *Q, F;* eleuen *Q2.*   155. coming-
in] *hyphened Theobald* (ii). 159. in the] *Q, F;* in a *Rowe* (iii). 160. twinkling] *Q,
F, Rowe* (iii); twinkling of an eye *Q2.*   S.D.] *Rowe subs.; Exit Clowne Q, F.*

150–2. *if...fortune*] This is probably
one of Launcelot's "confusions": it has
been variously interpreted: (1) there
is an abrupt break after *book* (so Johnson), (2) Launcelot "says the very
Reverse of what he should do: which
is, *That if* no *Man in* Italy, ..." (Theobald), or (3) for the natural conclusion "he shall have good fortune,"
Launcelot substitutes "I shall have
good fortune," the thought nearest his
heart (so Pooler).
151. *table*] part of the palm of a
hand (a term of palmistry).
which] i.e., the *table* and/or *man.*
offer to swear] "The act of ex-
pounding his hand puts him in mind of
the action in which the palm is shewn,
by raising it to lay it on the book, in
judicial attestations" (Johnson).
152. *go to*] an exclamation of protest, impatience, or disparagement.
simple] unremarkable, humble.
154. *aleven*] Q's "a leuen" was a
common form of eleven. Wilson called
it a "Shakespearian spelling" (*Shakespeare's Hand in* Sir Thomas More
(1923), pp. 126 and 136); it is found
elsewhere in good texts (i.e., *LLL.,*III.

i. 172; *Troil.,*III. ii. 296; *Rom.,*I. iii. 34;
and *Ham.,* I. ii. 252) and in "Addition
D" of *More.* On each occasion, except
in *Ham.,* the speaker is a "low" character, viz. Costard, Thersites, the
Nurse, and John Lincoln, the broker.
155. *coming-in*] income, revenue.
156. *drowning*] Professor Sisson has
referred me to *The Works of John
Metham* (ed. 1916), pp. 114–15 for the
lines signifying *drowning* and "pereel of
water". Here *drowning,* following
coming-in, may have a quibbling sense
of going bankrupt; cf. Greene, *A Quip
for an Upstart Courtier* (1592), *Wks,* xi.
238: "A clownes sonne must be clapt
in a Veluet pontophle, and a veluet
breech, though ye presumptuous asse
be drownd in the Mercers booke, &
make a con[v]ey of all his lands to the
vsurer for commodities."
157. *edge ... bed*] "A cant phrase to
signify the danger of marrying" (Warburton).
158. *gear*] business, purpose.
159–60. *the twinkling*] There is no
need to depart from Q; cf. *Every
Woman in her Humour* (1609), I. i:
"Heere and there in the twinckling."

These things being bought and orderly bestowed
Return in haste, for I do feast to-night
My best-esteem'd acquaintance, hie thee go.

Leon. My best endeavours shall be done herein.   165
                                        [*He leaves Bassanio.*]

Enter GRATIANO.

Gra. Where's your master?
Leon.   Yonder sir he walks.   *Exit.*
Gra. Signior Bassanio!
Bass. Gratiano!
Gra. I have suit to you.
Bass.   You have obtain'd it.
Gra. You must not deny me, I must go with you to Belmont.
Bass. Why then you must—but hear thee Gratiano,   171
Thou art too wild, too rude, and bold of voice,
Parts that become thee happily enough,
And in such eyes as ours appear not faults—
But where thou art not known;—why there they show
Something too liberal,—pray thee take pain   176

---

164. best-esteem'd] *hyphened Theobald (ii).*   165. *He . . . Bassanio*] *N.C.S. subs.;*
Exit Leonardo Q, F; om. Rowe, Theobald.   165.] S.D., *Scene* III (*at end of line*)
Pope.   166. Where's] *Q, F; Where is Pope.*   master?] Maister. *Q, F.*
S.D.] *Theobald subs.; om. Q, F.*   167. Bassanio!] Bassanio. *Q, F;* Bassanio,—
Theobald.   168. Gratiano!] Gratiano. *Q, F;* Gratiano? *Q2.*   169. I have] *Q;*
I haue a *Q2,F.*   170. You] *Q, F;* Nay, you *Hanmer.*   You . . . Belmont] as *Q;*
. . . to / Belmont *F;* . . . go / With . . . *Hanmer;* . . . you / To . . . *Kittredge.*
171. thee] *Q, F;* me *Q3.*   174. faults] *Q;* faults; *F.*   175. thou art] *Q;* they
are *F.*   known;] *Q;* knowne. *Q2;* knowne, *F.*

---

162. *bestowed*] i.e., on board ship (so
Furness).

165. S.D. He . . . Bassanio] His exit
is delayed by Gratiano's entry.

169. *have suit*] Elsewhere Shakespeare uses an article, as in Q2 and F,
but there is no need for emendation,
for the phrase was current without one.

170. *You . . . Belmont*] This may be
verse (as Hanmer), but short, single
speeches in prose are found elsewhere
(e.g. II. iv. 10–11, and II. v. 8–9).

171. *Why . . . must*] Cf. *John*, IV. i. 55:
"If heaven be pleased that you must

use me ill, / Why then you must"; the
idea was proverbial (cf. Tilley,
M1331).

thee] Abbott (¶231) noted the
change to the singular pronoun as
Bassanio becomes more familiar.

176. *liberal*] unrestrained; Desde-
mona describes Iago's humour as
"most profane and liberal" (*Oth.*, II. i.
165).

pain] Shakespeare usually used
"pains" as in IV. i. 7 and V. i. 182, but
the singular occurs in *H 8*, III. ii. 72 and
is a common variant of the phrase.

To allay with some cold drops of modesty
Thy skipping spirit, lest through thy wild behaviour
I be misconst'red in the place I go to,
And lose my hopes.

Gra.   Signior Bassanio, hear me,—   180
If I do not put on a sober habit,
Talk with respect, and swear but now and then,
Wear prayer-books in my pocket, look demurely,
Nay more, while grace is saying hood mine eyes
Thus with my hat, and sigh and say "amen":   185
Use all the observance of civility
Like one well studied in a sad ostent
To please his grandam, never trust me more.

Bass. Well, we shall see your bearing.

Gra. Nay but I bar to-night, you shall not gauge me   190
By what we do to-night.

Bass.   No that were pity,
I would entreat you rather to put on
Your boldest suit of mirth, for we have friends
That purpose merriment: but fare you well,
I have some business.   195

Gra. And I must to Lorenzo and the rest,
But we will visit you at supper-time.   *Exeunt.*

---

177. To] *Q, F;* T' *Pope.*   179. misconst'red] *Q;* misconsterd *F;* miscon-
stru'd *Rowe.*   182. then] *F2;* than *Q, F.*   183. pocket] *Q, F;* Pockets *Rowe.*

177. *allay*] temper, qualify (from L.
alligare); cf. *H 8,* I. i. 148–9: "If with
the sap of reason you would quench, /
Or but allay, the fire of passion . . ."
   modesty] decorum; cf. *Shr.,* Ind. i. 94.
   179. *misconst'red*] i.e., misconstrued;
the vb. was often spelt -ster.
   181. *habit*] bearing, disposition.
There is a quibble on the primary
sense of clothes, dress; cf. ll. 192–3
below. Gratiano does not promise to
be sober, but only to appear so.

183. *prayer-books . . . pocket*] Pooler
compared Greene, *Groatsworth of Wit*
(1592), *Wks,* xii. 104: "he was religious too, neuer without a booke at his
belt."
   184–5. *hood . . . hat*] Hats were worn
during dinner (so Malone).
   186. *observance of civility*] respect due
to good manners.
   187. *ostent*] appearance, show.
   189–90. *bearing . . . bar*] a jingle (cf.
Kökeritz, p. 70).

[SCENE III.—*Venice.*]

Enter JESSICA *and* [LAUNCELOT] *the clown.*

Jes. I am sorry thou wilt leave my father so,
Our house is hell, and thou (a merry devil)
Didst rob it of some taste of tediousness,—
But fare thee well, there is a ducat for thee,
And Launcelot, soon at supper shalt thou see   5
Lorenzo, who is thy new master's guest,
Give him this letter,—do it secretly,—
And so farewell: I would not have my father
See me in talk with thee.

Laun. Adieu! tears exhibit my tongue, most beautiful   10
pagan, most sweet Jew!—if a Christian do not play
the knave and get thee, I am much deceived; but
adieu! these foolish drops do something drown my
manly spirit: adieu!   [*Exit.*]

Jes. Farewell good Launcelot.   15
Alack, what heinous sin is it in me
To be ashamed to be my father's child!
But though I am a daughter to his blood

Scene III

Scene III] *Capell; om. Q, F; Scene* IV *Pope.*   *Venice*] *om. Q, F; Shylock's house
Theobald; The same. A Room in Shylock's House Capell.*   Launcelot] *Rowe; om.
Q, F.*   1. I am] *Q, F;* I'm *Pope.*   9. in] *Q; om. F.*   10. Laun.] *Q2;
Clowne. Q, F.*   Adieu!] Adiew, *Q, F.*   11. Jew!] Iewe, *Q, F.*   do] *Q, F;*
did *F2.*   13. adieu!] adiew, *Q, F.*   something] *Q;* somewhat *F.*   14.
adieu!] adiew. *Q, F.*   S.D.] *Q2, F; om. Q; after l. 15 Capell.*   17. child!]
child, *Q, F;* Child? *Rowe.*

---

5. *soon*] early.

10. *exhibit*] Eccles paraphrased "My
tears serve to express what my tongue
should, if sorrow would permit it," but
probably it is Launcelot's blunder for
prohibit (Halliwell) or inhibit (Clarendon).

11. *pagan*] This may have a scur-
rilous undertone: cf. *2 H 4,* II. ii.
168.

do] Malone upheld the reading of
Qq and F by comparing II. vi. 23:
"When you shall please to play the

thieves for wives"; Launcelot seems
fond of hinting at what is going to
happen (cf. II. v. 22–3). If F2's "did" is
accepted, *get* is used for beget, as in
III. v. 9.

13–14. *foolish . . . spirit*] "tears do not
become a man" (*AYL.,* III. iv. 3); cf.
also *H 5,* IV. vi. 28–32.

18–19. *daughter . . . manners*] There is
probably word-play on "man"; cf.
Lyly, *Campaspe* (1584), IV. i. 28–9:
"Yee tearme me an hater of menne;
no, I am a hater of your manners."

I am not to his manners: O Lorenzo
If thou keep promise I shall end this strife,   20
Become a Christian and thy loving wife!   *Exit.*

[SCENE IV.—*Venice.*]

Enter GRATIANO, LORENZO, SALERIO, *and* SOLANIO.

Lor. Nay, we will slink away in supper-time,
Disguise us at my lodging, and return
All in an hour.
Gra. We have not made good preparation.
Sal. We have not spoke us yet of torch-bearers,—   5
Sol. 'Tis vile unless it may be quaintly ordered,
And better in my mind not undertook.

21. wife!] wife. *Q, F.*

Scene IV

Scene IV] *Capell; om. Q, F;* Scene v *Pope.   Venice] om. Q, F; the Street Theo-bald; The same. A Street Capell.   Salerio] N.C.S.; Salaryno Q; Slarino F; Solarino Rowe; Salerino Capell.   Solanio] Capell; Salanio Q, F; Solania F2.* 1–3. Nay . . . hour] *as Capell;* . . . time, / Disguise . . . *Q, F; as prose Pope.* 5. *Sal.] F; Salari. Q.   *us] Q, F; as F4.   *torch-bearers,] Q; Torch-bearers. F.* 6. *Sol.] F; Solanio. Q; Salanio. Q2.*

20. *strife*] The strife/wife rhyme was frequent in popular literature and the sense of the former was consequently weakened (cf. *O.E.D.*, 1d).

Scene IV

1. *slink . . . supper-time*] Here, and in other plays, Shakespeare used the masque of the early Tudor period; the masquers made a formal entry and then joined the other guests in a dance. In *Ado* (II. i) the masque is after supper and in *H 8* (I. iv) it is a surprise to guests and host alike. Masquers wore visors (as in *Ado*) and disguised themselves fantastically (as in *H 8* and *LLL.*, v. ii).

in] during (cf. Abbott, ¶161).

3. *All . . . hour*] This "broken line" suggests that "a passage about the masque has been 'cut'; we do not

actually learn that a masque is afoot until l. 22" (*N.C.S.*). If the line is an imperfection, it could equally well be a sign of foul-paper copy (see Introduction, p. xvi), but Shakespeare may have adopted an indirect exposition to stimulate interest or give the illusion of casual conversation (cf. l. 21, note, below).

5. *spoke us*] Capell paraphrased "bespoke us", but F4 may be right, for "a" and "u" were easily confused in Elizabethan secretary hand (so *N.C.S.*).

torch-bearers] a common feature of masques; cf. *Rom.*, I. iv. S.D. Henry VIII had 16 torchbearers when his masquers arrived at Wolsey's banquet (so Holinshed, *Chronicles*, ed. 1808, iii. 763).

6. *quaintly*] skilfully, elegantly.

7. *undertook*] an Elizabethan form of the past participle.

Lor. 'Tis now but four of clock, we have two hours
      To furnish us;

          Enter LAUNCELOT[, *with a letter*].

                friend Launcelot what's the news?
Laun. And it shall please you to break up this, it shall   10
      seem to signify.
Lor. I know the hand, in faith 'tis a fair hand,
      And whiter than the paper it writ on
      Is the fair hand that writ.
Gra.   Love-news in faith.
Laun. By your leave sir.   15
Lor. Whither goest thou?
Laun. Marry sir to bid my old master the Jew to sup to-
      night with my new master the Christian.
Lor. Hold here—take this, tell gentle Jessica
      I will not fail her,—speak it privately. *Exit* [*Launcelot*]. 20
      Go gentlemen,
      Will you prepare you for this masque to-night?
      I am provided of a torch-bearer.
Sal. Ay marry, I'll be gone about it straight.
Sol. And so will I.
Lor.   Meet me and Gratiano   25

8. of] *Q, F;* a *Q2.*   9. S.D.] *as Johnson; at end of line Q, F; after l. 8 Q2.*
with a letter] F; om. Q.   news?] *Q2;* newes. *Q, F.*   10–11. it shall seem] *Q;*
shall it seeme *F.*   13. it] *Q, F;* it is *Rowe (iii);* that it *Hanmer.*   14. Is] *Q;*
I *F.*   Love-news] *F2;* Loue, newes *Q;* Loue newes, *Q2;* Loue newes *F.*
16. thou?] *Q2, F;* thou. *Q.*   20. privately.] *Q2;* priuatly, *Q.*   S.D.] *as
White (ii); after l. 23 Q, F; after l. 21 Capell; after l. 22 Staunton.   Launcelot*]
Rowe subs.; Clowne Q, F.   20-2. I . . . to-night] *as Collier; . . .* priuatly, /
Goe . . . *Q, F; . . .* go.— / Gentlemen, / Will . . . *Capell.*   21. Go] *Q,F;* Go,
Rowe; Go.— *Theobald.*   22. to-night?] to night, *Q, F.*   24. Sal.] *Q, F;*
Salar. Q2.   25. Sol.] *Q, F; Salan. Q2.*   25-6. Meet . . . hence] *as Pope;*
. . . lodging / Some . . . *Q, F.*

   10. *And*] If.
   break up] open; cf. *Wint.*, III. II.
132.
   13. *it writ on*] Hanmer's emendation
would regularize the metre (and Furness noted that "yt" and "yt" were
easily confused), but in this context *on*
may well take the stress and so point
the antithesis with *writ* in l. 14 (so
Pooler).

   21. *Go gentlemen*] Here, and at l. 27
below, *N.C.S.* suggested the short line
was a sign of a "cut", but in both cases
there is a change in the tone of the
dialogue and the short line might be
intended to emphasize this. The whole
scene seems designed to give the impression of casual and fragmentary
conversation, of many things about to
happen.

At Gratiano's lodging some hour hence.
Sal. 'Tis good we do so.   [*Exeunt Salerio and Solanio.*]
Gra. Was not that letter from fair Jessica?
Lor. I must needs tell thee all,—she hath directed
    How I shall take her from her father's house,   30
    What gold and jewels she is furnish'd with,
    What page's suit she hath in readiness,—
    If e'er the Jew her father come to heaven,
    It will be for his gentle daughter's sake,
    And never dare misfortune cross her foot,   35
    Unless she do it under this excuse,
    That she is issue to a faithless Jew:
    Come go with me, peruse this as thou goest,—
    Fair Jessica shall be my torch-bearer.   [*Exeunt.*]

[SCENE V.—*Venice. Before Shylock's House.*]

Enter [SHYLOCK *the*] *Jew and* [LAUNCELOT] *his man*
that was the clown.

Shy. Well, thou shalt see, thy eyes shall be thy judge,
    The difference of old Shylock and Bassanio;—

27. *Sal.*] *Q*, *F*; *Salar. Q2.*   S.D.] *N.C.S. subs.*; *Exit Q*, *F*; *Exeunt Sal. and Sol*
Capell.   28. Jessica?] *Q2*, *F*; *Iessica. Q.*   39. S.D.] *Rowe*; *Exit Q*, *F*.

Scene v

Scene v] *Capell*; *om. Q*, *F*; Scene vi *Pope.   Venice . . . House*] *Malone subs.*; *om.*
Q, *F*; *Shylock's house Theobald*; *The same. Before Shylock's Door Capell.*   Shylock
the] *om. Q*, *F*; *Shylock Rowe.*   Launcelot] *Q2*; *om. Q*, *F*, *Capell.*   *his . . .*
clown] *Q*, *F*; *om. Q2*; *Clown Capell.*   1. *Shy.*] *Q2*; *Iewe. Q*, *F*.   shalt] *Q*; shall
F.   thy judge] *Q*, *F*; the judge *Keightley conj.*

34. *gentle*] a pun on Gentile, as in
II. vi. 51; the words were not completely distinguished in spelling at this
time.

35. *dare*] i.e., will dare, or possibly a
subjunctive (cf. Abbott, ¶364).
  her foot] "i.e., her path" (*N.C.S.*).
37. *faithless*] unbelieving.

Scene v

S.D. his . . . clown] Either (1) there
should be a comma after *was*, and *the*
clown be a further description of the

character (cf. Introduction, p. xv), or
(2) Launcelot has ceased to be merely
a rustic "clown" and now appears in
the long motley "guarded" coat of a
fool of Bassanio's household (cf. II. ii.
148, note).
  The fact that Launcelot continues to be called Clown in S.D.s
and speech prefixes need not invali-
date the second interpretation; Feste is
so called in *Tw.N.*—he was a fool in
the play, but the clown of the theatre
company.

What Jessica!—thou shalt not gormandize
As thou hast done with me:—what Jessica!—
And sleep, and snore, and rend apparel out.   5
Why Jessica I say!

Laun.   Why Jessica!

Shy. Who bids thee call? I do not bid thee call.

Laun. Your worship was wont to tell me, I could do
   nothing without bidding.

Enter JESSICA.

Jes. Call you? what is your will?   10

Shy. I am bid forth to supper Jessica,
   There are my keys:—but wherefore should I go?
   I am not bid for love, they flatter me,
   But yet I'll go in hate, to feed upon
   The prodigal Christian. Jessica my girl,   15
   Look to my house,—I am right loath to go,
   There is some ill a-brewing towards my rest,
   For I did dream of money-bags to-night.

Laun. I beseech you sir go, my young master doth expect
   your reproach.   20

Shy. So do I his.

Laun. And they have conspired together,—I will not say
   you shall see a masque, but if you do, then it was not
   for nothing that my nose fell a-bleeding on Black-

3. Jessica!] Iessica, *Q*, *F*.   4. Jessica!] Iessica, *Q*; Iessica? *Q2*, *F*.   6. say!]
say. *Q*, *F*.   *Laun.*] *Rowe; Clowne. Q*, *F*.   Jessica!] Iessica. *Q*, *F*.   7. do]
Q, *F*; did *Rowe*.   8. *Laun.*] *Rowe; Clow. Q*, *F*.   8–9. Your . . . bidding] *as
Q2*; . . . me, / I . . . *Q*, *F*.   19, 22, 39. *Laun.*] *Rowe; Clowne. Q*, *F*.   19–20. I
. . . reproach] *as Pope*; . . . Maister / doth . . . *Q*; . . . go, / My . . . *Q2*; . . .
Master / Doth . . . *F*.

3. *gormandize*] Launcelot says he
was "famish'd" (II. ii. 101).

14–15. *to . . . Christian*] Shakespeare
meant to "heighten the malignity" of
Shylock "by making him depart from
his most settled resolve [cf. I. iii. 29–
33], for the prosecution of his revenge"
(Steevens).

17. *ill*] The interpretation of dreams
was notoriously difficult; *money-bags*
might bode good or ill. Shylock
guards against the worst interpreta-

tion. Cf. Nashe, *Terrors of the Night*
(1594), *Wks*, i. 358: "Dreames to none
are so fearfull, as to those whose
accusing priuate guilt expects mis-
chiefe euerie hower for their merit."
See also *Gernutus*, st. v (Appendix II).

18. *to-night*] i.e., last night (cf.
Abbott, ¶190).

24. *a-bleeding*] Reed compared Webster, *Duchess of Malfi* (1623), II. iii. 58–
60: "My nose bleedes, / One that were
superstitious, would count / This

Monday last, at six o'clock i' th' morning, falling out   25
that year on Ash-Wednesday was four year in th'
afternoon.

Shy. What are there masques? Hear you me Jessica,
Lock up my doors, and when you hear the drum
And the vile squealing of the wry-neck'd fife   30
Clamber not you up to the casements then
Nor thrust your head into the public street
To gaze on Christian fools with varnish'd faces:
But stop my house's ears, I mean my casements,
Let not the sound of shallow fopp'ry enter   35
My sober house. By Jacob's staff I swear
I have no mind of feasting forth to-night:
But I will go: go you before me sirrah,
Say I will come.

35. fopp'ry] *Q;* foppery *Q 2, F.*

ominous." Launcelot is mocking
Shylock's superstition or fear.

24–5. *Black-Monday*] Dreams [and
omens] happening on great feast days
of the church "shewe maruelous matters to follow, . . ." (T. Hill, *Interpretation of Dreams* (1576), E2); Launcelot,
mocking Shylock's superstition, has
chosen the day *after* Easter day. It was
so called because in 1360 it "was full
darke of mist and haile, and so bitter
cold, that many men dyed on their
horsebacks with the cold" (Stowe,
Chronicle, ed. 1631, p. 264b; quoted
Gray, *ap.* Johnson).

25–7. *at six . . . afternoon*] a jumble
of details which guys the manner of
prognostications.

29–30. *drum . . . fife*] Masquers were
usually accompanied by musicians; a
drum is used in *Rom.* (cf. I. iv. 114) and
Henry VIII's masque had several
(Holinshed, *op. cit.*).

30. *wry-neck'd fife*] Boswell quoted
Barnaby Riche, *Irish Hubbub* (1616),
"A fife is a wry-neckt musician, for
he always looks away from his in-
strument." Malone suggested that
Shakespeare imitated Horace, *Carm.*,
III. vii: "Prima nocte domum claude;

neque in vias / Sub cantu querulae
despice tibiæ."

32. *public street*] Masquers would
sometimes parade through the streets
before entering the place of revelry; so
did the masquers from the Middle
Temple when they visited the court on
Twelfth Night, 1598 (cf. *Elizabethan
Stage*, I. 169).

33. *varnish'd*] Explained as, (1)
painted (Halliwell quoted Coryat, i.
404: "Cortezans . . . doe varnish their
faces . . . with these kinde of sordid
trumperies"), or (2) "a reference to
the visors of the masquers" (*N.C.S.*).
In either case, Shylock is probably
hinting at Christian duplicity; Clarendon compared *Tim.*, IV. ii. 36: "But
only painted, like his varnish'd
friends."

35. *fopp'ry*] foolery, stupidness.

36. *Jacob's staff*] a suitable oath; cf.
G. Babington, *Notes upon . . . Genesis*
(1592), S1ᵛ: (on *Genesis*, xxxii. 10) "I
cannot omit this godly remembrance
that *Iacob* here maketh of his first estate
when he came into the countrey, and of
his estate present now when hee doth
returne. *With my staffe* saith he, *came I
ouer this Iorden & now haue I gotten two*

Laun.   I will go before sir.
  Mistress look out at window for all this,—   40
      There will come a Christian by
      Will be worth a Jewes eye.   [*Exit.*]
Shy. What says that fool of Hagar's offspring? ha?
Jes. His words were "Farewell mistress," nothing else.
Shy. The patch is kind enough, but a huge feeder,   45
      Snail-slow in profit, and he sleeps by day
      More than the wild-cat: drones hive not with me,
      Therefore I part with him, and part with him
      To one that I would have him help to waste
      His borrowed purse. Well Jessica go in,—   50
      Perhaps I will return immediately,—
      Do as I bid you, shut doors after you,

39–40. I . . . this] *as Q, F; as prose Collier.*   42. Jewes] *Q, F;* Jew's *F3;* Jewess'
Pope; Jewès *Keightley.*   S.D.] Rowe *subs.; om. Q, F.*   43. ha?] ha. *Q, F.*
46. Snail-slow] *hyphened Q2, F.*   and] *Q;* but *F.*   52–3. Do . . . find] *as Q2;
one line Q, F;* Shut . . . find / *Pope;* . . . you.— / Shut . . . *Theobald.*   52. shut]
Q, F; Shut the *Pope.*

bandes. A notable meditation morning
and euening for rich marchantes . . .
whom God hath exalted from litle
too much, . . ."
  39–40. *I . . . this*] l. 40 is difficult as
verse; Launcelot may complete the
verse line of the previous speaker (as in
l. 6 above) and then introduce his
couplet with a line of prose, his normal
idiom.
  42. *Jewes eye*] So Q's spelling is elsewhere to be understood, and to read
"Jewess" amounts to emendation.
Although *Jew's* is monosyllabic elsewhere (e.g. II. viii. 41), here, in a proverb and jigging verse, it might well be
disyllabic; Pooler compared *Travels of
the Three English Brothers* (1607), ed.
Bullen, pp. 60 and 62: "A Christian's
torture is a Jewes blisse" and "No
more of this, weele have a Jewes
Jigge." "Jew" is of common gender
elsewhere (II. iii. 11). For the proverb,
Dowden compared G. Harvey, *Pierce's
Supererogation* (1593), ed. Grosart, ii.
146: "as deare as a Iewes eye."
  43. *Hagar's offspring*] Hagar was a

Gentile and bondwoman to Sarah, Abraham's wife; her son was an outcast.
  45. *patch*] Sir T. Wilson (*Art of
Rhetoric* (ed. 1585), pp. 173–4) cited
the custom of calling one "Patche or
Coulson, whom we see to doe a thing
foolishly, because these two in their
tyme were notable fooles." *O.E.D.*
derived the name from It. *pazzo,* fool,
or from a jester's patched dress or face.
Bottom speaks of a "patched fool"
(*MND.,* IV. i. 215) and Trinculo is
called "pied ninny" and "patch"
(*Tp.,* III. ii. 71).
  kind] perhaps, "natural" (cf. I. iii.
138, note); i.e., Launcelot makes a
"natural" fool (cf. II. ii. 148, note).
  46. *profit*] improvement; cf. *AYL.,*
I. i. 7.
  sleeps by day] Cf. Salerno, *Regimen
Sanitatis* (tr. 1557), B6v: "after none
slepe causeth man to be slouthful . . .
for grosse humors & undigested cause
mans spirites slowely to moue the
bodi."
  47. *wild-cat*] Prowling at night, it
sleeps all day (so Clarendon).

Fast bind, fast find,—
A proverb never stale in thrifty mind.   *Exit.*
Jes. Farewell,—and if my fortune be not crost,   55
I have a father, you a daughter, lost.   *Exit.*

[SCENE VI.—*The Same.*]

Enter the masquers, GRATIANO *and* SALERIO.

Gra. This is the penthouse under which Lorenzo
Desired us to make stand.
Sal.   His hour is almost past.
Gra. And it is marvel he out-dwells his hour,
For lovers ever run before the clock.
Sal. O ten times faster Venus' pigeons fly   5
To seal love's bonds new-made, than they are wont
To keep obliged faith unforfeited!

53. find,] *Q2,F;* find. *Q.*   56. daughter,] daughter *Q,F.*

Scene VI

Scene VI] *Capell; om. Q,F, Halliwell;* Scene VII *Pope.   The Same*] *Capell; om. Q,F; the Street Theobald; Behind Shylock's House Collier* (iii).   Salerio] *N.C.S.;* Salerino *Q;* Salarino *Q2;* Salino *F;* Salanio *Rowe.*   1–2. This . . . stand] *as Q,F;* . . . which / Lorenzo . . . *Q2; as prose Rowe.*   2. make] *Q;* make a *F.*   5. pigeons] *Q,F;* Widgeons *Warburton.*   6. seal] *Q;* steale *F.*   7. unforfeited!] vnforfaited. *Q,F.*

53. *Fast . . . find*] For the proverb, see Tilley, B352. The lining is difficult, but a couplet with a short first line is found elsewhere (e.g. *Gent.*, II. ii. 20–1 and *1 H 6,* V. iii. 108–9).

Scene VI

1. *penthouse*] porch, or shelter with sloping roof; the balcony of the upper stage or the "heavens" (or roof) over the stage could do service as a *penthouse* in the Elizabethan theatre. There is a similar reference in *Ado,* III. iii. 111.

1–2. *Lorenzo . . . stand*] a secret arrangement; when we last saw them, they arranged to meet at Gratiano's lodging, and it must be to that rendezvous that they hurry at l. 59 below. In view of this, *masquers* of the S.D. cannot imply that others taking part in

the masque are meant to be present; it describes how Gratiano and Salerio are dressed.

5. *Venus' pigeons*] Probably an allusion to the doves which drew Venus' chariot (see, for example, *Tp.*, IV. i. 94); they are more ready to take Venus to preside at a betrothal, than at a marriage (so Pooler). Since a *pigeon* was primarily a young dove, Salerio may imply that Venus is drawn by youth.

Another interpretation is that *pigeons* are lovers, who were often called "turtles" or "doves" (so Johnson); the joke then would be that *pigeon* (as Warburton's "widgeon") was also used of a simpleton or gull (cf. *O.E.D.*, 3b).

7. *obliged faith*] "faith bound by contract" (Clarendon).

Gra. That ever holds: who riseth from a feast
    With that keen appetite that he sits down?
    Where is the horse that doth untread again   10
    His tedious measures with the unbated fire
    That he did pace them first?—all things that are,
    Are with more spirit chased than enjoy'd.
    How like a younger or a prodigal
    The scarfed bark puts from her native bay—   15
    Hugg'd and embraced by the strumpet wind!
    How like the prodigal doth she return
    With over-weather'd ribs and ragged sails—
    Lean, rent, and beggar'd by the strumpet wind!

Enter LORENZO.

Sal. Here comes Lorenzo, more of this hereafter.   20
Lor. Sweet friends, your patience for my long abode
    (Not I but my affairs have made you wait):
    When you shall please to play the thieves for wives
    I'll watch as long for you then: approach—

12. first?] *Q2;* first: *Q, F.*   are,] *Q2, F;* are *Q.*   14. younger] *Q, F;*
Younker *Rowe.*   16. wind!] wind, *Q.*   17. the] *Q;* a *F.*   18. over-
weather'd] *Q3;* ouer-wetherd *Q;* ouer-wither'd *F.*   19. wind!] wind? *Q, F.*
S.D.] *as Q, F; after l. 20 Dyce.*   20. *Sal.*] *Q; Salino. F.*

10. *untread*] retrace.

11. *measures*] Horses were put
through their paces in a formal "manage"; cf. T. Blunderville, *Horsemanship*
(ed. 1597), II–Iᵛ: ". . . beware that in
maneging your horse, ye gallop him
not at the first to swiftlie: for so shall he
neuer be able to continue with one time
and mesure, . . . for after a while euery
one shall be slower than another."

14. *younger*] younger son (so
Schmidt), usually used in apposition to
elder. The word could easily be confused with "younker" which Shakespeare used elsewhere (e.g., *3 H 6*, II. i.
24) and some editors read here; this
word was originally from Dutch or
German (modern, *jonker* or *junker*) and
meant young nobleman. Cf. l. 16, note,
for an allusion which makes *younger*
the more likely reading here.

15. *scarfed*] i.e., decorated with flags,

as a gallant with scarves; cf. *All's W*,
II. iii. 214 (so Steevens). It may also
allude to a ship's hull which is *scarfed* or
jointed together.

16. *strumpet wind*] "The reference,
of course, is to the harlots with whom
the 'younger', or Prodigal, wasted
his substance" (*N.C.S.*); cf. *Luke*, xv.
H. T. Price compared the proverb,
"Free as air" (Tilley, A88) and *H 5*, I.
i. 48 and *Oth.*, IV. ii. 78.

18. *over-weather'd*] worn or damaged
by exposure to the weather; the word
ribs continues the comparison between
a ship and the prodigal (cf. ll. 15 and
16, notes, above).

24. *I'll . . . approach*] The irregular
metre of this line, and the short lines
below (28 and 46), may suggest pauses
in delivery. They may, however, be
due to "cuts" (so *N.C.S.*) or foul-paper
copy (see Introduction, p. xvi).

Here dwells my father Jew. How! who's within?   25

[Enter] JESSICA *above[, in boy's clothes]*.

Jes. Who are you?—tell me for more certainty,
   Albeit I'll swear that I do know your tongue.
Lor. Lorenzo and thy love.
Jes. Lorenzo certain, and my love indeed,
   For who love I so much? and now who knows   30
   But you Lorenzo whether I am yours?
Lor. Heaven and thy thoughts are witness that thou art.
Jes. Here catch this casket, it is worth the pains.
   I am glad 'tis night—you do not look on me,—
   For I am much asham'd of my exchange: 35
   But love is blind, and lovers cannot see
   The pretty follies that themselves commit,
   For if they could, Cupid himself would blush
   To see me thus transformed to a boy.
Lor. Descend, for you must be my torch-bearer.   40
Jes. What, must I hold a candle to my shames?—
   They in themselves (goodsooth) are too too light.
   Why, 'tis an office of discovery (love),
   And I should be obscur'd.
Lor.   So are you (sweet)
   Even in the lovely garnish of a boy.   45
   But come at once,

25. How!] Howe *Q;* Ho, *Q2;* Hoa, *F.*   Enter] *Capell; om. Q, F.*   in . . .
clothes] *Rowe; om. Q, F.*   30. For who] *Q, F;* For whom *Johnson.*   33. pains.]
paines, *Q, F.*   34. I am] *Q, F;* I'm *Pope.*   41. shames?] *F;* shames, *Q;* shame?
F2.   44. are you] *Q;* you are *F.*   45-7. Even . . . runaway] *as Pope;* . . . once, /
[F]or . . . *Q, F;* . . . boy, / But . . . night / Doth . . . *Q2.*   45. boy.] boy, *Q.*

25. *How!]* an exclamation to attract attention, as Ho! (cf. *O.E.D.*).

30. *who]* occasionally used for whom.

37. *pretty]* perhaps, artful, ingenious (often ironical as in *2 H 6*, I. iv. 59, and *Ado*, v. i. 202).

41. *hold a candle]* i.e., stand by and see something happening; cf. *Rom.*, I. iv. 38 and T. Tyro, *Tyro's Roaring Megge* (1598), B3ᵛ—from an epigram by a rejected lover: "Base-minded thing, shall asses trapt in gold / Haue free accesse, while I the candle hold?"

Some quotations in Tilley, C40, suggest a bawdy application, as in "to keep the door" (so J. C. Maxwell, privately).

42. *light]* for the pun, cf. v. i. 129.

43. *of discovery]* i.e., which reveals, or brings to light; cf. *Troil.*, v. ii. 5.

44. *obscur'd]* hid, darkened; Lorenzo puns on a further sense, disguised (as in *Wint.*, IV. iv. 8).

45. *garnish]* The verb was used occasionally in the sense, to clothe, or adorn; cf. III. v. 63; and *O.E.D.*, 3 and 4.

For the close night doth play the runaway,
And we are stay'd for at Bassanio's feast.

Jes. I will make fast the doors and gild myself
With some moe ducats, and be with you straight.   50
                                    [*Exit above.*]

Gra. Now (by my hood) a gentle, and no Jew.
Lor. Beshrew me but I love her heartily,
For she is wise, if I can judge of her,
And fair she is, if that mine eyes be true,
And true she is, as she hath prov'd herself: 55
And therefore like herself, wise, fair, and true,
Shall she be placed in my constant soul.

Enter JESSICA.

What, art thou come?—on gentlemen, away!
Our masquing mates by this time for us stay.
Exit [with Jessica and Salerio; Gratiano is about to follow them].

Enter ANTONIO.

Ant. Who's there?   60
Gra. Signior Antonio?
Ant. Fie, fie Gratiano! where are all the rest?
'Tis nine o'clock, our friends all stay for you,—
No masque to-night,—the wind is come about—
Bassanio presently will go aboard,—   65
I have sent twenty out to seek for you.
Gra. I am glad on't,—I desire no more delight
Than to be under sail, and gone to-night.   *Exeunt.*

50. moe] *Q;* more *F.*   S.D.] *Theobald subs.; om. Q, F.*   51. gentle] *Q, F;* Gentile *Q2.*   58. come?] *Q2, F;* come *Q,*   gentlemen] *Q2, F;* gentleman *Q.*   away!] away, *Q, F.*   59. S.D.] *Exit Q, F; Exit, with Jessica | Hanmer; Exit, with Jessica, and Salerino Capell; he departs with Jessica and Salerio N.C.S.*   61. Antonio?] *Q, F;* Antonio, *Pope (ii).*   62. fie] *Q, F; om. Pope.*   Gratiano!] Gratiano, *Q, F.*   66. I ... you] *Q, F; om. Q2.*   67. Gra.] *Q, F; om. Q2.* I am] *Q, F;* I'm *Pope.*

47. *close*] secretive; cf. *Rom.*, I. i. 155.
doth ... runaway] "is stealing away" (Clarendon).

51. *by my hood*] an asseveration dating back to M.E. (so *O.E.D.*). Malone suggested that Gratiano alludes to a

hood which was part of his "masqued habit", but normally the asseveration seems to have had no precise meaning. *gentle*] Cf. II. iv. 34, and note.

52. *Beshrew*] lit., evil befall, but often used light-heartedly.

[SCENE VII.—*Belmont.*]

[*Flourish Cornets.*] *Enter* PORTIA *with* MOROCCO
and both their trains.

Por. Go, draw aside the curtains and discover
    The several caskets to this noble prince:
    Now make your choice.
Mor.   This first of gold, who this inscription bears,
    "Who chooseth me, shall gain what many men desire."
    The second silver, which this promise carries,   6
    "Who chooseth me, shall get as much as he deserves."
    This third, dull lead, with warning all as blunt,
    "Who chooseth me, must give and hazard all he hath."
    How shall I know if I do choose the right?   10
Por. The one of them contains my picture prince,
    If you choose that, then I am yours withal.
Mor. Some god direct my judgment! let me see,
    I will survey th'inscriptions back again,—
    What says this leaden casket?   15
    "Who chooseth me, must give and hazard all he hath,"
    Must give,—for what? for lead, hazard for lead!

Scene VII

Scene VII] *Capell; om. Q,F;* Scene III *Rowe;* Scene VIII *Pope;* Scene VI *Halliwell.*
Belmont] *Rowe; om. Q,F; Belmont. A Room in Portia's House Capell.*   *Flourish
Cornets*] *om. Q,F; Flourish | Capell; Flourish of Cornets Malone.*   1. curtains] *Q,
F;* Curtain *F4.*   3.] S.D., *Three Caskets are discovered.* (*at end of line*) *Rowe.*
4. This] *Q;* The *Q2, F.*   who] *Q,F;* which *Pope.*   5. many] *Q; om. F.*
10. How . . . right] *printed twice F.*   13. judgment!] iudgement, *Q,F.*   14.
th'inscriptions] *Q2;* th' inscriptions, *Q;* the inscriptions, *F.*   17. lead,] *Q,F;*
lead? *Q3.*   lead!] lead? *Q,F.*

S.D. Flourish Cornets] F seems to
have printed this at the beginning of
the wrong scene (II. viii). Some editors
repeat the direction at the close of this
scene; but although F has cornets at
the beginning and end of Morocco's
previous appearance (II. i), this time
he leaves in a hurry and a state exit
is hardly appropriate. F marks a
"Flourish Cornets" at Arragon's entry, not at his exit (II. ix. 3).

  1. *discover*] reveal.

  4. *who*] sometimes used for "which"

with no idea of personification;
euphony sufficiently explains the
change to *which* in l. 6.

  8. *dull . . . blunt*] a double pun; *dull*
could mean blunt of edge (as in *Ham.*,
I. iii. 77) and *blunt* meant (1) plain-
spoken, and (2) base (as in Spenser,
Colin Clout (1595), l. 710: "base, or
blunt, unmeet for melodie").

  11. *The one*] This might imply that
there were only two caskets (cf. I. ii.
92, note), but *contains* may = which
contains (so Pooler).

This casket threatens—men that hazard all
Do it in hope of fair advantages:
A golden mind stoops not to shows of dross,   20
I'll then nor give nor hazard aught for lead.
What says the silver with her virgin hue?
"Who chooseth me, shall get as much as he deserves."
As much as he deserves,—pause there Morocco,
And weigh thy value with an even hand,—   25
If thou be'st rated by thy estimation
Thou dost deserve enough, and yet enough
May not extend so far as to the lady:
And yet to be afeard of my deserving
Were but a weak disabling of myself.   30
As much as I deserve,—why that's the lady.
I do in birth deserve her, and in fortunes,
In graces, and in qualities of breeding:
But more than these, in love I do deserve,—
What if I stray'd no further, but chose here?   35
Let's see once more this saying grav'd in gold:
"Who chooseth me shall gain what many men desire":
Why that's the lady, all the world desires her.
From the four corners of the earth they come
To kiss this shrine, this mortal breathing saint.   40

24. deserves.] *Q;* deserves? *Pope.*   34. deserve] *Q, F;* deserve her *Capell conj.,*
Collier (ii).

19. *advantages*] This echoes the commercial talk of Venice; cf. I. iii. 65, and note.

20. *to shows of dross*] for tokens (or promise) of rubbish; for *to* = for cf. *Ham.*, III. ii. 160, for *shows* cf. *Cæs.*, IV. ii. 24, and for *dross*, cf. *Err.*, II. ii. 179.

22. *her*] by association with *virgin* (so Allen, quoted Furness).

23. *deserves*] *N.C.S.* noted the many full stops in this speech; Morocco, the self-styled man of action, seems to speak with difficulty, his speech lunging forward.

25. *even*] impartial; cf. *Mac.*, I. vii. 10, and R. Southwell, *St Peter's Complaint* (1595), To the Reader: "equities euen-hand the ballance held . . ."

26. *estimation*] probably, valuation,

estimate; cf. IV. i. 160 and *1 H 4,* I. iii. 272: "I speak not this in estimation,/ As what I think might be, . . ." So Morocco says "if I am valued at my own valuation . . ." But *estimation* also means reputation (as in *Err.,* III. i. 102).

30. *disabling*] disparagement.

34. *deserve*] Capell may be right; with *here* at the end of the next line, a compositor might easily overlook "her" (so *N.C.S.*).

40. *shrine*] image of a saint or god, as in *Cym.*, V. v. 164.

breathing] living; cf. *R 2*, IV. i. 48.

saint] The lover's service of his lady was often likened to the worship of a saint; cf., for example, *Lucr.*, l. 85, *Rom.*, I. v. 95–112, and *Mer.V.*, I. i. 120.

The Hyrcanian deserts, and the vasty wilds
Of wide Arabia are as throughfarès now
For princes to come view fair Portia.
The watery kingdom, whose ambitious head
Spets in the face of heaven, is no bar   45
To stop the foreign spirits, but they come
As o'er a brook to see fair Portia.
One of these three contains her heavenly picture.
Is't like that lead contains her?—'twere damnation
To think so base a thought, it were too gross   50
To rib her cerecloth in the obscure grave,—
Or shall I think in silver she's immur'd
Being ten times undervalued to try'd gold?
O sinful thought! never so rich a gem
Was set in worse than gold. They have in England   55
A coin that bears the figure of an angel
Stamp'd in gold, but that's insculp'd upon:

41. The] Q, F; Th' Pope.   vasty] Q; vaste F; vast F3.   44. watery] Q, F;
watry Q2.   45. Spets] Q, F; Spits Rowe.   49. her?] F; her, Q.   53. gold?]
gold, Q.   54. thought!] thought, Q, F.   57. Stamp'd] Q, F; Stamped
Rowe (iii).

41. Hyrcanian deserts] an area south
of the Caspian Sea, famed for its wildness; Shakespeare alludes three times
to the tigers of Hyrcania (e.g., 3 H 6,
I. iv. 155).

vasty] vast. Spenser and other Elizabethan poets varied the form of adjectives by the suffix -y; it seems to have
had a poetic, and probably, archaic
effect (so hugy, stilly, etc.). Shakespeare seems to have originated vasty;
the poet, Glendower, uses it in I H 4,
III. i. 53 and it recurs three times in
H 5.

44–5. whose . . . heaven] Oth.,II.i.11–
15 describes a storm in similar terms,
but the phrase was often used of vain
ambition (cf. Tilley, H355) as in
Stubbes, Anatomy of Abuses (1583), ed.
Furnival, i. 139: "Els we spit against
heauen, we striue against the stream,
and we contemn him in his ordin-
ances."

46. spirits] "There is a quibble

here, inasmuch as according to the
superstition of the age 'spirits' were
unable to travel easily across water"
(N.C.S.).

50. base] a pun; lead is a base metal.
51. rib] en close.
cerecloth] a waxed cloth used for em-
balming; cf. "cerements" (Ham.,I. iv.
48). Corpses were normally wrapped
in lead at this period; Morocco's
speech is in something like Marlowe's
idiom, and there may be an allusion to
Tamburlaine who decreed that Zeno-
crate should be "Not lapt in lead, but
in a sheet of gold" (2 Tam.,II. iv. 131).

53. ten . . . gold] In 1600, gold was, in
fact, ten times more valuable than
silver (so Clarendon).

56–7. coin . . . gold] The "angel" was
a gold coin in current use; it bore the
device of the archangel Michael tread-
ing on the dragon.

57. insculp'd] engraved.
upon] adv., on it, on the surface.

But here an angel in a golden bed
Lies all within. Deliver me the key:
Here do I choose, and thrive I as I may.   60
Por. There take it prince, and if my form lie there
    Then I am yours!   [*He unlocks the golden casket.*]
Mor.   O hell! what have we here?
A carrion Death, within whose empty eye
There is a written scroll,—I'll read the writing.

> *All that glisters is not gold,*   65
> *Often have you heard that told,—*
> *Many a man his life hath sold*
> *But my outside to behold,—*
> *Gilded tombs do worms infold:*
> *Had you been as wise as bold,*   70
> *Young in limbs, in judgment old,*
> *Your answer had not been inscroll'd,—*
> *Fare you well, your suit is cold.*

62. yours!] yours? *Q.*   S.D.] *Rowe subs.; om. Q, F.*   62-4. O . . . writing] *as
Capell; . . . death, /* [W]ithin . . . scroule, / Ile . . . *Q, F.*   62. here?] heare, *Q,
F.*   63. Death] *Rowe;* death *Q, F.*   69. *tombs do*] *Johnson conj., Capell;* timber
doe *Q, F;* wood may *Pope;* timber *Staunton conj.;* woods do *Keightley.*   72. *Your*] *Q,
F; This Johnson conj.*   73. *Fare you well*] *Q2; Fareyouwell Q, F.*

58. *angel . . . bed*] "Portia's picture in
a golden casket" (Pooler).

59-60. *key . . . may*] a rhyme;
Kökeritz (p. 455) compared key/sur-
vay (*Sonn.*, lii. 3). There were probably
two pronunciations for *key*, for it also
rhymed with "be" and "thee" (cf.
Kökeritz, p. 178).

61. *form*] image, likeness.

63. *Death*] i.e., death's head. Miss
M. C. Bradbrook pointed out that
this was appropriate for one more
bold than wise, for it was "Mortality"
that conquered Tamburlaine (*Shakespeare and Elizabethan Poetry* (1951),
p. 176).

65. All . . . gold] a common proverb
(Tilley, A146).

68. my outside] Variously explained
as the golden casket or the beautiful
face that once covered the skull; it also
suggests "all the 'outward shows' of
life upon which Bassanio comments

in III. ii. 73-101" (*N.C.S.*).

69. tombs] Q's "timber" might be
used as a plural noun (so Douce), but
emendation is also desirable on metri-
cal grounds. Supporting Johnson's
conjecture, Malone compared *Sonn.*,
ci. 11: "gilded tomb". *N.C.S.* compared *Matthew*, xxiii. 27: "whited
[marg. "or, painted"] tombes, which
appeare beautiful outward, but are
within full of dead mens bones and of
all filthines" (Genevan version); Q's
Gilded and the marginal "painted" are
linked in *R 2*, 1. i. 179. Capell noted
that a compositor might easily misread
"tombes" as "timber".

72. Your answer] i.e., such an
answer as you have now received (so
Eccles).

73. suit is cold] a common saying.
The meaning of *cold* is doubtful;
O.E.D. (Cold, 11) suggested "Without
power to move or influence" and com-

Cold indeed and labour lost,
Then farewell heat, and welcome frost: 75
Portia adieu! I have too griev'd a heart
To take a tedious leave: thus losers part.

Exit [with his train].

Por. A gentle riddance,—draw the curtains, go,—
Let all of his complexion choose me so.   *Exeunt.*

[SCENE VIII.—*Venice.*]

Enter SALERIO *and* SOLANIO.

Sal. Why man I saw Bassanio under sail,
With him is Gratiano gone along;
And in their ship I am sure Lorenzo is not.
Sol. The villain Jew with outcries rais'd the duke,
Who went with him to search Bassanio's ship.   5
Sal. He came too late, the ship was under sail,
But there the duke was given to understand
That in a gondola were seen together

74. Cold] *Capell; Mor.* Cold *Q, F.*   76. adieu!] adiew, *Q, F.*   77. *with . . .
train*] *Dyce; om. Q, F.*   S.D.] *Cornets. (added) Dyce.*

Scene VIII

Scene VIII] *Capell; om. Q, F;* Scene IV *Rowe;* Scene IX *Pope;* Scene VII *Halliwell.
Venice*] *Rowe; om. Q, F; Venice. A Street Capell.*   Salerio] *N.C.S.;* Salarino *Q.
F;* Solarino *Rowe;* Salerino *Capell.*   Solanio] *Q;* Salanio *Q2;* Solanio. *Flo.
Cornets F.*   1. *Sal.*] *Q, F;* Salar. *Q2.*   3. I am] *Q, F;* Ime *Q2.*   4. *Sol.*] *F;
Sola. Q; Salan. Q2.*   6. *Sal.*] *Q, F; Salar. Q2.*   came] *Q;* comes *F.*   8. gondola] *Theobald;* Gondylo *Q.*

pared *Gent.,* IV. iv. 186. There may be
a quibble on *cold*=dead; Pooler compared *Fair Maid of the Exchange* (1607),
IV. i: "For well I wot, his suit is cold:
't must die."

75. *farewell . . . frost*] an inversion of
the old saying "Farewell frost", used on
parting with anything that was unwelcome (so Halliwell; cf. Tilley, F769).

77. *part*] depart.

79. *complexion*] originally used of the
constitution or "temperament" of a
person; the proportion in which the
four humours (choler, blood, phlegm,

and melancholy) were combined.
"Complexion" was first used of the
skin (as in modern usage) because its
appearance was thought to indicate
this "temperament".

Scene VIII

7–9. *given . . . Jessica*] presumably a
false report to cover their tracks; Jessica should not have been recognizable
in her page's suit, and, as Knight remarked, a gondola was constructed so
that its passengers could be hidden
from view.

Lorenzo and his amorous Jessica.
Besides, Antonio certified the duke   10
They were not with Bassanio in his ship.

Sol. I never heard a passion so confus'd,
So strange, outrageous, and so variable
As the dog Jew did utter in the streets,—
"My daughter! O my ducats! O my daughter!   15
Fled with a Christian! O my Christian ducats!
Justice, the law, my ducats, and my daughter!
A sealed bag, two sealed bags of ducats,
Of double ducats, stol'n from me by my daughter!
And jewels, two stones, two rich and precious stones,   20
Stol'n by my daughter! Justice!—find the girl,
She hath the stones upon her, and the ducats!"

Sal. Why all the boys in Venice follow him,
Crying his stones, his daughter, and his ducats.

Sol. Let good Antonio look he keep his day   25
Or he shall pay for this.

Sal.   Marry well rememb'red,—
I reason'd with a Frenchman yesterday,
Who told me, in the narrow seas that part
The French and English, there miscarried
A vessel of our country richly fraught: 30
I thought upon Antonio when he told me,

And wish'd in silence that it were not his.

Sol. You were best to tell Antonio what you hear,—
Yet do not suddenly, for it may grieve him.

Sal. A kinder gentleman treads not the earth,—   35
I saw Bassanio and Antonio part,
Bassanio told him he would make some speed
Of his return: he answered, "Do not so,
Slubber not business for my sake Bassanio,
But stay the very riping of the time,   40
And for the Jew's bond which he hath of me—
Let it not enter in your mind of love:
Be merry, and employ your chiefest thoughts
To courtship, and such fair ostents of love
As shall conveniently become you there."   45
And even there (his eye being big with tears),
Turning his face, he put his hand behind him,
And with affection wondrous sensible
He wrung Bassanio's hand, and so they parted.

Sol. I think he only loves the world for him,—   50
I pray thee let us go and find him out
And quicken his embraced heaviness
With some delight or other.

Sal.   Do we so.   *Exeunt.*

33. *Sol.*] *Q, F; Salan. Q2.*   35. *Sal.*] *Q, F; Salar. Q2.*   39. Slubber] *Q2, F;*
slumber *Q.*   45. there.] *Q2;* there, *Q.*   46. there] *Q, F;* then *Dyce (ii).*
50. *Sol.*] *Q, F; Salan. Q2.*   53. *Sal.*] *Q, F; Salar. Q2.*

39. *Slubber*] Q's "slumber" gives no
satisfactory sense; the compositor
might have mistaken "sluber" for
"slūber". *Slubber* = perform hurried-
ly or carelessly; it is used in its original sense of to smear in *Oth.*, I. iii.
228.

40. *stay . . . time*] i.e., wait for time to
bring your business to ripeness, or
completion (cf. *2 H 4*, IV. i. 13) or perhaps, stay until the time is most suitable (cf. *1 H 4*, I. iii. 294).

42. *mind of love*] intention, or
thought, about love (cf. II. v. 37 and
O.E.D., Mind, 7 and 10); *N.C.S.* paraphrased "love-schemes".

44. *ostents*] expressions, shows.

46. *there*] then, thereupon (as often);
Dyce supposed that *there* was caught in
error from the previous line.

48. *sensible*] evident (cf. *Mac.*, II. i.
36), or sensitive (Pooler compared
LLL., IV. iii. 337).

50. *I . . . him*] This echoes Valentine's avowal of friendship: "I . . .
count the world a stranger for thy
sake" (*Gent.*, v. iv. 69–70).

52. *embraced*] "We say of a man now,
that he hugs *his sorrows,* and why may
not *Anthonio embrace heaviness*?" (Johnson); cf. "rash-embrac'd despair"
(III. ii. 109).

[SCENE IX.—*Belmont.*]

Enter NERISSA *and a Servitor.*

Ner. Quick, quick I pray thee, draw the curtain straight,—
          The Prince of Arragon hath ta'en his oath,
          And comes to his election presently.

          [*Flourish Cornets.*] *Enter* [*the Prince of*] ARRAGON,
                    his train, and PORTIA.

Por. Behold, there stand the caskets noble prince,
          If you choose that wherein I am contain'd   5
          Straight shall our nuptial rites be solemniz'd:
          But if you fail, without more speech my lord
          You must be gone from hence immediately.
Ar. I am enjoin'd by oath to observe three things,—
          First, never to unfold to any one   10
          Which casket 'twas I chose; next, if I fail
          Of the right casket, never in my life
          To woo a maid in way of marriage:
          Lastly,
          If I do fail in fortune of my choice,   15
          Immediately to leave you, and be gone.
Por. To these injunctions every one doth swear
          That comes to hazard for my worthless self.

Scene IX

Scene IX] *Capell; om. Q, F;* Scene V *Rowe;* Scene X *Pope;* Scene VIII *Halliwell.*
Belmont] *Rowe; om. Q, F; Belmont. A Room in Portia's House Capell.*   3. *Flourish
Cornets*] *om. Q; Flor. Cornets (after* Portia) *F; Flourish | Capell.*   the . . . *of*]
Capell; om. Q, F.   his train] *Q, F; and their Trains (after* Portia) *Capell
S.D.*] *The Caskets are discover'd. (added) Rowe.*   6. rites] *Pope;* rights *Q, F.*
7. you] *Q;* thou *F.*   9. to] *Q, F;* t' *Pope.*   13–15. To . . . choice] *as Cambridge;* . . . marriage: / [L]astly . . . *Q, F, Pope;* . . . lastly, / If . . . *Capell.*
14. Lastly] *Q, F;* Last *Pope.*   15. do] *Q, F; om. Pope.*

          S.D. Servitor] *N.C.S.* suggested that
this referred to a playhouse attendant,
but the term was in general use (=
servant).
          1. *straight*] immediately.
          2. *ta'en his oath*] i.e., at the temple;
cf. II. i. 44.
          3. *election*] choice; cf. *All's W.,* II. iii.
61.

          14. *Lastly*] If this word did not begin
a new line in the copy, it is hard to see
why the compositor did not set it at the
end of l. 13 where there was plenty of
space for it; *marriage* (l. 13) is probably
trisyllabic as in *Shr.,* III. ii. 142. Cf.
I. iii. 120 for a similar two-syllable line.
          18. *hazard*] probably a substantive
(so Clarendon); cf. *H 5,* III. vii. 93.

Ar. And so have I address'd me,—fortune now
     To my heart's hope!—gold, silver, and base lead.   20
     "Who chooseth me, must give and hazard all he hath."
     You shall look fairer ere I give or hazard.
     What says the golden chest? ha! let me see,
     "Who chooseth me, shall gain what many men desire,"
     What many men desire,—that "many" may be meant
     By the fool multitude that choose by show,   26
     Not learning more than the fond eye doth teach,
     Which pries not to th' interior, but like the martlet
     Builds in the weather on the outward wall,
     Even in the force and road of casualty.   30
     I will not choose what many men desire,
     Because I will not jump with common spirits,
     And rank me with the barbarous multitudes.
     Why then to thee (thou silver treasure house),
     Tell me once more what title thou dost bear;   35
     "Who chooseth me shall get as much as he deserves,"
     And well said too; for who shall go about
     To cozen Fortune, and be honourable
     Without the stamp of merit?—let none presume
     To wear an undeserved dignity: 40

20. hope!] hope: *Q, F.*   23. chest?] *Q2;* chest, *Q, F.*   ha!] ha, *Q, F.*
25. "many"] many *Q,F;* om. *Pope.*   26. fool multitude] *Q,F;* fool-multitude
Q2.   28. pries] *Q,F;* pry *Pope (ii).*   33. multitudes] *Q,F;* multitude *Walker*
conj., Dyce (ii).   39. merit?] merrit, *Q, F.*

19. *address'd*] prepared, as in *MND.*,
v. i. 106; Steevens paraphrased, "I
have prepared my self by the same
ceremonies."

fortune] good luck.

26. *By*] For; cf. *O.E.D.*, Mean, *vb.*,
1e.

fool] used adjectivally as in 1. i.
102.

27. *fond*] infatuated, foolish; cf.
MND., III. ii. 114 and 317.

28. *martlet*] swift, "formerly often
confused with the swallow and the
house-martin" (*O.E.D.*). According
to Shakespeare, it builds its nest in
situations which look fair, but are in
fact dangerous. Shakespeare again
refers to the *martlet* when he wishes to

"emphasise the irony of the deceptive-
ness of appearances" (*Mac.*, I. vi. 4; so
C. Spurgeon, *Shakespeare's Imagery*
(1935), pp. 187–90). If *martlet* = martin, there may be a quibble on the
slang use of martin = a dupe; it was so
used by Greene and Fletcher (so
Spurgeon, *ibid.*).

29. *in the weather*] in an exposed situation (cf. *O.E.D.*, 2d).

30. *force*] power (so Steevens).

casualty] mischance.

32. *jump*] agree, as in *1 H 4*, I. ii. 78.

39. *stamp*] official mark certifying a
document; cf. *Cym.*, v. v. 366. Arragon
will not attempt to cheat Fortune by
aspiring to honour without a proper
claim based on merit.

O that estates, degrees, and offices,
Were not deriv'd corruptly, and that clear honour
Were purchas'd by the merit of the wearer!—
How many then should cover that stand bare!
How many be commanded that command!   45
How much low peasantry would then be gleaned
From the true seed of honour! and how much honour
Pick'd from the chaff and ruin of the times,
To be new-varnish'd!—well, but to my choice.
"Who chooseth me shall get as much as he deserves,"—
I will assume desert; give me a key for this,   51
And instantly unlock my fortunes here.

[He opens the silver casket.]

Por. Too long a pause for that which you find there.
Ar. What's here? the portrait of a blinking idiot

---

42. and] *Q, F; om. Pope.*   43. wearer!] wearer, *Q.*   44. bare!] bare? *Q, F.*
45. command!] commaund? *Q, F.*   46. peasantry] *Q;* pleasantry *F.*
gleaned] *Q, F;* pick'd *Johnson conj.*   47. honour!] honour? *Q, F.*   and] *Q,*
F; om. Pope.   48. Pick'd] *Q, F;* Glean'd *Johnson conj.*   chaff] chaft *Q;*
chaffe *Q2, F.*   49. new-varnish'd!] *Dyce;* new varnist; *Q;* new vernish'd? *Q2;*
new varnisht: *F;* new vanned? *Warburton.*   well,] *Q2, F;* well *Q.*   52. S.D.]
Delius subs.; om. Q, F; after l. 53 Rowe subs.   53. Too . . . there] *as aside*
Capell.   54. here?] heere, *Q, F.*

---

41. *estates, degrees*] Both words mean
status, social rank, but here, perhaps,
estates = property, possessions.

42. *deriv'd*] gained; also inherited
(cf. *All's W.,* ii. iii. 143).

clear] unsullied (cf. *Tp.,* iii. i. 82), or,
perhaps, bright (Pooler compared
"bright honour" (*1 H 4,* i. iii. 202) and
Furness, *Lr.,* iv. vi. 73, for which see
Muir's note, New Arden edn.).

43. *purchas'd*] acquired, as in *R 2,*
i. iii. 282.

44. *cover . . . bare*] i.e., be masters
who are now servants; the head was
uncovered in the presence of a superior (cf. iii. v. 48–9).

47. *seed*] a quibble on the (biblical)
sense of offspring, progeny (cf. *Mac.,*
iii. i. 70); Arragon implies that among
the true sons of the nobility (i.e., of
honour) there are those who should
rank as peasants.

48. *ruin*] usually glossed as refuse,

rubbish, but perhaps, "those who have
been 'ruined', or made destitute, by
the times" (cf. *H 8,* ii. i. 114 and
O.E.D., 2b and 6). Arragon adds a
rider to his previous claim, and says
that there is honour among the reput-
edly worthless (i.e., *chaff*) and those
who have been ruined.

times] A quibble on "temse" (=
sieve for bolting meal) has been suggested (so Bailey, *Received Text,* ii
(1866), 209.)

49. *be new-varnish'd*] i.e., regain the
outward appearance of nobility. For
varnish'd, Pooler compared *LLL.,* iv.
iii. 244: "Beauty doth varnish age, as
if new-born." Warburton emended in
order to avoid mixed metaphors;
"vanned" = winnowed.

51. *assume*] invest myself with, take
to myself (so Furness who compared
Ham., iii. iv. 160: "Assume a virtue, if
you have it not").

Presenting me a schedule! I will read it: 55
How much unlike art thou to Portia!
How much unlike my hopes and my deservings!
"Who chooseth me, shall have as much as he deserves"!
Did I deserve no more than a fool's head?
Is that my prize? are my deserts no better?   60

Por. To offend and judge are distinct offices,
And of opposed natures.

Ar.   What is here?

The fire seven times tried this:
Seven times tried that judgment is,
That did never choose amiss.   65
Some there be that shadows kiss,
Such have but a shadow's bliss:
There be fools alive (Iwis)
Silver'd o'er, and so was this.
Take what wife you will to bed,   70
I will ever be your head:
So be gone, you are sped.

Still more fool I shall appear
By the time I linger here,—

55. schedule!] shedule, *Q*, *F*.   56. Portia!] Portia? *Q*, *F*.   57. deservings!]
deseruings. *Q*.   58. have] *Q*, *F;* get *Knight.*   deserves"!] deserues? *Q*.
59. head?] *Q2;* head, *Q*, *F*.   60. prize?] *Q2;* prize, *Q*, *F*.   62.] S.D., *Hee*
reads. (*at end of line*) *Q2*.   63. *this:*] *Q2; this*, *Q*, *F*.   65. *amiss.*] *Q2; amis*, *Q*,
F.   66. *kiss*,] *Q2*, *F; kis*. *Q*.   73. Still] *Q2; Arrag.* Still *Q*, *F*.

58. *have*] The change in wording
may hint that Arragon quotes the inscription from memory (so Furness).

61–2. *To . . . natures*] The thought
was proverbial (cf. Tilley, M341).

63. this] i.e., the maxims on the
scroll.

66. shadows] "Shadow" was used of
anything unsubstantial and fleeting,
but Pooler also saw an allusion to the
practice of kissing portraits, or
shadows; he compared *Gent.*, IV. ii. 121–
6 and IV. iv. 202–3, and Webster,
White Devil (1612), II. ii. 25–8: " 'twas
her custome nightly, / . . . to go and
visite / Your picture, and to feed her
eyes and lippes / On the dead shadow."

68. Iwis] certainly; often used as an
almost meaningless rhyming tag.

69. Silver'd o'er] i.e., silver-haired
and, therefore, appearing wise (cf.
Cæs., II. i. 144); or possibly, "whose
wealth conceals their folly" (Pooler).

70. Take . . . bed] Johnson supposed
that Shakespeare forgot the condition
never to "woo a maid."

71. I . . . head] The husband should
be the "head" of the wife: cf. *Ephesians*,
v. 23.

72. sped] This has a range of meanings: well-satisfied, dealt with, "done
for" (Pooler). It is used ambiguously
here, as perhaps, in *Shr.*, v. ii. 185.

With one fool's head I came to woo,   75
But I go away with two.
Sweet adieu! I'll keep my oath,
Patiently to bear my wroth.
        [*Exit Arragon with his train.*]

Por. Thus hath the candle sing'd the moth:
O these deliberate fools! when they do choose,   80
They have the wisdom by their wit to lose.

Ner. The ancient saying is no heresy,
Hanging and wiving goes by destiny.

Por. Come draw the curtain Nerissa.

Enter Messenger.

Mess. Where is my lady?
Por.   Here, what would my lord?   85
Mess. Madam, there is alighted at your gate
A young Venetian, one that comes before
To signify th'approaching of his lord,
From whom he bringeth sensible regreets;
To wit, (besides commends and courteous breath)   90
Gifts of rich value; yet I have not seen

77. adieu!] adiew, *Q, F.*   78. wroth] *Q 3;* wroath *Q, F;* wrath *Theobald (ii);*
roth *Dyce;* ruth *Sisson.*   S.D.] *Capell subs.; om. Q, F; Exit Rowe.*   79. moth]
Q2; moath *Q, F.*   80. fools!] fooles *Q, F.*   83. goes] *Q, F;* go *Hanmer.*
85. lady?] *Q2, F;* Lady. *Q.*   90. (besides . . . breath)] *Q, F.*

78. *wroth*] Q's "wroath" was a current spelling for wroth (= wrath), but
this would not give satisfactory sense.
"Ruth" (= misfortune, grief) seems
to be meant (so Onions); *wroth* was a
current spelling and may be read here
to emphasize the rhyme. Q's "a" may
have been added to give an eye-
rhyme.

79. *moth*] Q's "moath" (a possible
Elizabethan spelling) suggests that
Portia pronounces a "difficult" rhyme
(so Capell; see also Kökeritz, pp. 227–
8). The saying was proverbial (cf.
Tilley, F394).

80. *deliberate*] "The right choice
depended not on reasoning but on
love" (Pooler).

83. *Hanging . . . destiny*] proverbial

saying (cf. Tilley, W232).

84. *Come . . . Nerissa*] The metre is
broken and this may be a single line
of prose (so *N.C.S.*); as such it might be
evidence of a cut or alteration during
composition (cf. Introduction, p. xvi).

85. *my lord*] Dyce compared *1 H 4,*
II. iv. 315 and *R 2,* v. v. 67 where
superiors address inferiors as equals;
in each case there is an additional
point to the retort and, here, Portia
may quibble on *lady* = wife and *lord* =
husband.

89. *sensible regreets*] substantial greet-
ings, i.e., not words only. For *sensible* =
evident to the senses cf. *Mac.,* II. i. 36.

90. *commends*] commendations.
breath] speech (as often); cf. *John,*
III. i. 8.

So likely an ambassador of love.
A day in April never came so sweet
To show how costly summer was at hand,
As this fore-spurrer comes before his lord.   95
Por. No more I pray thee, I am half afeard
Thou wilt say anon he is some kin to thee,
Thou spend'st such high-day wit in praising him:
Come, come Nerissa, for I long to see
Quick Cupid's post that comes so mannerly.   100
Ner. Bassanio, Lord Love, if thy will it be!   *Exeunt.*

97. Thou wilt] *Q, F;* Thou'lt *Pope.*   98. high-day] *hyphened F.*   99. Come,]
Q2, F; Come *Q.*   101. Bassanio, Lord Love,] *Rowe;* Bassanio Lord, loue *Q,*
F; Bassanio, Lord, Love *Q3;* Bassanio Lord, love, *F4;* Bassanio lord, Love!
Pope.   be!] be. *Q, F.*

92. *likely*] promising; cf. *2 H 4*, III.
ii. 186. Although not found in Shakespeare, the sense "good looking" was
current and may be implied here (cf.
O.E.D., 5).

94. *costly*] lavish, rich (so Onions);
cf. *Ado*, II. i. 341.

98. *high-day*] high-flown (lit., be-
fitting a festival): Steevens compared
Wiv., III. ii. 69: "he writes verses, he
speaks holiday, . . ."

100. *post*] messenger, as in v. i. 46.

101. *Lord Love*,] Since Cupid is mentioned in the preceding line, Rowe's
punctuation is probably right; Nerissa
wishes that Bassanio will be the new
suitor. It is just possible that Q's
"Bassanio Lord" stands for Lord Bassanio, and that Nerissa, apostrophiz-
ing, says that he may love if he wishes,
because it is clear, from her eagerness,
that Portia would reciprocate; if
this were so, Q's punctuation could
stand.

[ACT III]

[SCENE I.—*Venice.*]

[*Enter*] SOLANIO *and* SALERIO.

Sol. Now what news on the Rialto?

Sal. Why yet it lives there uncheck'd, that Antonio hath a
ship of rich lading wrack'd on the narrow seas; the
Goodwins I think they call the place, a very dangerous flat, and fatal, where the carcases of many a   5
tall ship lie buried, as they say,—if my gossip Report
be an honest woman of her word.

Sol. I would she were as lying a gossip in that, as ever
knapp'd ginger, or made her neighbours believe she
wept for the death of a third husband: but it is true,   10
without any slips of prolixity, or crossing the plain
highway of talk, that the good Antonio, the honest
Antonio;—O that I had a title good enough to keep
'his name company!—

ACT III

Scene 1

Act III] *om. Q.;* Actus Tertius *F.*   Scene 1] *Rowe; om. Q., F.*   Venice] *Rowe;
om. Q., F; a Street in Venice Theobald.*   Enter] *Q2, F; om. Q.*   Solanio] *Q, F;*
Salanio *Q2.*   Salerio] *N.C.S.;* Salarino *Q, F;* Solarino *F4;* Salerino *Capell.*
1. *Sol.*] *F; Solanio. Q; Salan. Q2.*   2. *Sal.*] *F; Salari. Q.*   6. gossip] *Q;*
gossips *Q2, F.*   Report] *Q3;* report *Q, F.*   8. *Sol.*] *F; Solanio. Q; Salan. Q2.*
14. company!—] company. *Q.*

3. *narrow seas*] Cf. II. viii. 28, note.

4. *Goodwins*] N. Nathan suggested
that Shakespeare knew *Goodwins*
meant 'good friends': Antonio is
wrecked on the hidden shoals of friendship (*Names*, vii (1959), 191).

6. *gossip Report*] i.e., Dame Rumour
(so Pooler, comparing *Shr.*, II. i. 246).

9. *knapp'd ginger*] Ginger seems to
have been associated with old women.

See also H. Buttes, *Diet's Dry Dinner*
(1599), O2ᵛ: "Greene Ginger, condite
with hony, warmes olde mens bellyes."
To knap = to bite, nibble.

11. *slips of prolixity*] i.e., words
which are the offspring of tediousness;
for *slips*, cf. *2 H 6*, II. ii. 58, and for
prolixity, *Rom.*, I. iv. 3. However, *slips*
may = faults, lapses (so Pooler), as in
Oth., IV. i. 9.

Sal. Come, the full stop.   15
Sol. Ha! what sayest thou?—why the end is, he hath lost
    a ship.
Sal. I would it might prove the end of his losses.
Sol. Let me say "amen" betimes, lest the devil cross my
    prayer, for here he comes in the likeness of a Jew.   20

Enter SHYLOCK.

    How now Shylock! what news among the merchants?
Shy. You knew, none so well, none so well as you, of my
    daughter's flight.
Sal. That's certain,—I (for my part) knew the tailor that
    made the wings she flew withal.   25
Sol. And Shylock (for his own part) knew the bird was
    fledge, and then it is the complexion of them all to
    leave the dam.
Shy. She is damn'd for it.
Sal. That's certain, if the devil may be her judge.   30
Shy. My own flesh and blood to rebel!
Sol. Out upon it old carrion! rebels it at these years?

15. *Sal.*] *F; Salari. Q*.   16. *Sol.*] *F; Solanio. Q; Sal. Q2.*   Ha!] Ha, *Q, F.*
thou?] *Q2;* thou, *Q, F.*   18. *Sal.*] *F; Salari. Q.*   19. *Sol.*] *F; Solanio Q;*
Salan. Q2.   my] *Q, F;* thy *Theobald.*   20. S.D.] *as Q2; after l. 21 Q, F.*
21. Shylock!] Shylocke, *Q, F.*   22–5. You . . . withal] *as Q, F; . . .* you, / Of
. . . flight. / *Salar. . . .* Taylor / That . . . *Q2.*   24. *Sal.*] *F; Salari. Q.*   26. *Sol.*]
F; Solan. Q; Salan. Q2.   27. fledge] *Q;* fledg'd *Q2, F;* fledge *Capell.*   30.
Sal.] *F; Salari. Q.*   31. rebel!] rebell. *Q, F.*   32. *Sol.*] *F; Sola. Q; Salan.*
Q2.   carrion!] carrion, *Q, F.*   years?] yeeres. *Q, F.*

15. *full stop*] "Salerio refers here not
only to the period but to the 'stop'
in the manage; Solanio is a colt
whose 'career' must be checked"
(*N.C.S.*).

19–20. *lest . . . comes*] For the word-
play, cf. Lodge, *Wit's Misery* (1596),
D2: "Beware . . . of this diuellish
Scandale, . . . and crosse you from this
Deuill, least he crosse you in your
walkes."

my prayer] i.e., the "amen" he has
just said (so Heath, *Revisal* (1765),
p. 116).

21–33. *How now . . .*] *N.C.S.* pointed
out that this passage needs little alteration to read as verse; cf. Q2's arrange-

ment of ll. 22–5, which Furness called
"metric prose".

25. *wings*] i.e., the page's suit; there
is a quibble on flight (l. 23).

27. *fledge*] a form of fledge (adj.),
meaning fit to fly, fledged.

complexion] nature, disposition; cf.
II. vii. 79, note.

31. *flesh and blood*] As Shylock uses it,
this means his own child, but as
Solanio chooses to understand it, sensual appetites and passion (cf. *Shr.*,
Ind. ii. 130).

32. *carrion*] a common term of
abuse; Pooler compared *Cæs.*, II. i.
130. It was also used of the "fleshly
nature of man" (cf. *O.E.D.*, 3b).

Shy. I say my daughter is my flesh and my blood.

Sal. There is more difference between thy flesh and hers,
than between jet and ivory, more between your   35
bloods, than there is between red wine and Rhenish:
but tell us, do you hear whether Antonio have had
any loss at sea or no?

Shy. There I have another bad match, a bankrupt, a prodigal, who dare scarce show his head on the Rialto, a   40
beggar that was us'd to come so smug upon the mart:
let him look to his bond! he was wont to call me
usurer, let him look to his bond! he was wont to lend
money for a Christian cur'sy, let him look to his bond!

Sal. Why I am sure if he forfeit, thou wilt not take his   45
flesh,—what's that good for?

Shy. To bait fish withal,—if it will feed nothing else, it
will feed my revenge; he hath disgrac'd me, and
hind'red me half a million, laugh'd at my losses,

33. my blood] *Q;* blood *Q2, F.*   34. *Sal.*] *F; Salari. Q.*   37. hear] *Q, F;* hear,
Q2.   40. dare] *Q, F;* dares *Rowe (iii).*   41. was] *Q, F; om. Rowe (iii).*   42,
43. bond!] bond, *Q, F.*   44. cur'sy] *Q;* curtsie *Q2, F;* courtesie *Rowe.*   bond!]
bond. *Q, F.*   45. *Sal.*] *F; Salari. Q.*   49. me] *Q, F;* me of *Theobald (ii).*

33. *my blood*] Q's repetition need not
be dismissed as a compositor's mistake; Shylock might alter the usual
phraseology in an effort to be unambiguous. In any case, the form "the . . .
the . . ." is found *Shr.,* Ind. ii. 130.

36. *red . . . Rhenish*] Red wine was
considered superior "in alcoholic
strength and in the important physio-
logical power of generating blood";
"the rich red blood of the young
Jessica" is contrasted with "the thin
feeble blood of her father" (D. C.
Boughner, *S.A.B.,* xiv (1939), 46–50).

39. *match*] bargain as in *Cor.,* II. iii.
86. Perhaps Shylock is quibbling on
the bad "match", or lack of similarity,
which has been alleged between himself and Jessica.

39–40. *prodigal*] "There could be, in
Shylock's opinion, no prodigality more
culpable than such liberality as that by
which a man exposes himself to ruin
for his friend" (Johnson).

41. *smug*] spruce, smooth, sleek;

Pooler compared G. Harvey, *Pierce's
Supererogation* (1593), *Wks,* ed. Grosart, ii. 301: "For his smug, and
Canonicall countenance, certainly he
mought have bene S. Boniface himselfe."

mart] market-place.

44. *cur'sy*] a current form of curtsy
or courtesy: these were, in fact, one
word with a wide range of meanings—
that of an act of generosity or benevolence may be most appropriate here.

47. *bait*] act as bait for; Shylock
could not eat (*take*) Antonio's flesh for
it is neither "fish" nor "flesh" (cf. *Err.,*
III. i. 2), but he could use it as a bait to
get some fish.

if . . . else] Stoll (*Shakespeare Studies*
(1927), p. 325, n. 135) suggested that
Shylock alludes to the superstition that
Jews ate Christian flesh; cf. Day,
Travels of Three English Brothers (1607),
ed. Bullen, ii. 60: "Sweet gold, sweete
Iewell! but the sweetest part / Of a
Iewes feast is a Christian's heart."

mock'd at my gains, scorned my nation, thwarted   50
my bargains, cooled my friends, heated mine
enemies,—and what's his reason? I am a Jew. Hath
not a Jew eyes? hath not a Jew hands, organs, dimensions, senses, affections, passions? fed with the same
food, hurt with the same weapons, subject to the   55
same diseases, healed by the same means, warmed
and cooled by the same winter and summer as a
Christian is?—if you prick us do we not bleed? if
you tickle us do we not laugh? if you poison us do we
not die? and if you wrong us shall we not revenge?—   60
if we are like you in the rest, we will resemble you in
that. If a Jew wrong a Christian, what is his humility?
revenge! If a Christian wrong a Jew, what should his
sufferance be by Christian example?—why revenge!
The villainy you teach me I will execute, and it shall   65
go hard but I will better the instruction.

Enter a [serving-]man from Antonio.

Serv. Gentlemen, my master Antonio is at his house, and
    desires to speak with you both.
Sal. We have been up and down to seek him.

52. his] *Q; the F.*   reason?] *F; reason, Q.*   Jew. Hath] *Q2;* Iewe: Hath *Q,
F.*   53. eyes?] *Q2, F;* eyes, *Q.*   54. passions?] *Q2;* passions, *Q, F.*   57.
winter and summer] *Q, F;* summer and winter *Hanmer.*   58. is?] *Q2;* is: *Q,
F.*   bleed?] *Q2, F;* bleede, *Q.*   59. laugh?] *Q2, F;* laugh, *Q.*   60. die?]
Q2, F; die, *Q.*   revenge?] *Q2, F;* reuenge, *Q.*   62. humility?] humillity,
Q, F.   63, 64. revenge!] reuenge? *Q, F.*   64. example?] example, *Q, F.*
66. *serving-*] *om. Q, F.*   67. *Serv.*] *Rowe; om. Q, F.*   69. *Sal.*] *F; Saleri. Q;
Salar. Q2.*

53–4. *dimensions*] bodily frame; cf.
Lr., I. ii. 7.
    54. *affections, passions*] not always
distinguished, but probably *passions* =
feelings, emotions, and *affections* are the
wishes or desires which prompt the
passions; Furness compared Greene,
Never Too Late (1590), *Wks*, VIII. 174:
"his hart was fuller of passions, than
his eyes of affections" and *Mer.V.*,
IV. i. 50–1.
    62. *humility*] Schmidt glossed as
"kindness, benevolence, humanity"

and compared *LLL.*, IV. iii. 349, *H 5*,
III. i. 4, and *R 3*, II. i. 72 (cf. *Shakespeare
Jahrbuch*, III (1868), 346–7). But for
the *LLL.* reference Halliwell quoted
Huloet, *Abecedarium* (1552): "*Humilitie* is a gentlenes of the mynde, or a
gentle patience withoute all angre or
wrathe."
    64. *sufferance*] Cf. I. iii. 105. Mar-
lowe's Barabas also justifies himself:
"This is the life we Jews are us'd to
lead;/And reason too,for Christians do
the like" (*Jew of Malta*, v. ii. 115–16).

Enter TUBAL.

Sol. Here comes another of the tribe,—a third cannot be   70
match'd, unless the devil himself turn Jew.

> *Exeunt gentlemen* [*(Solanio and*
> *Salerio) with servant*].

Shy. How now Tubal! what news from Genoa? hast thou
found my daughter?

Tub. I often came where I did hear of her, but cannot
find her.   75

Shy. Why there, there, there, there! a diamond gone cost
me two thousand ducats in Frankfort,—the curse
never fell upon our nation till now, I never felt it till
now,—two thousand ducats in that, and other precious, precious jewels; I would my daughter were   80
dead at my foot, and the jewels in her ear: would she
were hears'd at my foot, and the ducats in her coffin:
—no news of them? why so!—and I know not what's
spent in the search: why thou—loss upon loss! the
thief gone with so much, and so much to find the   85
thief, and no satisfaction, no revenge, nor no ill luck
stirring but what lights o' my shoulders, no sighs but

S.D.] *Q*, *F*; *om. Collier* (i).   70. *Sol.*] *F*; *Solanio. Q*; *Salan. Q2*.   71. *(Solanio*
. . . *servant*] *N.C.S. subs.; Enter* Tuball. *Q*, *Collier* (i); *om. F*.   72. Tubal!]
Tuball, *Q*, *F*.   Genoa?] *Q2*, *F*; Genowa, *Q*.   74. her] *Q*; ster *F*.   76.
there!] there, *Q*, *F*.   79–80. precious,] *F*; precious *Q*.   83. them?]
them, *Q*, *F*.   so!] so? *Q*, *F*.   what's] *Q*; how much is *F*.   84. thou] *Q*, *F*;
then *F2*.   loss!] losse, *Q*, *F*.   87, 88. o'] *Rowe* (ii); a *Q*, *F*.

69. Enter *Tuball*] Q's repetition of
this entry after l. 71 is discussed, Introduction p. xv. It was probably due to
printing from Shakespeare's uncorrected papers; perhaps Shylock's conversation with Tuball was grafted on
to the earlier part of this scene late in
the composition of the play. A speech
prefix is missing at l. 67 and this also
may suggest an alteration in the copy
to provide transition between the two
parts of the scene.

70–1. *cannot be match'd*] i.e., cannot
be found to match them.

71. Exeunt gentlemen] Cf. *"Exeunt
Gent."* for Rosencrantz and Guilden-
stern in Q2 *Ham.*, III. iii. 26; the S.D.s

of *Mer.V.*, like those of Q2 *Ham.*, are
authorial rather than theatrical (cf.
Introduction, p. xiv).

77. *Frankfort*] An international fair
was held there, twice a year.

82. *hears'd*] buried, coffined; cf.
Ham., I. iv. 47 (so Pooler).

83. *why so!*] In Q, question marks
are often used to mark exclamations;
Furness preferred to read a query here,
but Pooler compared the use of "so" at
I. iii. 165, and of *why so* elsewhere in
Shakespeare (e.g., *R 2*, II. ii. 87).

84. *thou*] F2's "then" makes better
sense, but in so "variable" a speech
there is not sufficient warrant to depart
from the copy text.

o' my breathing, no tears but o' my shedding.

Tub. Yes, other men have ill luck too,—Antonio (as I
    heard in Genoa)—   90

Shy. What, what, what? ill luck, ill luck?

Tub. —hath an argosy cast away coming from Tripolis.

Shy. I thank God, I thank God! is it true, is it true?

Tub. I spoke with some of the sailors that escaped the
    wrack.   95

Shy. I thank thee good Tubal, good news, good news: ha
    ha! heard in Genoa!

Tub. Your daughter spent in Genoa, as I heard, one
    night, fourscore ducats.

Shy. Thou stick'st a dagger in me,—I shall never see my   100
    gold again,—fourscore ducats at a sitting, fourscore
    ducats!

Tub. There came divers of Antonio's creditors in my
    company to Venice, that swear, he cannot choose
    but break.   105

Shy. I am very glad of it,—I'll plague him, I'll torture
    him,—I am glad of it.

Tub. One of them showed me a ring that he had of your
    daughter for a monkey.

Shy. Out upon her!—thou torturest me Tubal,—it was   110
    my turquoise, I had it of Leah when I was a bachelor:

90. Genoa)—] Genowa? *Q, F;* Genowa, *F2.*   91. what?] what, *Q, F;* what
Q2.   luck?] *Q2;* lucke. *Q, F.*   92. —hath] Hath *Q, F.*   93. God!] God,
Q, F.   true?] *Q2, F;* true. *Q.*   97. ha!] ha, *Q, F.*   heard] *Kellner conj.,
Neilson and Hill;* heere *Q, F;* where? *Rowe.*   Genoa!] Genowa. *Q, F;*
Genoua? *Rowe.*   98. one] *Q, F;* in one *Q2.*   99. night,] *Q2;* night *Q, F.*
102. ducats!] *Q2;* ducats. *Q, F.*   104. swear,] *comma is uncertain reading in Q.*
107. it.] *Q; it, F.*   110. her!] her, *Q, F.*   111. turquoise] *Rowe;* Turkies *Q, F.*

97. *heard*] Furness defended Q and
F, interpreting "here" as here in Italy,
but this interpretation is very forced.
Final "e" and "d" are easily confused
in Elizabethan secretary handwriting,
and so Q's "heere" could be a misreading of the copy's *heard* or "herd"
(a possible form); Shylock repeats
Tubal's words as he does in l. 101.

98-9. *one night*] There was a tendency to omit prepositions "in adverbial expressions of time, manner, &c"
(Abbott, ¶202).

105. *break*] become bankrupt.

111. *turquoise*] The stone had special
properties; Steevens quoted E. Fen-
ton, *Secret Wonders of Nature* (1569),
p. 51b: "The *Turkeys* doth moue when
there is any peril prepared to him that
weareth it" and T. Nichols, *Lapidary*:
it "is likewise said to take away all
enmity, and to reconcile man and
wife."

Leah] the name meant painful, or
wearied (so R. F. H[errey], *Two Right
Profitable and Fruitful Concordances*

I would not have given it for a wilderness of monkeys.

Tub. But Antonio is certainly undone.

Shy. Nay, that's true, that's very true,—go Tubal, fee me   115
an officer, bespeak him a fortnight before,—I will
have the heart of him if he forfeit, ior were he out of
Venice I can make what merchandise I will: go
Tubal, and meet me at our synagogue,—go good
Tubal,—at our synagogue Tubal.   *Exeunt.*   120

[SCENE II.—*Belmont.*]

Enter BASSANIO, PORTIA, GRATIANO, [NERISSA,]
and all their trains.

Por. I pray you tarry, pause a day or two
Before you hazard, for in choosing wrong
I lose your company; therefore forbear a while,—
There's something tells me (but it is not love)
I would not lose you, and you know yourself,   5
Hate counsels not in such a quality;
But lest you should not understand me well,—
And yet a maiden hath no tongue, but thought,—

115. Tubal,] *Q2, F;* Tuball *Q.*

Scene II

Scene II] *Rowe; om. Q, F.*   Belmont] *Rowe; om. Q, F; Belmont. A Room in
Portia's House Capell.*   Nerissa] *Capell; om. Q, F.*   trains] *Q; traine F.*
S.D.] *The Caskets are set out. (added) Rowe.*   4. (but ... love)] *Q, F.*   5. lose]
Q2; loose *Q, F.*

(1578); quoted, E. N. Alder, *Jewish
Forum,* xvi (1933), 25–32).

116. *officer*] Sheriff's officer, or
catchpole; it was his duty to make
arrests (as Fang tries to do in *2 H 4*,
II. i).

118. *make ... merchandise*] drive what
bargain (cf. *O.E.D.*, Merchandise, Ic).

Scene II

4. *but . . . love*] Pooler compared
Ado, IV. i. 274; like Beatrice, Portia
tries to confess nothing and deny

nothing, but soon the whole truth is
out (ll. 16–18). Note also that at first
she asks for only a *day or two*, but by l. 9,
it is some *month or two*.

6. *quality*] manner.

8. *And yet . . . thought*] Portia probably alludes to the proverb: "Maidens
should be seen and not heard" (cf.
Tilley, M45); the parenthesis is half
apology for not being more explicit
and half acknowledgement that she is
speaking out of turn (cf. *Troil.*, III. ii.
135–7). Or perhaps Portia means,

I would detain you here some month or two
Before you venture for me. I could teach you   10
How to choose right, but then I am forsworn,
So will I never be,—so may you miss me,—
But if you do, you'll make me wish a sin,
That I had been forsworn. Beshrew your eyes,
They have o'erlook'd me and divided me,   15
One half of me is yours, the other half yours,—
Mine own I would say: but if mine then yours,
And so all yours; O these naughty times
Put bars between the owners and their rights!
And so though yours, not yours,—prove it so,   20
Let Fortune go to hell for it, not I.
I speak too long, but 'tis to peise the time,

14. forsworn. Beshrew] *Q2;* forsworne: Beshrow *Q, F.*   16. the] *Q, F;* th'
Johnson.   half yours] *Q, F, Johnson;* halfe *F2;* yours *Capell.*   17. if] *Q;* of *F.*
19. Put] *F2;* puts *Q, F.*   rights!] rights, *Q, F.*   20. not] *Q, F;* I'm not
Johnson conj.   prove it so,] (proue it so) *Q, F;* Prove it not so! *Capell.*   22.
peise] *Dyce;* peize *Q, F;* poize *Rowe;* peece *Rowe (iii).*

"You should understand me because
I must say, quite simply, what I
think"; cf. *AYL.,* III. ii. 263–4 and
Speeches Delivered to her Majesty (1592),
Lyly, *Wks,* i. 474: "Thus weomens
tongues are made of the same flesh that
their harts are, and speake as they
thinke."

10. *venture*] a word which echoes the
commercial talk of Venice (e.g.,I. i. 15
and I. iii. 86).

14. *Beshrew*] Cf. II. vi. 52, note.

15. *o'erlook'd*] bewitched, looked on
with the "evil eye" (so Eccles); cf.
Wiv., v. v. 87.

17–18. *but if . . . yours*] Cf. *H 5,* v. ii.
185–6: "when France is mine and I
am yours, then yours is France and you
are mine" and *Meas.,* v. i. 543.

18. *naughty*] wicked, worthless, as in
III.iii. 9 and v. i. 91.

19. *Put*] Abbott (¶333) defended
Q's "Puts" as an old form of the
plural, but euphony seems to require
the change and final "s" is particularly liable to error (cf. I. iii. 157, note).
A regular plural verb is used with
times, l. 100 below.

20. *And so . . . so*] Editors have tried
to provide ten syllables but a pause
before the last three is appropriate to
the sense.

yours, not yours] yours *de jure* not *de
facto* (Pooler).

prove it so] i.e., if it prove so.

21. *not I*] i.e., for being forsworn.

22. *peise*] Usually explained as from
O. Fr. *peser,* hence retard by hanging
weights on (so Steevens) or "weigh
with deliberation each precious moment" (Clarendon). But no satisfactory parallel has been found and the
usual senses of weigh, weight, or balance are unsatisfactory.

Rowe (ed. 3) suggested the verb to
piece; since "z" is often found for "s"
in "good" Shakespeare Quartos (cf.
Shakespeare's Hand in Sir Thomas More
(1923), p. 136), Q's "peize" could
easily represent the variant form *peise*
(see *O.E.D.*). Its primary sense is to
mend or patch, but it was used figur-
atively—to augment, complete, extend, etc. Shakespeare usually used
this verb with "out", as in *H 5,* Prol.
23: "Peece out our imperfections with

> To eche it, and to draw it out in length,
> To stay you from election.
> *Bass.*   Let me choose,
> For as I am, I live upon the rack.   25
> *Por.* Upon the rack Bassanio? then confess
> What treason there is mingled with your love.
> *Bass.* None but that ugly treason of mistrust,
> Which makes me fear th'enjoying of my love,—
> There may as well be amity and life   30
> 'Tween snow and fire, as treason and my love.
> *Por.* Ay, but I fear you speak upon the rack
> Where men enforced do speak any thing.
> *Bass.* Promise me life, and I'll confess the truth.
> *Por.* Well then, confess and live.
> *Bass.*   "Confess and love"   35
> Had been the very sum of my confession:
> O happy torment, when my torturer
> Doth teach me answers for deliverance!
> But let me to my fortune and the caskets.
> *Por.* Away then! I am lock'd in one of them,—   40
> If you do love me, you will find me out.

23. eche] *Rowe;* ech *Q;* eck *Q2;* ich *F;* eech *Q3;* eke *Johnson.*   26. Bassanio?]
Bassanio, *Q, F.*   29. th'enjoying] *Q;* the enioying *F.*   30. life] *Q, F;*
league *Walker conj., Dyce* (ii).   32. Ay,] I, *F;* I *Q.*   33. do] *Q;* doth *F.*
38. deliverance!] deliuerance: *Q, F.*   40. then!] then, *Q, F.*

your thoughts" (Folio text)—which is exactly parallel with the use of "eech" elsewhere in *H 5* (see next note). Cf. also *Ant.,* I. v. 45: "I will peece / Her opulent Throne, with King-domes" (Folio text), and *Cor.,* II. iii. 220.

23. *eche*] augment, increase; this verb (from O.E. *écan*) has been super-seded in Mod. E. by the cognate eke (cf. *O.E.D.*). In *H 5,* III. Prol. 35 it is used with "out": "Still be kind, / And eech out our performance with your mind" (Folio text).

29. *fear*] be apprehensive about, doubt; cf. *Ven.,* 642.

30. *life*] Walker suggested "league" thinking that the compositor's eye caught *life* from l. 34 ("league and

amity" occurs *R 3,* I. iii. 281); but *amity and life* is an acceptable phrase, as in *1 Tam.,* II. i. 22.

33. *Where . . . thing*] Cf. Lopez (cf. Introduction, p. xxiii) who "pleaded . . . he had much belied him-self in his confession to save himself from racking" (noted Palmer, *Comic Characters* (1946), p. 54, n. 1).

35. *confess and live*] denying the com-mon proverb "Confess and be hang-ed"; cf. *Jew of Malta,* IV. ii. 18–19 and *Oth.,* IV. i. 38.

live . . . love] a common quibble.

41. *If . . . out*] However much Portia wishes to delay the choice, she knows that the lottery will not deny her a husband who truly loves her; cf. I. ii. 27–32 and II. ix. 79–81.

Nerissa and the rest, stand all aloof,—
Let music sound while he doth make his choice,
Then if he lose he makes a swan-like end,
Fading in music. That the comparison   45
May stand more proper, my eye shall be the
    stream
And wat'ry death-bed for him:—he may win,
And what is music then? Then music is
Even as the flourish, when true subiects bow
To a new-crowned monarch: such it is,   50
As are those dulcet sounds in break of day,
That creep into the dreaming bridegroom's ear,
And summon him to marriage. Now he goes
With no less presence, but with much more love
Than young Alcides, when he did redeem   55
The virgin tribute, paid by howling Troy
To the sea-monster: I stand for sacrifice,
The rest aloof are the Dardanian wives,
With bleared visages come forth to view
The issue of th' exploit: go Hercules!   60
Live thou, I live—with much much more dismay,
I view the fight, than thou that mak'st the fray.

*A song [to music] the whilst Bassanio comments on the
caskets to himself.*

48. then] *Q2;* than *Q, F.*   Then] *Q2;* Than *Q, F.*   58. wives,] *Q2;* vviues:
Q, F.   60. Hercules!] Hercules, *Q, F.*   61. live] *Q, F;* live. *Johnson.*
much much] *Q;* much *Q2, F.*   62. I] *Q, F;* To *Q2.*   *to music] om. Q; Here
Musicke. (before A song ...) F; Musick within. (before A song ...) Rowe.*

44. *swan-like end*] "E.K." glossed
Spenser's *Shepherd's Calendar* (1579),
Oct. 90: "it is sayd of the learned, that
the swan, a little before hir death,
singeth most pleasantly, as prophecy-
ing by a secrete instinct her neere des-
tinie." He also quoted Spenser (from
an otherwise unknown sonnet): "The
silver swanne doth sing before her
dying day, / As shee that feeles the
deepe delight that is in death." Shakespeare called it a "sad dirge" (*Lucr.*,
1612) or "doleful hymn" (*John*, v. vii.
22).

49–50. *flourish . . . monarch*] Cf. Introduction, p. xxv.

51–3. *dulcet . . . marriage*] It was customary to play music under a bridegroom's window on the morning of
his wedding (so Halliwell).

54. *presence*] nobleness, dignity.
with . . . love] Hercules rescued
Hesione not for love, but for the sake of
the horses which Laomedon, her
father and King of Troy, had promised
to him; see Ovid, *Met.*, xi. 199 ff.

58. *Dardanian*] Trojan.

59. *bleared*] i.e., with weeping eyes.

> *Tell me where is Fancy bred,*
> *Or in the heart, or in the head?*
> *How begot, how nourished?*   65
> All. *Reply, reply.*
>
> *It is engend'red in the eyes,*
> *With gazing fed, and Fancy dies*
> *In the cradle where it lies:*
> *Let us all ring Fancy's knell.*   70
> *I'll begin it. Ding, dong, bell.*

63. *Tell*] Q, F; I.V. *Tell Capell.*   64. *head?*] Q2; *head,* Q.   66. All.] *Lawrence conj., N.C.S.; om.* Q, F.   *Reply, reply*] *as Pope; printed to right of l. 65* Q, F; *om. Rowe; Reply (as S.D.) Hanmer.*   67. *It*] Q, F; 2.V. *It Capell.*   *eyes*] F; *eye* Q.   68. *dies*] *dies:* Q.   69. *lies:*] F; *lies* Q.   71. *I'll . . . it*] *as Johnson; roman type* Q, F.   *I'll . . . bell*] *as Johnson; . . . it. | Ding . . .* Q, F.

63. Fancy] Pooler quoted Greene, *Tritameron* (1584), *Wks,* iii. 60: "fancie is *Vox equiuoca,* which either may be taken for honest loue, or fond [i.e., foolish] affection." Here the sense is "fond affection"; cf. Raleigh (*Davidson's Poetical Rhapsody* (1602), ed. Bullen, ii. 112–13):

> "Conceit, begotten by the eyes,
>   Is quickly born, and quickly dies;
>   For while it seeks our hearts to have,
>   Meanwhile there reason makes his
>   grave;
>   For many things the eyes approve,
>   Which yet the heart doth seldom
>   love . . ."

Some critics (e.g., J. Weiss, *Wit, Humour, and Shakespeare* (1876), p. 312) believed that the song tells Bassanio which casket he should choose; (1) Bassanio's next words sound like a "comment . . . inspired by the song" (R. Noble, *Shakespeare's Use of Song* (1923), pp. 45–8); (2) in *Il Pecorone* (cf. Introduction, p. xxviii) the maid gives a hint to the successful wooer, and (3) the song rhymes on "lead". However there are strong reasons against these: (1) Portia has said she will not direct Bassanio (cf. ll. 10–12, above); (2) she believes the lottery will find the right husband (cf. l. 41, and note above); (3) the S.D. (which is probably Shakespeare's own; cf. Introduction, p. xiv) says Bassanio comments "*to himself*"; and (4) it would belittle Bassanio and Portia and cheapen the themes of the play (cf. Introduction, pp. xlvi–lviii). Granville-Barker did not think that Shakespeare would use such a "slim trick" or that there was any suitable way to let an audience into such a secret (*Prefaces,* 2nd series (1930), p. 74, note). In other plays where a character *sings* a secret that he is forbidden to *speak,* the hint is very much broader than here (cf. Heywood, *Rape of Lucrece* (1608), iv. vi and Middleton and Rowley, *Fair Quarrel* (1617), v. i). The song prevents a third recital of the mottoes on the caskets, dignifies and adds expectation to the dramatic context, and prepares the audience for Bassanio's following speech (his thirty-four lines would be an odd elaboration if he believed that the song had given him the secret).

67. engend'red . . . eyes] Portia and Bassanio are both aware that they have kindled each other's "fancy" (cf. i. i. 163–4, and iii. ii. 14–15); the song warns that there must be a deeper love.

69. In the cradle] i.e., "in the eye" (Capell), or in its infancy (so Eccles).

All. *Ding, dong, bell.*

Bass. So may the outward shows be least themselves,—
    The world is still deceiv'd with ornament—
    In law, what plea so tainted and corrupt,   75
    But being season'd with a gracious voice,
    Obscures the show of evil? In religion,
    What damned error but some sober brow
    Will bless it, and approve it with a text,
    Hiding the grossness with fair ornament?   80
    There is no vice so simple, but assumes
    Some mark of virtue on his outward parts;
    How many cowards whose hearts are all as false
    As stairs of sand, wear yet upon their chins
    The beards of Hercules and frowning Mars,   85
    Who inward search'd, have livers white as milk?—
    And these assume but valour's excrement
    To render them redoubted. Look on beauty,
    And you shall see 'tis purchas'd by the weight,
    Which therein works a miracle in nature,   90
    Making them lightest that wear most of it:
    So are those crisped snaky golden locks

77. evil?] *F;* euill. *Q.*   religion,] *F;* religion *Q.*   80. ornament?] ornament:
Q, F.   81. vice] *F2;* voyce *Q;* voice *Q2, F.*   84. stairs] *F4;* stayers *Q, F.*
86. milk?] milke, *Q, F.*

73. *So*] He begins abruptly, the first
part of the argument having passed in
his mind (so Johnson); but cf. l. 63,
note, above.

74. *still*] continually.

75-6. *plea...season'd*] For this metaphor, cf. *Ado*, IV. i. 144 (so Pooler).

79. *approve*] show to be true, confirm; cf. *2 H 4*, I. ii. 180 and *Lr.*, II. ii.
167.

81. *vice*] Q's "voyce" is possibly due
to the levelling in pronunciation of *oi*
and *i* (see Kökeritz, p. 217); *vice* is so
spelt *Cym.*, II. iii. 33 (Folio text) and
"smoyle" for "smile" is found in *Lr.*,
II. ii. 88 (Q1).

84. *stairs*] Q's "stayers" is a variant
spelling; Knight explained it as
"banks, bulwarks of sand", and Hudson as "props, supports, or stays"

but no parallel has been found.

86. *search'd*] probed; a term of sur-
gery (so Pooler); cf. *AYL.*, II. iv. 44.

livers ... milk] When the blood is
"cold and settled", the liver is left
"white and pale, which is the badge of
pusillanimity" (*2 H 4*, IV. iii. 112-14);
cf. also, *Mac.*, v. iii. 15.

87. *excrement*] outgrowth; often used
of hairs, as in *LLL.*, v. i. 109-10.

88. *Look on beauty*] i.e., judging it by
"outward shows".

89. *'tis ... weight*] i.e., it is bought at
so much an ounce.

91. *lightest*] a common quibble; cf.
v. i. 129.

92. *crisped*] curled.

snaky] long, sinuous, but also an
allusion to a snake's poison, deceit,
etc.

Which make such wanton gambols with the wind
Upon supposed fairness, often known
To be the dowry of a second head,   95
The skull that bred them in the sepulchre.
Thus ornament is but the guiled shore
To a most dangerous sea: the beauteous scarf
Veiling an Indian beauty; in a word,
The seeming truth which cunning times put on   100
To entrap the wisest. Therefore thou gaudy gold,
Hard food for Midas, I will none of thee,
Nor none of thee thou pale and common drudge
'Tween man and man: but thou, thou meagre lead
Which rather threaten'st than dost promise aught,   105
Thy paleness moves me more than eloquence,

93. make] *Pope;* maketh *Q;* makes *F.*   97. guiled] *Q, F;* guilded *F2.*
99. Indian beauty;] *Q, F;* Indian dowdy; *Hanmer;* Indian: beauty, *Collier (ii).*
101. To] *Q, F;* T' *Pope.*   Therefore] *Q2;* Therefore then *Q, F;* Then *Pope.*
103. pale] *Q, F;* stale *Farmer conj., Rann.*   105. threaten'st] *Q;* threatnest *Q2,*
F.   106. paleness] *Q, F;* plainness *Theobald.*

93. *make*] The plural in "-th" (Q) is unusual in Shakespeare except in "doth" and "hath" (cf. Abbott, ¶¶332 and 334); emendation also seems to improve the metre.

94. *Upon…fairness*]i.e.,"surmounting fictitious beauty" (Clarendon), or on the strength of their fictitious beauty (so Rolfe).

95–6. *To . . . sepulchre*] Cf. *Sonn.,* lxviii. 5–7: ". . . the golden tresses of the dead, / The right of sepulchres, were shorn away, / To live a second life on second head."

95. *dowry*] endowment; cf. *Per.,* I. i. 9.

97. *guiled*] treacherous, full of guile; cf. *1 H 4,* I. iii. 183: "the jeering and disdain'd contempt / Of this proud king", where "disdain'd" means full of disdain (so Clarendon). Cf. also Abbott, ¶294.

99. *Indian beauty*] Some editors tried to emend because of the jingle and lack of contrast with *beauteous,* but the Elizabethan aversion to dark skins gives sufficient meaning to the passage; cf. "brow of Egypt" (*MND.,* v. i. 11)

and "Ethiope" (*Ado,* v. iv. 38 and elsewhere). The emphasis is on *Indian.*

101. *Therefore thou*] "The misprint and the correction have been left side by side in Q" (*N.C.S.*). Perhaps this Alexandrine should be printed as two short lines, indicating a break in delivery.

102. *Midas*] All he touched, including what he tried to eat or drink, was turned to gold; cf. Ovid, *Met.,* xi.

103. *pale*] Farmer suggested "stale" to avoid emendation at l. 106.

106. *paleness*] Q has been emended because *paleness* does not distinguish lead from "pale" silver (so Warburton), while "plainness" is contrasted with *eloquence* and continues the idea of the preceding line (to threaten is to speak plainly). Sir Walter Greg suggested that the copy's "plaines" was "accidentally misprinted 'palines' and was then wrongly corrected" (quoted *N.C.S.*).

But Farmer showed that pale was often used of lead (e.g., *Rom.,*II. v. 17). Moreover it was a commonplace to talk of the "colours of rhetoric", and

And here choose I,—joy be the consequence!
Por. [*Aside.*] How all the other passions fleet to air:
As doubtful thoughts, and rash-embrac'd despair,
And shudd'ring fear, and green-eyed jealousy.   110
O love be moderate, allay thy extasy,
In measure rain thy joy, scant this excess!
I feel too much thy blessing, make it less
For fear I surfeit.
Bass.   What find I here?
                    [*He opens the leaden casket.*]
Fair Portia's counterfeit! What demi-god   115
Hath come so near creation? move these eyes?
Or whether (riding on the balls of mine)
Seem they in motion? Here are sever'd lips
Parted with sugar breath,—so sweet a bar
Should sunder such sweet friends: here in her hairs   120
The painter plays the spider, and hath woven

107. consequence!] consequence. *Q, F.*   108. S.D.] *Cambridge; om. Q, F.*
air:] ayre, *Q, F.*   109. rash-embrac'd] *hyphened Theobald.*   despair,]
despaire: *Q, F.*   110. shudd'ring] *F;* shyddring *Q.*   111. O love] *as Q, F;*
separate line Walker conj., Globe.   112. rain] raine *Q, F;* reine *Q 3;* rein *Johnson*
conj., Collier (ii).   excess!] excesse, *Q, F.*   114. S.D.] *Malone subs.; om. Q, F;*
after surfeit *Rowe subs.*   115. counterfeit!] counterfeit. *Q, F.*   117. whether]
F; whither *Q.*

so coloured *eloquence* might be contrasted with *paleness.* This would be in
keeping with Bassanio's line of thought
about "beauty . . . purchas'd by the
weight", "ornament", and "seeming
truth". For the contrast, cf. *Ham.,* iii.
i. 51–3: "The harlot's cheek, beautied
with plastering art, / Is not more
ugly . . . / Than is my deed to my most
painted word," or Sir J. Davies, *Epi-*
grams (*c.* 1598), no. 45: "Dacus with
some good colour and pretence, /
Tearmes his love's beauty 'silent eloquence': / For she doth lay more
colour on her face / Than ever Tully
us'd his speech to grace." *Paleness* also
continues the idea of the previous
line, for the face goes pale when me-
nacing (cf., for example, *R 3,* i. iv.
175–7).
The passage makes good sense
therefore without emendation; *Thy*

(l. 106) should be stressed (so Malone).
    109. *As*] such as.
    111. *O love*] possibly a separate,
extra-metrical line (so Globe), but
this would break the couplet.
    112. *rain*] Cf. *Tp.,* iii. i. 75, but Q's
"raine" was also a common form of
"rein".
    scant] diminish, withhold.
    excess] a synonym for interest, or
usury; cf. i. iii. 57 and note.
    115. *counterfeit*] likeness, portrait.
    116. *Hath . . . creation*] has painted a
counterfeit so nearly indistinguishable
from its subject. Life-likeness was the
commonest criterion in painting; cf.
the description of pictures offered to
Sly (*Shr.,* Ind. ii. 51–62), and R. W.
Zandvoort, *Rivista di Letterature Mod-*
erne, v (1951), 351–6.
    117. *Or whether*] or (cf. Abbott,
¶136).

A golden mesh t'entrap the hearts of men
Faster than gnats in cobwebs,—but her eyes!
How could he see to do them? having made one,
Methinks it should have power to steal both his   125
And leave itself unfurnish'd: yet look how far
The substance of my praise doth wrong this shadow
In underprizing it, so far this shadow
Doth limp behind the substance. Here's the scroll,
The continent and summary of my fortune.   130

> *You that choose not by the view*
> *Chance as fair, and choose as true:*
> *Since this fortune falls to you,*
> *Be content, and seek no new.*
> *If you be well pleas'd with this,*   135
> *And hold your fortune for your bliss,*
> *Turn you where your lady is,*
> *And claim her with a loving kiss.*

A gentle scroll: fair lady, by your leave,
I come by note to give, and to receive,—   140

123. eyes!] eyes *Q*.   126. unfurnish'd] *Q, F;* unfinish'd *Rowe*.   139. *A*] *Q;*
Bass. A *F*.   139.] S.D., *Kissing her. (at end of line) Rowe; after l. 140 Collier.*

122. *golden . . . men*] Cf. Spenser,
Amoretti (1595), xxxvii: ". . . her golden tresses / She doth attyre under a
net of gold; . . . / Is it that men's frayle
eyes, which gaze too bold, / She may
entangle in that golden snare; / And,
being caught, may craftily enfold /
Theyr weaker harts, which are not
wel aware? / Take heed . . . / . . . if ever
ye entrapped are, / Out of her bands
ye by no meanes shall get . . ."

124. *How . . . them*] Steevens quoted
J. de Flores, *Bellora and Fidelio* [tr.
R. Greene], (1606), B2: "If Apelles
had beene tasked to have drawne her
counterfeit, her two bright-burning
Lampes, would haue so dazled his
quicke-seeing sences that quite dis-
pairing to expresse . . . so admirable a
worke of Nature, he had beene in-

forced to haue . . . left this earthly
Venus unfinished."

126. *unfurnish'd*] i.e., without the
other eye.

127. *shadow*] picture; cf. II. ix. 66,
note.

129. *limp*] Steevens compared *Tp.*,
IV. i. 10–11: "she will outstrip all
praise / And make it halt behind her."

substance] i.e., original; cf. l. 116,
note above, and *Gent.*, IV. ii. 123–5.

130. *continent*] "That which com-
prises or sums up" (*O.E.D.*, 1b).

139. *A*] l. 139 begins F1ᵛ in Q, but
the catchword on F1 is "*Bass.*".

140. *by note*] an allusion to a bill, or
note, of dues; the metaphor is continued in l. 148 (so Halliwell). See also
Tim., II. ii. 16, and Introduction,
p. lvi.

Like one of two contending in a prize
That thinks he hath done well in people's eyes,
Hearing applause and universal shout,
Giddy in spirit, still gazing in a doubt
Whether those peals of praise be his or no,   145
So (thrice-fair lady) stand I even so,
As doubtful whether what I see be true,
Until confirm'd, sign'd, ratified by you.

Por. You see me Lord Bassanio where I stand,
Such as I am; though for myself alone   150
I would not be ambitious in my wish
To wish myself much better, yet for you,
I would be trebled twenty times myself,
A thousand times more fair, ten thousand times
          more rich,
That only to stand high in your account,   155
I might in virtues, beauties, livings, friends
Exceed account: but the full sum of me
Is sum of something: which to term in gross,
Is an unlesson'd girl, unschool'd, unpractised,
Happy in this, she is not yet so old   160

---

142. eyes,] eyes: *Q, F*.   145. peals] *Q, F;* pearles *Q2*.   149. me] *Q;* my *F*.
154–5. A ... account] *as Collier; ...* times / [M]ore rich ... *Q, F; ...* times /
More rich, / That ... *Malone*.   155. only] *Q, F;* om. *F2*.   158. sum of something] *Theobald;* sume of something *Q;* sum of nothing *F;* some of something
Warburton; sum of—something *Clarendon*.   159. unlesson'd] *Q;* vnlessoned *F*.
unpractised] *Q;* vnpractiz'd *F*.

141. *prize*] contest at fencing or wrestling etc.

154. *more rich*] This would not be significant as a short line and it is probably best to accept an Alexandrine and assume that the compositor altered his copy in order to avoid a single long line.

156. *livings*] possessions.

158. *sum of something*] There are two difficulties: (1) Q's "sume" might represent modern *sum* or "some", and (2) several editors have objected to the jingle. Those who read "sum of nothing" have thought this was appropriate to Portia's exaggeration; those

who read *sum of something*, that it was the modest assertion of an *unlesson'd girl*; and those who read "some of something" explained the phrase as the "portion of a portion" (*N.C.S.*, quoting *O.E.D.*, 2). Since this is part of a sequence of commercial terms, started by *account*, Portia may be varying the common phrase "sum of all" (cf. e.g., *Ado*, I. i. 147 and *John*, II. i. 151) which is equivalent to *the full sum*, and *to term in gross*; this point could be accentuated by pausing slightly before *something* (see Clarendon's pointing). The phrase is varied again in "sum of sums" (*Sonn.*, iv. 8).

But she may learn: happier than this,
She is not bred so dull but she can learn;
Happiest of all, is that her gentle spirit
Commits itself to yours to be directed,
As from her lord, her governor, her king.   165
Myself, and what is mine, to you and yours
Is now converted. But now I was the lord
Of this fair mansion, master of my servants,
Queen o'er myself: and even now, but now.
This house, these servants, and this same myself   170
Are yours,—my lord's!—I give them with this ring,
Which when you part from, lose, or give away,
Let it presage the ruin of your love,
And be my vantage to exclaim on you.
Bass. Madam, you have bereft me of all words,   175
Only my blood speaks to you in my veins,
And there is such confusion in my powers,
As after some oration fairly spoke
By a beloved prince, there doth appear
Among the buzzing pleased multitude,   180
Where every something being blent together,
Turns to a wild of nothing, save of joy
Express'd, and not express'd: but when this ring
Parts from this finger, then parts life from hence,—
O then be bold to say Bassanio's dead!   185
Ner. My lord and lady, it is now our time
That have stood by and seen our wishes prosper,

161. happier than this,] happier then this, *Q, F;* happier then in this, *F2;* more happy then in this, *Pope;* and happier than this, *Johnson;* happier than this, in that *Capell;* then happier in this, *Dyce* (ii).   163. is] *Q, F;* in *Collier* (ii). 167. lord] *Q, F;* Lady *Rowe.*   168. master] *Q, F;* Mistress *Rowe.*   171. lord's!] *N.C.S.;* Lords, *Q;* Lord, *Q2, F.*   180. multitude,] *F;* multitude. *Q.* 185. dead!] dead. *Q, F.*

161. *than*] Some editors have wished to improve the metre, but there is probably a pause before *happier.* The construction changes; Portia is happy in her youth, and a happier circumstance is that she can learn (so Pooler).

169. *even now, but now*] i.e., at this very moment (cf. Abbott, ¶38).

171. *my lord's*] Q's reading "under-

lines Portia's act of fealty" (*N.C.S.*); but the reading is not very secure, for final "s" is particularly liable to error (cf. I. iii. 157, note).

174. *vantage*] opportunity.

exclaim on] accuse, protest against; cf. *I H 6,* III. iii. 60.

182. *wild*] a figurative use of the word, often used of deserts and waste places, as in II. vii. 41.

To cry good joy,—good joy my lord and lady!
Gra. My Lord Bassanio, and my gentle lady,
    I wish you all the joy that you can wish: 190
    For I am sure you can wish none from me:
    And when your honours mean to solemnize
    The bargain of your faith, I do beseech you
    Even at that time I may be married too.
Bass. With all my heart, so thou canst get a wife.   195
Gra. I thank your lordship, you have got me one.
    My eyes my lord can look as swift as yours:
    You saw the mistress, I beheld the maid:
    You lov'd, I lov'd—for intermission
    No more pertains to me my lord than you;   200
    Your fortune stood upon the caskets there,
    And so did mine too as the matter falls:
    For wooing here until I sweat again,
    And swearing till my very roof was dry
    With oaths of love, at last, (if promise last)   205
    I got a promise of this fair one here
    To have her love, provided that your fortune
    Achiev'd her mistress.
Por.   Is this true Nerissa?
Ner. Madam it is, so you stand pleas'd withal.
Bass. And do you Gratiano mean good faith?   210
Gra. Yes—faith my lord.

188. lady!] Lady. *Q*, *F*.   193. faith,] fayth: *Q*, *F*.   196. have] *Q*; gave *F*.
199. lov'd] *Q*, *F*; lov'd: *Theobald*.   intermission] *Theobald*; intermission, *Q*,
F; intermission. *Q 3*.   201. caskets] *Q*, *F*; Casket *Q2*.   203. here] *Q*, *F*;
Her *Rowe (iii)*.   204. roof] *Q2*; rough *Q*, *F*; tongue *Collier (ii) conj.*, *Delius*;
ruff *Flatter conj.*   207. love,] loue: *Q*, *F*.   209. is] *Q*; is so *F*.

191. *none from me*] i.e., no more than
I wish you; cf. Lyly, *Euphues and his
England* (1580), Epistle: "To the
Ladies . . . Iohn Lyly wisheth what
they would." Or perhaps, Gratiano
means "nothing away from me" (so
Johnson).
198. *maid*] This might describe a
"wayting-Gentlewoman"(Q3, Actors'
Names); her status seems much like
Maria's in *Tw.N.*, or Ursula's and
Margaret's in *Ado*.
199. *intermission*] respite (cf. *AYL.*,

II. vii. 32–3: "I did laugh sans intermission / An hour by his dial"), or
delay (cf. *Lr.*, II. iv. 33). Q's pointing
is defensible if *intermission* can mean
relief, pastime; then l. 200 would
mean "my lot is the same as yours".
204. *roof*] i.e., of his mouth; cf. *R 2*,
v. iii. 31, and *O.E.D.*, 3. Conjectural
emendations were discussed in *T.L.S.*
9, 30 Dec. 1949, and 3, 17 Feb. and
17 Mar. 1950; "tongue" was suggested
on the assumption that the copy read
"tonge".

Bass. Our feast shall be much honoured in your marriage.
Gra. We'll play with them the first boy for a thousand
    ducats.
Ner. What! and stake down?   215
Gra. No, we shall ne'er win at that sport and stake down.
    But who comes here? Lorenzo and his infidel!
    What! and my old Venetian friend Salerio?

    Enter LORENZO, JESSICA, *and* SALERIO (*a messenger
            from Venice*).

Bass. Lorenzo and Salerio, welcome hither,
    If that the youth of my new int'rest here   220
    Have power to bid you welcome:—by your leave
    I bid my very friends and countrymen
    (Sweet Portia) welcome.
Por.   So do I my lord,
    They are entirely welcome.
Lor. I thank your honour,—for my part my lord   225
    My purpose was not to have seen you here,
    But meeting with Salerio by the way
    He did entreat me (past all saying nay)
    To come with him along.
Sal.   I did my lord,
    And I have reason for it,—Signior Antonio   230

215. What!] What *Q, F.*   217. infidel!] infidell? *Q, F.*   218. What!]
vvhat, *Q.*   218, 219. Salerio] *Q, F;* Salanio *Rowe;* Solanio *Knight.*   218.]
S.D., Scene III *Pope.*   S.D.] *as Q, F; after l. 216 N.C.S.*   Salerio] *Q, F;*
Salanio *Rowe;* Salerino *Capell;* Solanio *Knight.*   a . . . *Venice*] *Q; om. F.*
220. int'rest] *Q;* interest *F.*   223–4. So . . . welcome] *as Capell; one line Q, F.*
227. Salerio] *Q, F;* Salanio *Rowe;* Solanio *Knight.*   230. I] *Q, F; om. F2.*
for it] *Q, F;* for't *Pope.*

215–16. *stake down*] For the lewd
quibble see *Wint.*, I. ii. 248 and Partridge, *Shakespeare's Bawdy* (1947), p.
193. The prose is appropriate to the
conversation and does not necessarily
imply an interpolation as suggested by
N.C.S.

217. *infidel*] Theobald and *N.C.S.*
noted that no one greets Jessica until
l. 236 below, and the latter, that
Lorenzo ignores Portia's greeting

(l. 224) which is an incomplete line
metrically. It has been suggested that
this is a sign of revision but with the
entry of three new characters, some
formalities might be glossed over in
the dialogue, so that the pace of the action is not lost; the formalities can
be more rapidly performed in dumb
show.

222. *very*] true.
224. *entirely*] sincerely.

Commends him to you.   [*Gives Bassanio a letter.*]
Bass.   Ere I ope his letter
      I pray you tell me how my good friend doth.
Sal. Not sick my lord, unless it be in mind,
      Nor well, unless in mind: his letter there
      Will show you his estate.   [*Bassanio*] *open*[*s*] *the letter.*
Gra. Nerissa, cheer yond stranger, bid her welcome.   236
      Your hand Salerio,—what's the news from Venice?
      How doth that royal merchant good Antonio?
      I know he will be glad of our success,
      We are the Jasons, we have won the fleece.   240
Sal. I would you had won the fleece that he hath lost.
Por. There are some shrewd contents in yond same paper
      That steals the colour from Bassanio's cheek,—
      Some dear friend dead, else nothing in the world
      Could turn so much the constitution   245
      Of any constant man: what worse and worse?
      With leave Bassanio, I am half yourself,
      And I must freely have the half of anything
      That this same paper brings you.
Bass.   O sweet Portia,
      Here are a few of the unpleasant'st words   250
      That ever blotted paper! Gentle lady
      When I did first impart my love to you,
      I freely told you all the wealth I had

231. S.D.] *Theobald; om. Q, F.*   235. S.D.] *Rowe; open the letter Q; He opens the
Letter Q2; Opens the Letter F.*   236. yond] *Q, F;* yon *Q2.*   237. Salerio] *Q,
F;* Salanio *Rowe;* Solanio *Knight.*   241. I] *Q, F; om. Pope.*   242. yond] *Q,
F;* yon *Q2.*   243. steals] *Q, F;* steal *Pope.*   247. Bassanio,] *Q2;* Bassanio *Q,
F.*   248. I] *Q, F; om. F2.*   freely] *Q, F; om. Q3.*   251. paper!] paper.
Q, F.

231. *Commends . . . you*] a habitual
phrase for sending remembrances.

234. *unless in mind*] unless he is comforted by fortitude (so Eccles).

235. *estate*] state, condition; cf. l. 315
below, and *H 5,* IV. i. 99.

238. *royal merchant*] "merchant
prince" (Pooler); one who can rise no
higher in his calling.

240. *We . . . Jasons*] i.e., not Antonio with his *argosy* (so Douce). See
also Introduction, p. lv.

241. *fleece*] a pun on fleets (so Daniel,
Notes and Conjectural Emendations (1870),
p. 37).

242. *shrewd*] evil, unfortunate; cf.
John, V. v. 14.

245. *turn*] change; cf. to turn colour,
as in *Ham.,* II. ii. 542–3. For the relation between the complexion and constitution, cf. II. vii. 79, note.

246. *constant*] steadfast, with a
settled and well-ordered constitution.

Ran in my veins,—I was a gentleman,—
And then I told you true: and yet dear lady   255
Rating myself at nothing, you shall see
How much I was a braggart,—when I told you
My state was nothing, I should then have told you
That I was worse than nothing; for indeed
I have engag'd myself to a dear friend,   260
Engag'd my friend to his mere enemy
To feed my means. Here is a letter lady,
The paper as the body of my friend,
And every word in it a gaping wound
Issuing life-blood. But is it true Salerio?   265
Hath all his ventures fail'd? what not one hit?
From Tripolis, from Mexico and England,
From Lisbon, Barbary, and India,
And not one vessel scape the dreadful touch
Of merchant-marring rocks?

Sal.   Not one my lord.   270
Besides, it should appear, that if he had
The present money to discharge the Jew,
He would not take it: never did I know
A creature that did bear the shape of man
So keen and greedy to confound a man.   275
He plies the duke at morning and at night,
And doth impeach the freedom of the state
If they deny him justice. Twenty merchants,
The duke himself, and the magnificoes

---

263. as] *Q*, *F*; is *Pope.*
Rowe; Solanio? *Knight.*
Q, *F.*   hit?] hit, *Q*, *F.*
'scap'd *Pope.*

265. Salerio?] *Q2;* Salerio *Q;* Salerio, *F;* Salanio?
266. Hath] *Q*, *F;* Have *Rowe.*   fail'd?] *Q2;* faild,
267. and] *Q*, *F;* from *Rowe.*   269. scape] *Q*, *F;*

---

261. *mere*] unqualified.

267. *Mexico*] Elze (*Shakespeare Jahr-buch*, xiv (1879), 179) cited this as one of the few inaccuracies in Shakespeare's picture of Venice. Venice had no direct communication with Mexico or America.

272. *present*] ready.

275. *keen*] savage, cruel; so used of wild animals (cf. *O.E.D.*, 2c and *MND.*, iii. ii. 323). Usurers were likened to ravenous beasts; cf., for

example, *Life and Death of a Miserable Usurer* (1584), B5v: "the vnreasonable beastes, . . . he resembled not in shape, yet was he lyke them in mind: . . ."

confound] destroy.

277. *impeach*] challenge, discredit; cf.iii.iii. 26–31, and iv. i. 35–9.

279. *magnificoes*] Cf. Minsheu, *Guide into Tongues* (1617): "the chiefe men of Venice are . . . called *Magnifici*, i. Magnificoes" (quoted Furness).

Of greatest port have all persuaded with him,   280
But none can drive him from the envious plea
Of forfeiture, of justice, and his bond.

Jes. When I was with him, I have heard him swear
To Tubal and to Chus, his countrymen,
That he would rather have Antonio's flesh   285
Than twenty times the value of the sum
That he did owe him: and I know my lord,
If law, authority, and power deny not,
It will go hard with poor Antonio.

Por. Is it your dear friend that is thus in trouble?   290

Bass. The dearest friend to me, the kindest man,
The best-condition'd and unwearied spirit
In doing courtesies: and one in whom
The ancient Roman honour more appears
Than any that draws breath in Italy.   295

Por. What sum owes he the Jew?

Bass. For me three thousand ducats.

Por.   What no more?
Pay him six thousand, and deface the bond:
Double six thousand, and then treble that,
Before a friend of this description   300
Shall lose a hair through Bassanio's fault.
First go with me to church, and call me wife,
And then away to Venice to your friend:
For never shall you lie by Portia's side
With an unquiet soul. You shall have gold   305
To pay the petty debt twenty times over.
When it is paid, bring your true friend along,—
My maid Nerissa, and myself meantime
Will live as maids and widows;—come away!
For you shall hence upon your wedding day: 310

---

292. best-condition'd] *hyphened Anon. 1734.*   and] *Q*, *F*; an *Warburton.*
297-8. What . . . bond] *as F; one line Q.*   297. more?] *F*; more, *Q*.   300.
this] *Q*, *F*; his *Walker conj.*   301. through] *Q*, *F*; through my *F2*; thorough
Var. '78.   309. away!] away, *Q*, *F*.

280. *port*] dignity.
persuaded] pleaded; cf. *Meas.*, v. i. 93.
281. *envious*] malicious.
292. *best-condition'd*] best natured.
293. *courtesies*] Cf. III. i. 44, note.

296. *What . . . Jew*] a short line; Bassanio may pause before replying and then Portia continue eagerly without further break. The gratuitous *For me* (l. 297) also indicates embarrassment.

Bid your friends welcome, show a merry cheer,—
Since you are dear bought, I will love you dear.
But let me hear the letter of your friend.

Bass. [*Reads.*] *Sweet Bassanio, my ships have all miscarried,*
my creditors grow cruel, my estate is very low, my bond to 315
the Jew is forfeit, and (since in paying it, it is impos-
sible I should live), all debts are clear'd between you and I,
if I might but see you at my death: notwithstanding, use
your pleasure,—if your love do not persuade you to come,
let not my letter. 320

Por. O love!—dispatch all business and be gone!
Bass. Since I have your good leave to go away,
　　　I will make haste; but till I come again,
　　　　No bed shall e'er be guilty of my stay,
　　　　　Nor rest be interposer 'twixt us twain.   *Exeunt.* 325

[SCENE III.—*Venice.*]

Enter [SHYLOCK] *the Jew, and* SOLANIO, *and* ANTONIO, *and the Gaoler.*

Shy. Gaoler, look to him,—tell not me of mercy,—
　　This is the fool that lent out money gratis.
　　Gaoler, look to him.
Ant.　　　　　　Hear me yet good Shylock.
Shy. I'll have my bond, speak not against my bond,—

314. *Bass.*] *Rowe; om. Q, F.*　　S.D.] *Rowe; om. Q, F.*　　317. *I,*] *F; I Q; me*
Pope.　　318. *but*] *Q; om. F.*　　321. *Por.*] *Q, F; om. Q2.*　　gone!] gone. *Q, F.*
325. Nor] *Q, F; No Q2.*

Scene III

Scene III] *Rowe; om. Q, F;* Scene IV *Pope.*　　*Venice*] *Rowe; om. Q, F; a Street in*
Venice Theobald.　　Shylock] *Rowe; om. Q, F.*　　Solanio] *F;* Salerio *Q;*
Salarino *Q2;* Salanio *F4;* Solarino *Rowe.*　　1, 4, 12. *Shy.*] *Rowe; Iew. Q, F.*
2. lent] *Q;* lends *F.*

311. *cheer*] disposition.

311–12. *Bid . . . dear*] Cf. Introduction, p. lvii. H. T. Price (*JEGP*, LV
(1956), 644) suggested an allusion to
the proverb "Dear bought and far-
fetched are dainties for ladies"
(Tilley, D12).

314. *Bass.*] The emendation is suggested by *hear* of the previous line.

Scene III

Solanio] "Salerio" (Q) is presumably at Belmont; Q's speech prefix Sol.
at l. 18 reinforces the emendation (so
N.C.S.).

I have sworn an oath, that I will have my bond: 5
Thou call'dst me dog before thou hadst a cause,
But since I am a dog, beware my fangs,—
The duke shall grant me justice,—I do wonder
(Thou naughty gaoler) that thou art so fond
To come abroad with him at his request.   10
Ant. I pray thee hear me speak.
Shy. I'll have my bond. I will not hear thee speak,
I'll have my bond, and therefore speak no more.
I'll not be made a soft and dull-ey'd fool,
To shake the head, relent, and sigh, and yield   15
To Christian intercessors: follow not,—
I'll have no speaking, I will have my bond.   *Exit.*
Sol. It is the most impenetrable cur
That ever kept with men.
Ant.   Let him alone,
I'll follow him no more with bootless prayers.   20
He seeks my life, his reason well I know;
I oft deliver'd from his forfeitures
Many that have at times made moan to me,
Therefore he hates me.
Sol.   I am sure the duke
Will never grant this forfeiture to hold.   25
Ant. The duke cannot deny the course of law:
For the commodity that strangers have

5. I have] *Q, F;* I've *Pope.*   17. S.D.] *Exit Iew Q, F.*   24. *Sol.*] *F; Sal. Q.*
24–5. I . . . hold] *as Pope;* . . . grant / this . . . *Q, F;* . . . grant / This . . . *Q2.*

9. *naughty*] wicked.
    fond] foolish, or "indulgent" (Knight).
    10. *come . . . request*] *N.C.S.* suggested that Antonio has just visited Shylock to make some request (cf. l. 20).
    14. *dull-ey'd*] easily deceived; Clarendon compared Fletcher, *Elder Brother* (1637), I. ii. 231: "Though I be dull-eyed, I see through this juggling."
    fool] To Shylock, kindness, compassion, and good feeling are synonymous with folly; cf. l. 2 above (so Cowden Clarke).
    19. *kept*] lived.

20. *bootless*] unavailing.
26. *deny*] refuse to accept, prevent.
27. *commodity*] convenience, benefit. Clarendon quoted Thomas, *History of Italy* (1549), Z1: "Al men, specially strangers, haue so muche libertee there, that though they speake verie ill by the Venetians, so they attempt nothyng in effecte against theyr astate, no man shall controll them for it. . . . If thou be a Jewe, a Turke, or beleeuest in the diuell (so thou spreade not thyne opinions abroade) thou arte free from all controllement . . ."

With us in Venice, if it be denied,
Will much impeach the justice of the state,
Since that the trade and profit of the city   30
Consisteth of all nations. Therefore go,—
These griefs and losses have so bated me
That I shall hardly spare a pound of flesh
To-morrow, to my bloody creditor.
Well gaoler, on,—pray God Bassanio come   35
To see me pay his debt, and then I care not.   *Exeunt.*

[SCENE IV.—*Belmont.*]

Enter PORTIA, NERISSA, LORENZO, JESSICA, *and*
[BALTHAZAR] (*a man of Portia's*).

Lor. Madam, although I speak it in your presence,
You have a noble and a true conceit
Of god-like amity, which appears most strongly
In bearing thus the absence of your lord.
But if you knew to whom you show this honour,   5
How true a gentleman you send relief,
How dear a lover of my lord your husband,
I know you would be prouder of the work
Than customary bounty can enforce you.

29. Will] *Q, F;* 'Twill *Theobald conj., Capell.*   35. gaoler,] *F;* Iaylor *Q.*

Scene IV

Scene IV] *Rowe; om. Q, F;* Scene V *Pope.*   Belmont] *Rowe; om. Q, F; Belmont.*
A Room in Portia's House *Capell.*   Balthazar] *Theobald; om. Q, F.*   3. most]
Q, F; om. Pope.

29. *Will . . . impeach*] The construction is loose; the subject is the denial of
commodity, or, possibly, of the course
of law.

30-1. *Since . . . nations*] a further
reason why the law must have its
course.

32. *bated*] (1) dejected (cf. *O.E.D.,*
2) and (2) reduced in weight (cf. IV. i.
72 and *1 H 4,* III. iii. 2).

Scene IV

2. *conceit*] conception.

3. *amity*] "Lorenzo and Portia have
evidently been discussing, in Renaissance fashion, the relations between
Love and Friendship" (*N.C.S.*).

6. *relief*] *gentleman* is dative (so
Clarendon).

9. *Than . . . you*] i.e., than ordinary
acts of kindness can incline you to be
(so Eccles), or, than ordinary benevolence can constrain you to be (so
Clarendon). For *bounty* = goodness,
benevolence, cf. *Gent.,*III. i. 65.

Por. I never did repent for doing good,   10
       Nor shall not now: for in companions
       That do converse and waste the time together,
       Whose souls do bear an egall yoke of love,
       There must be needs a like proportion
       Of lineaments, of manners, and of spirit;   15
       Which makes me think that this Antonio
       Being the bosom lover of my lord,
       Must needs be like my lord. If it be so,
       How little is the cost I have bestowed
       In purchasing the semblance of my soul,   20
       From out the state of hellish cruelty!—
       This comes too near the praising of myself,
       Therefore no more of it: hear other things—
       Lorenzo I commit into your hands,
       The husbandry and manage of my house,   •   25
       Until my lord's return: for mine own part
       I have toward heaven breath'd a secret vow,
       To live in prayer and contemplation,
       Only attended by Nerissa here,
       Until her husband and my lord's return,—   30
       There is a monast'ry two miles off,
       And there we will abide. I do desire you
       Not to deny this imposition,
       The which my love and some necessity

15. lineaments,] *Q, F;* lineaments *Warburton.*   20. soul,] *Q2;* soule; *Q, F.*
21. cruelty!] cruelty, *Q, F;* misery. *Q2.*   31. monast'ry] *Q;* Monastery *Q2, F.*

12. *waste*] spend; improvidence is
not necessarily implied. Pooler compared *Tp.*, v. i. 302 and *Gent.*, ii. iv. 63:
"conversed and spent our hours together".

13. *egall*] equal; from O. Fr. *egal.*

14. *needs*] of necessity (cf. Abbott,
¶25).

proportion] harmony, balance (cf.
Wiv., v. v. 235), but Pooler's gloss
"shape or appearance" may be right
(cf. *2 H 6*, i. iii. 57).

15. *lineaments*] lit., features of the
body or face. Warburton's punctuation avoided the "nonsense" of two
friends having to be alike physically;

Steevens quoted *2 H 4*, ii. iv. 265–6 to
show that, in a general sense, this
might have been implied. However,
the word may be interpreted figura-
tively, as "characteristics" (so Verity).

17. *bosom*] intimate, confidential; cf.
substantive use *Cæs.*, v. i. 7, and *Lr.*,
iv. v. 26.

20. *my soul*] i.e., Bassanio; Cæsario
would so call Olivia (*Tw.N.*, i. v.
288).

25. *husbandry and manage*] ordering
and management.

30. *her . . . lord's*] the genitive applies
to both nouns (cf. Abbott, ¶397).

33. *imposition*] command, charge.

Now lays upon you.

Lor.   Madam, with all my heart,   35
I shall obey you in all fair commands.

Por. My people do already know my mind,
And will acknowledge you and Jessica
In place of Lord Bassanio and myself.
So fare you well till we shall meet again.   40

Lor. Fair thoughts and happy hours attend on you!

Jes. I wish your ladyship all heart's content.

Por. I thank you for your wish, and am well pleas'd
To wish it back on you: fare you well Jessica.
                    Exeunt [Jessica and Lorenzo].

Now Balthazar,   45
As I have ever found thee honest-true,
So let me find thee still: take this same letter,
And use thou all th'endeavour of a man
In speed to Padua, see thou render this
Into my cousin's hand (Doctor Bellario),   50
And look what notes and garments he doth give thee,—
Bring them (I pray thee) with imagin'd speed
Unto the traject, to the common ferry
Which trades to Venice; waste no time in words
But get thee gone,—I shall be there before thee.   55

Bal. Madam, I go with all convenient speed.   [*Exit.*]

35. lays] *Q, F;* lay *Hanmer.*   41. you!] you. *Q, F.*   44. fare you well] *Q;* farewell *Q2;* faryouwell *F.*   *Jessica and Lorenzo*] *Rowe subs.; om. Q, F.*   45–6. Now
... honest-true] *as Pope; one line Q, F.*   46. honest-true] *hyphened Dyce;* honest,
true *Rowe.*   48. th'endeavour] *Q;* the indeauor *F.*   man] *Q2;* man, *Q, F.*
49. Padua] *Theobald;* Mantua *Q, F.*   50. cousin's hand] *F;* cosin hands *Q;*
Cosins hands *Q2.*   53. traject] *Rowe;* Tranect *Q, F.*   56. S.D.] *Q2; om. Q, F.*

45. *Now Balthazar*] *N.C.S.* thought
this short line showed that the text had
been "adapted", but it probably indicates that Portia pauses until the others
are clear of the stage before speaking
to Balthazar.

49. *Padua*] Theobald's emendation
is necessitated by IV. i. 109 and 119,
and V. i. 268. Civil Law was studied in
the university of Padua.

50. *cousin's hand*] The compositor
probably added the "s" to the wrong
word; Shakespeare usually used the
singular in such contexts, e.g., *John,*

I. i. 14.   *cousin's* = kinsman's.

52. *imagin'd*] imaginable (cf.
Abbott, ¶375).

53. *traject*] Q's "Tranect" is probably a misreading of "traiect"; this
would represent It. *traghetto,* a ferry,
which is found in Florio's *World of
Words* (1598). Steevens identified
"Tranect" with It. *tranare,* to draw,
pass over, swim, but the sense is strained and the "-ect" ending is not
explained.

54. *trades to*] communicates with.
56. *convenient*] appropriate, due.

Por. Come on Nerissa, I have work in hand
       That you yet know not of; we'll see our husbands
       Before they think of us!
Ner.   Shall they see us?
Por. They shall Nerissa: but in such a habit,   60
       That they shall think we are accomplished
       With that we lack; I'll hold thee any wager
       When we are both accoutered like young men,
       I'll prove the prettier fellow of the two,
       And wear my dagger with the braver grace,   65
       And speak between the change of man and boy,
       With a reed voice, and turn two mincing steps
       Into a manly stride; and speak of frays
       Like a fine bragging youth: and tell quaint lies
       How honourable ladies sought my love,   70
       Which I denying, they fell sick and died:
       I could not do withal:—then I'll repent,
       And wish for all that, that I had not kill'd them;
       And twenty of these puny lies I'll tell,
       That men shall swear I have discontinued school   75
       Above a twelvemonth: I have within my mind
       A thousand raw tricks of these bragging Jacks,
       Which I will practise.
Ner.   Why, shall we turn to men?
Por. Fie! what a question's that,
       If thou wert near a lewd interpreter!   80
       But come, I'll tell thee all my whole device
       When I am in my coach, which stays for us
       At the park gate; and therefore haste away,
       For we must measure twenty miles to-day.   *Exeunt.*

59. us!] us? *Q*, *F*.   63. accoutered] *Q*, *F*; accoutred *Q3*.   71. died:] *Q2*; dyed. *Q*, *F*.   75. I have] *Q*, *F*; I've *Pope*.   79. Fie!] Fie, *Q*, *F*.   80. near] *F3*; nere *Q*, *F*.   interpreter!] interpreter: *Q*, *F*.   81. my] *Q2*, *F*; my my *Q*.

60. *habit*] dress.
61. *accomplished*] equipped; cf. *H 5,* IV. Prol. 12.
67–8. *turn . . . stride*] i.e., "my stride then will be two of my present steps" (Pooler).
69. *quaint*] ingenious.
72. *I . . . withal*] I could not help it (cf. *O.E.D.*, Do, vb., 54).
77. *Jacks*] fellows; used contemptuously e.g., *Ado*, v. i. 91 and *R 3*, I. iii. 53.
78. *turn to men*] Cf. I. iii. 76.

[SCENE V.—*Belmont*.]

Enter [LAUNCELOT *the*] *clown and* JESSICA.

Laun. Yes truly, for look you, the sins of the father are to
  be laid upon the children, therefore (I promise you),
  I fear you,—I was always plain with you, and so now
  I speak my agitation of the matter: therefore be o'
  good cheer, for truly I think you are damn'd,—there   5
  is but one hope in it that can do you any good, and
  that is but a kind of bastard hope neither.

Jes. And what hope is that I pray thee?

Laun. Marry, you may partly hope that your father got
  you not, that you are not the Jew's daughter.   10

Jes. That were a kind of bastard hope indeed,—so the
  sins of my mother should be visited upon me.

Laun. Truly then I fear you are damn'd both by father
  and mother: thus when I shun Scylla (your father),
  I fall into Charybdis (your mother); well, you are   15
  gone both ways.

Jes. I shall be sav'd by my husband,—he hath made me
  a Christian!

Scene v

Scene v] *Capell; om. Q, F;* Scene vi *Pope.   Belmont*] *om. Q, F; The same.
A Garden Capell.*   Launcelot *the*] *om. Q, F;* Launcelot *Rowe.*   1, etc. *Laun.*]
Rowe; Clowne. Q, F.   4. o'] *Capell; a Q; of F.*   9. Marry,] Marry *Q, F.*
13. damn'd] *Q;* damned *F.*   14-15. I . . . I] *Q, F;* you . . . you *Rowe.*
18. Christian!] Christian? *Q.*

III. v.] The authenticity of this scene
has been doubted (cf. *N.C.S.*) but, as
the annotations show, it contains
Shakespearian phrases and ideas; it
also marks the passage of time, and
contains eloquent praise of Portia
which is in keeping with the ideas of
the play.

1-2. *sins . . . children*] according to
Mosaic Law.

3. *fear you*] i.e., for you (cf. Abbott,
¶200).

4. *agitation*] probably a blunder for
cogitation (so Eccles).

5. *damn'd*] Touchstone jests with
Corin to the same effect (*AYL.*, III. ii.
36-40).

7. *neither*] used to emphasize the
asseveration (cf. *O.E.D.*, 3a, and b).

14-15. *Scylla . . . Charybdis*] Scylla
was a nymph whom Amphitrite
transformed into a monster; she then
preyed on mariners who attempted to
pass between her cave and the whirl-
pool of *Charybdis* in the Straits of
Messina. Cf. Homer, *Od.*, xii. 235 ff.;
the proverbial use probably derives
from Philippe Gualtier's *Alexandreis*, v.
301: "Incidis in Scyllam, cupiens
vitare Charybdim" (so Malone). It is
found in Erasmus, *Adagia*, and many
Elizabethan writers (cf. Tilley, S169).

17. *I . . . husband*] Cf. *1 Corinthians*,
vii. 14.

Laun. Truly the more to blame he, we were Christians
    enow before, e'en as many as could well live one by   20
    another: this making of Christians will raise the price
    of hogs,—if we grow all to be pork-eaters, we shall
    not shortly have a rasher on the coals for money.

Enter LORENZO.

Jes. I'll tell my husband (Launcelot) what you say,—
    here he comes!   25

Lor. I shall grow jealous of you shortly Launcelot, if you
    thus get my wife into corners!

Jes. Nay, you need not fear us Lorenzo, Launcelot and I
    are out,—he tells me flatly there's no mercy for me in
    heaven, because I am a Jew's daughter: and he says   30
    you are no good member of the commonwealth, for
    in converting Jews to Christians, you raise the price
    of pork.

Lor. I shall answer that better to the commonwealth than
    you can the getting up of the negro's belly: the Moor   35
    is with child by you Launcelot!

Laun. It is much that the Moor should be more than

20. e'en] *Q2, F;* in *Q.*   23. S.D.] *as Q, F; after l.* 25 *Dyce.*   25. comes!]
come? *Q;* comes. *Q2, F.*   27. corners!] corners? *Q, F.*   29. there's] *Q;*
there is *F.*   36. Launcelot!] Launcelet? *Q, F.*

20. *enow*] a variant form of enough.
    e'en] A similar misprint is found in
Troil., I. iii. 355 (Folio text) and, perhaps, in *Err.,* II. ii. 103. Q2 *Ham.,* I. i.
108 has "enso" for "*e'en so*".

20–1. *one by another*] together (*by =*
beside); Pooler compared Marston,
Malcontent (1604), IV. iv: "do not
turne player, theres more of them than
can well live one by another already."
Perhaps there is a quibble on *by =* by
means of, upon.

23. *rasher*] i.e., of bacon, which was
often broiled before a fire. It seems to
have been a poor man's diet; cf. R.
Wilson, *Pedlar's Prophecy* (1595), B4:
". . . our cheare is but small, / But yet
he shall be sure of bacon and a peece of
sowse."

27. *corners*] secret or remote places;
cf. Peele, *Arraignement of Paris* (1584),
I. ii. 74: "kisse in corners"; and *Arden
of Feversham* (1592), M.S.R., l. 514:
"Yet doth he keepe in euery corner
trulles."

29. *are out*] have quarrelled; cf.
Cæs., I. i. 17–18 (so Pooler).

34. *answer . . . commonwealth*] It was
one's duty to beget children who would
be profitable to the commonwealth;
this is made a matter for jest in *LLL.,*
IV. i. 41 and IV. ii. 79.

35–6. *negro's . . . Launcelot*] This passage has not been explained; it might
be an outcrop of a lost source, or a
topical allusion. Perhaps it was introduced simply for the sake of the elaborate pun on Moor/more.

reason: but if she be less than an honest woman, she
is indeed more than I took her for.

Lor. How every fool can play upon the word! I think the   40
best grace of wit will shortly turn into silence, and
discourse grow commendable in none only but par-
rots: go in sirrah, bid them prepare for dinner!

Laun. That is done sir, they have all stomachs!

Lor. Goodly Lord, what a wit-snapper are you! then bid   45
them prepare dinner!

Laun. That is done too sir, only "cover" is the word.

Lor. Will you cover then sir?

Laun. Not so sir neither, I know my duty.

Lor. Yet more quarrelling with occasion! wilt thou show   50
the whole wealth of thy wit in an instant? I pray thee
understand a plain man in his plain meaning: go to
thy fellows, bid them cover the table, serve in the
meat, and we will come in to dinner.

Laun. For the table sir, it shall be serv'd in,—for the meat   55
sir, it shall be cover'd,—for your coming in to dinner
sir, why let it be as humours and conceits shall
govern.   *Exit.*

Lor. O dear discretion, how his words are suited!
The fool hath planted in his memory   60
An army of good words, and I do know

40. the word] *Q, F;* a word *Hanmer.*   word!] word, *Q, F.*   43. dinner!]
dinner? *Q, F.*   44. stomachs!] stomacks? *Q, F.*   45. Lord,] *F;* Lord *Q.*
you!] you, *Q, F.*   then] *Q2, F;* than *Q.*   46. dinner!] dinner? *Q.*   48.
then] *F4;* than *Q, F.*   50. occasion!] occasion, *Q, F.*   51. instant?] *Q2;*
instant; *Q, F.*   56. cover'd] *Q;* couered *Q2, F.*   58. S.D.] *Exit Clowne Q, F.*
59. suited!] suted, *Q, F.*

38. *reason*] what is reasonable; cf.
Ado, v. iv. 74 (so Onions).

44. *stomachs*] appetites; cf. *Ado,* i. iii.
16.

47. *cover*] lay the cloth; at l. 49,
Launcelot puns upon *cover* = cover the
head (cf. ii. ix. 44, and note).

50. *quarrelling with occasion*] i.e.,
"disputing at every opportunity"
(Pooler; cf. *Tw.N.,* i. v. 95), or, being
at odds with the matter in question (so
Schmidt).

55. *table*] This time Launcelot

means fare, supply of food (cf. *O.E.D.,*
6c), so *serve in* is appropriate.

56. *cover'd*] i.e., it will be served in a
covered dish.

57. *humours and conceits*] inclinations
and personal opinions.

59. *dear discretion*] Pooler thought
this was an apostrophe, but Onions
that *dear* was ironical, = precious (cf.
Ado, i. i. 130). *discretion* = discrimina-
tion.

suited] made suitable, adapted to the
matter in hand (cf. *O.E.D.,* 10b).

A many fools that stand in better place,
Garnish'd like him, that for a tricksy word
Defy the matter: how cheer'st thou Jessica?
And now (good sweet) say thy opinion,   65
How dost thou like the Lord Bassanio's wife?

Jes. Past all expressing,—it is very meet
The Lord Bassanio live an upright life
For having such a blessing in his lady,
He finds the joys of heaven here on earth,   70
And if on earth he do not merit it,
In reason he should never come to heaven!
Why, if two gods should play some heavenly match,
And on the wager lay two earthly women,
And Portia one, there must be something else   75
Pawn'd with the other, for the poor rude world
Hath not her fellow.

Lor.   Even such a husband
Hast thou of me, as she is for a wife.

---

64. Jessica?] *Q2; Iessica, Q, F.*   71. merit it,] *Pope;* meane it, it *Q, F;*
meane it, then *Q2;* meane it, *Q3.*   72. In] *Q, Q2-3, Pope;* Is *F.*   heauen!]
heauen? *Q, F.*   75. one,] one: *Q, F.*   78. for a] *F;* for *Q.*

62. *A many*] i.e., many (cf. Abbott, ¶87).

stand . . . place] have a better position, or employment (cf. *Gent.*, I. ii. 45); Touchstone alludes to his "place" at court (*AYL.*, II. iv. 18) so the word would be appropriate for a professional fool (cf. II. ii. 148, note).

63. *Garnish'd*] "furnished with a supply of words" (Verity) or, clothed (cf. II. vi. 45, and note) since Launcelot may now be dressed as a "fool" (cf. II. ii. 148, note).

tricksy] artful, capricious.

64. *Defy the matter*] disdain to make sense; in discussions of style, *matter* was often opposed to "words" or manner (e.g., *1 H 4*, II. iv. 479 and *Rom.*, II. vi. 30). For *Defy*, cf. *1 H 4*, I. iii. 228. It is not clear whether Launcelot is supposed to be superior to other fools on this account.

how . . . thou] what cheer.

71-2. *merit . . .*] F and Q2 tried to correct Q, but the line still remained unsatisfactory. Pope's reading makes good sense, and is palaeographically simple, "merryt" being taken for "mean yt" (so *N.C.S.*). The sense is that heaven is (1) a reward for an upright life, and (2) a compensation for an unhappy one; Bassanio cannot claim the compensation, so he must earn the reward (so Pooler). Cf. the parable of Dives and Lazarus; Pooler compared North, "Pelopidas", *Plutarch's Lives* (1579), Temple edn., iii. 252, where at the height of success, Diagoras is told "die presently, else thou shalt never come to heaven."

Hilda Hulme would retain "mean" = "avoid extremes"; she compared the *O.E.D.* quotation for the adj. of *c.* 1540: "If he coulde not lyue chast . . . he shoulde tak a wif and lyue a meane lyf" (cf. *Neophil.*, xli (1957), 50).

76. *Pawn'd*] staked.

Jes. Nay, but ask my opinion too of that.
Lor. I will anon,—first let us go to dinner.   80
Jes. Nay, let me praise you while I have a stomach.
Lor. No pray thee, let it serve for table-talk,
          Then howsome'er thou speak'st, 'mong other things
          I shall digest it.
Jes.   Well, I'll set you forth.   [*Exeunt.*]

79. that.] *Q2;* that? *Q , F.*   80. dinner.] *Q2;* dinner? *Q, F.*   81. stomach.]
Q2; stomack? *Q, F.*   83. howsome'er] how so mere *Q;* howsoere *Q2;* how
som ere *F.*   speak'st,] speakst *Q, F.*   things] things, *Q, F.*   84. it.] *Q2;*
it? *Q, F.*   S.D.] *F; Exit Q.*

81. *stomach*] a quibble; (1) appetite (as l. 44 above), (2) inclination (cf. *Shr.,* I. i. 38).

83. *howsome'er*] in whatever manner, a "parallel formation" to howsoever (*O.E.D.*); it recurs *Ham.,* I. v. 84 (Q2) and *All's W.,* I. iii. 57.

Q's "mere" suggests a pun on adv. mere; cf. *All's W.,* III. v. 58 and R. Wilson, *Pedlar's Prophecy* (1595), A2ᵛ: "lewdnesse shall be exiled, / And

other things spoken of very merely." Mere = pure, unmixed; it was often used of wine, meaning unmixed with water, and so this pun would be apt to Lorenzo's conclusion, *'mong other things ... digest it.*

84. *set you forth*] extol, praise greatly (cf. *Lucr.,* 32; so Onions). The phrase also refers to "the setting forth, or preparing, a table for a feast" (Clarendon).

[ACT IV]

[SCENE I.—*Venice. A Court of Justice.*]

Enter the DUKE, *the Magnificoes,* ANTONIO, BASSANIO,
and GRATIANO[, SALERIO *and others*].

Duke. What, is Antonio here?
Ant. Ready, so please your grace!
Duke. I am sorry for thee,—thou art come to answer
    A stony adversary, an inhuman wretch,
    Uncapable of pity, void, and empty   5
    From any dram of mercy.
Ant.   I have heard
    Your grace hath ta'en great pains to qualify
    His rigorous course; but since he stands obdurate,
    And that no lawful means can carry me
    Out of his envy's reach, I do oppose   10
    My patience to his fury, and am arm'd
    To suffer with a quietness of spirit,
    The very tyranny and rage of his.
Duke. Go one and call the Jew into the court.

ACT IV

Scene 1

Act IV] *om. Q;* Actus Quartus *F.*   Scene I] *Rowe; om. Q, F.*   Venice . . .
Justice] *Capell; om. Q, F; Venice Rowe; the Senate-house in Venice Theobald.*
Salerio *and others*] *Cambridge; om. Q, F; at the Bar Theobald;* Salerino, Solanio,
and others Capell; and others Var. '73; Salarino, Salanio, *and others Malone;* Solanio,
officers, clerks, attendants, and a concourse of people N.C.S.   2. grace!] grace? *Q, F.*
3. I am] *Q, F;* I'm *Pope.*   5. void,] *Q, F;* voide *Q2.*

Entry] The constitution of this court
bears little relation to historical fact;
the Doge had not presided over a
Court of Justice since the 14th century
and magnificoes did not act as judges
(so Elze, *Shakespeare Jahrbuch,* xiv
(1879), 178).

2. *Ready*] "used in replying to a call
or summons = here!" (Onions, who
compared *MND.,* I. ii. 20).

7. *qualify*] moderate.

10. *envy's*] malice's; cf. *R 3,* IV. i. 100.

13. *tyranny*] violence; cf. *All's W.,*
I. i. 58.

Sal. He is ready at the door,—he comes my lord.   15

Enter SHYLOCK.

Duke. Make room, and let him stand before our face.
    Shylock the world thinks, and I think so too,
    That thou but leadest this fashion of thy malice
    To the last hour of act, and then 'tis thought
    Thou'lt show thy mercy and remorse more strange   20
    Than is thy strange apparent cruelty;
    And where thou now exacts the penalty,
    Which is a pound of this poor merchant's flesh,
    Thou wilt not only loose the forfeiture,
    But touch'd with human gentleness and love,   25
    Forgive a moiety of the principal,
    Glancing an eye of pity on his losses
    That have of late so huddled on his back,
    Enow to press a royal merchant down,
    And pluck commiseration of his state   30
    From brassy bosoms and rough hearts of flint,
    From stubborn Turks, and Tartars never train'd
    To offices of tender courtesy:
    We all expect a gentle answer Jew!
Shy. I have possess'd your grace of what I purpose,   35

15. *Sal.*] *Q2, F; Salerio. Q.*   He is] *Q, F;* He's *Pope.*   17. too,] *Q2;* to *Q, F.*
18. leadest] *Q, F;* lead'st *Rowe.*   20. strange] strange, *Q, F.*   21. strange
apparent] *as Q, F;* hyphened *Walker conj., Dyce (ii).*   22. exacts] *Q;* exact'st *F.*
24. loose] *Q, F;* lose *F4.*   25. love,] *Q2;* loue: *Q, F.*   29. down,] *Q2;*
downe; *Q, F.*   30. his state] *Q2,F;* this states *Q.*   31. flint] *Q2;* flints *Q, F.*
34. Jew!] Iewe? *Q, F.*   35. *Shy.*] *Rowe; Iewe. Q, F.*

20. *remorse*] pity, compassion.
21. *apparent*] seeming (so Johnson), but the usual sense was manifest, conspicuous (cf. *R 2,* IV. i. 124).
22. *where*] whereas (cf. Abbott, ¶134).
exacts] 2nd person sing., as often in verbs ending with *-t* (cf. Abbott, ¶340).
24. *loose*] release; but "lose" may be meant, for the two verbs were not clearly distinguished in spelling (there is a similar ambiguity in *LLL.,* IV. iii. 73). For "lose" = forget, cf. *H 8,* II. i. 57.

26. *moiety*] portion (not necessarily a half); Pooler compared *Ham.,* I. i. 90.
30. *his state*] Q is easily explained as a misreading; for "this" / "his" errors, cf. *Ham.,* (Q2) IV. v. 89 and v. ii. 148.
31. *brassy*] Cf. "brass impregnable" (*R 2,* III. ii. 168).
flint] Final -*s* is very liable to error; for singular cf. *Tw.N.,* I. v. 305 and *Per.,* IV. iv. 43 (in rhyme).
33. *offices*] duties (L. *officium*).
34. *gentle*] Cf. II. iv. 34, and note.
35. *possess'd*] informed.

And by our holy Sabbath have I sworn
To have the due and forfeit of my bond,—
If you deny it, let the danger light
Upon your charter and your city's freedom!
You'll ask me why I rather choose to have   40
A weight of carrion flesh, than to receive
Three thousand ducats: I'll not answer that!
But say it is my humour,—is it answer'd?
What if my house be troubled with a rat,
And I be pleas'd to give ten thousand ducats   45
To have it ban'd? what, are you answer'd yet?
Some men there are love not a gaping pig!
Some that are mad if they behold a cat!
And others when the bagpipe sings i'th'nose,
Cannot contain their urine—for affection   50

36. Sabbath] *Q2, F;* Sabaoth *Q.*   39. freedom!] freedome? *Q.*   42. that!]
that? *Q.*   43. answer'd] *Q;* answered *Q2, F.*   47. pig!] pigge? *Q.*
48. cat!] Cat? *Q.*   50. urine—] vrine *Q, F;* urine, *Johnson;* urine; *Thirlby
conj., Capell;* urine. *Var '73, Var. '78.*   affection] affection. *Q, F;* affection,
Thirlby conj., Capell; affection; *Johnson;* affections, *Var. '78.*

36. *Sabbath*] Commonly confused
with "Sabaoth" (= armies, hosts);
the metre seems to require two syllables only.

38. *danger*] harm, damage (so
Onions); cf. *Cæs.*, II. i. 17.

39. *your . . . freedom*] This would be
applicable to an English town rather
than the sovereign state of Venice. Cf.
Introduction, p. xvi.

43. *humour*] whim, caprice (cf. III. v.
57). "Shylock refuses to give a direct
answer; 'but suppose,' he says, 'it is just
my humour—wouldn't that serve for
an answer?'" (*N.C.S.*). Johnson noted
that the answer is given gratuitously
"to aggravate the pain" of his adver-
saries.

D. H. Bishop (*S.A.B.*, xxiii (1948),
174–80) argued for the primary sense
of *humour* "derived directly from the
mediæval conception of the four phy-
siological humours . . . [and] indicating a fixation in character." He considered it synonymous with *affection*
(l. 50). Perhaps Shylock is intention-
ally ambiguous in his use of the word.

47. *gaping pig*] Malone compared
Nashe, *Pierce Penniless* (1592), *Wks*,
i. 188: "Some will take on like a mad
man, if they see a pigge come to the
table" and Fletcher, *Elder Brother*
(1637), II. ii: "they stand gaping like a
roasted pig."

49. *bagpipe*] Cf. *Everyman in his
Humour* (1616), IV. ii. 19–22: ". . . can
he not hold his water, at reading of a
ballad? / —O, no: a rime to him, is
worse then cheese, or a bag-pipe."

50–1. *affection . . . sways*] This seems
the simplest way of giving satisfactory
sense.

Warburton interpreted "Masters of
passion" as musicians, and Grant
White as such "agencies" as those he
had just mentioned, but all attempts at
keeping Q's punctuation obscure the
distinction between *affection* and *passion*
(cf. III. i. 54, and note) and make
difficulties over *it* of l. 52 which would
presumably refer to "Masters".

Professor Wilson finally preferred
"Mistress" on the grounds that "Mistress" and "Masters" would both be

(Master of passion) sways it to the mood
Of what it likes or loathes,—now for your answer:
As there is no firm reason to be rend'red
Why he cannot abide a gaping pig,
Why he a harmless necessary cat,   55
Why he a woollen bagpipe, but of force
Must yield to such inevitable shame,
As to offend himself being offended:
So can I give no reason, nor I will not,
More than a lodg'd hate, and a certain loathing   60
I bear Antonio, that I follow thus
A losing suit against him!—are you answered?
Bass. This is no answer thou unfeeling man,
    To excuse the current of thy cruelty.
Shy. I am not bound to please thee with my answers!   65
Bass. Do all men kill the things they do not love?
Shy. Hates any man the thing he would not kill?
Bass. Every offence is not a hate at first!
Shy. What! wouldst thou have a serpent sting thee twice?
Ant. I pray you think you question with the Jew,—   70
    You may as well go stand upon the beach
    And bid the main flood bate his usual height,

---

51. Master of] *Thirlby conj., Johnson;* Maisters of *Q, F, Var. '73, Var. '78;* Masterless *Rowe;* Mistress of *Thirlby conj., Capell, Keightley.* sways] *Q, F;* sway *Warburton.* it] *Q, F;* us *Hanmer.* 52. it] *Q, F;* she *Keightley.* 54. pig,] pigge? *Q, F.* 55. cat,] Cat? *Q, F.* 56. woollen] *Q, F;* swoln *Hawkins conj. (quoted Johnson);* swollen *Var. '93;* wawling *Capell conj.;* bollen *Dyce.* bagpipe,] bagpipe: *Q, F.* 58. offend himself] *Q, F;* offend, himself *Q2;* offend himself, *F4.* 62. him!] him? *Q, F.* 64. To] *Q, F;* T' *Pope.* cruelty.] *Q2, F;* cruelty? *Q.* 65, 67, 69. *Shy.*] *Q2; Iewe. Q, F.* 65. answers!] answers? *Q;* answere. *Q2, F.* 66. things] *Q, F;* thing *F2.* 68. first!] first? *Q.* 69. What!] What *Q, F.* 70. the] *Q, F;* a *F3.*

---

contracted as "Mrs" (*N.C.S.*, 2nd edn., 1953).

55. *harmless . . . cat*] Cf. *All's W.*, IV. iii. 267, and *Tarleton's Jests* (1638), Sh. Soc., ed., p. 38: "How Tarleton could not abide a cat" (so Pooler). Devils were thought to "possess" cats (cf., for example, Harsnet, *Declaration* (1603), E1v), hence, perhaps, the distinguishing epithets *harmless, necessary*.

56. *woollen*] Emendation is un-

necessary, for the "bags" are quite commonly wrapped in baize or flannel (so *N.C.S.*).

60. *lodg'd*] "deep-seated" (Pooler). *certain*] determined, fixed; cf. "certainly" *1 H 6*, v. i. 37.

62. *losing suit*] If his case is upheld, Shylock will lose three thousand ducats, receiving only a "weight of carrion flesh."

70. *question*] dispute.
72. *main flood*] high tide.

You may as well use question with the wolf,
Why he hath made the ewe bleak for the lamb:
You may as well forbid the mountain pines   75
To wag their high tops, and to make no noise
When they are fretten with the gusts of heaven:
You may as well do any thing most hard
As seek to soften that—than which what's harder?—
His Jewish heart! Therefore (I do beseech you)   80
Make no moe offers, use no farther means,
But with all brief and plain conveniency
Let me have judgment, and the Jew his will!
Bass. For thy three thousand ducats here is six!
Shy. If every ducat in six thousand ducats   85
Were in six parts, and every part a ducat,
I would not draw them, I would have my bond!
Duke. How shalt thou hope for mercy rend'ring none?
Shy. What judgment shall I dread doing no wrong?
You have among you many a purchas'd slave,   90
Which (like your asses, and your dogs and mules)
You use in abject and in slavish parts,
Because you bought them,—shall I say to you,
Let them be free, marry them to your heirs?
Why sweat they under burthens? let their beds   95
Be made as soft as yours, and let their palates
Be season'd with such viands? you will answer

---

73. You may as] *Q (correct), Q2; om Q (incorrect);* Or euen as *F.*   wolf,] *Q (incorrect), Q2, F;* Woolfe *Q (correct).*   74. Why . . . made] *Q (correct), Q2; om. Q (incorrect), F.*   bleak] bleake *Q;* bleate *F.*   75. mountain] *F;* mountaine of *Q.*   77. fretten] *Q;* fretted *F.*   79. what's] *Q;* what *F.*   harder?] *F;* harder: *Q.*   80. heart!] hart? *Q.*   81. moe] *Q;* more *F.*   83. will!] will? *Q.*   84. six!] sixe? *Q.*   85, 89. *Shy.*] *Rowe; Iewe. Q, F.*   87. bond!] bond? *Q, F.*   95. burthens?] *F;* burthens, *Q.*   97. viands?] viands, *Q.*

74. *bleak*] Craig (quoted Pooler) compared Somerset dialect blake = to bleat. Q's "bleake" might, however, be a misprint for "bleate"; cf. J. D. Wilson, *The Manuscript of Shakespeare's Hamlet* (1934), I. 111 which cites "kyth" for "tythe" in Q2, *Ham.* and other *k/t* confusions.

76. *no*] Either "bid" is implied from *forbid* of the previous line (for similar ellipses, cf. Abbott, ¶382)

or this is a double negative.

77. *fretten*] an archaic form of fretted (cf. Abbott, ¶344).

81. *moe*] more (in number).

82. *conveniency*] convenience, propriety.

87. *draw*] take, receive; cf. *Lr.*, I. i. 87.

92. *parts*] duties.

95. *burthens*] a common form of burdens.

"The slaves are ours,"—so do I answer you:
The pound of flesh which I demand of him
Is dearly bought, 'tis mine and I will have it: 100
If you deny me, fie upon your law!
There is no force in the decrees of Venice:
I stand for judgment,—answer, shall I have it?
Duke. Upon my power I may dismiss this court,
Unless Bellario (a learned doctor,   105
Whom I have sent for to determine this)
Come here to-day.
Sal.   My lord, here stays without
A messenger with letters from the doctor,
New come from Padua.
Duke. Bring us the letters! call the messenger!   110
Bass. Good cheer Antonio! what man, courage yet!
The Jew shall have my flesh, blood, bones and all,
Ere thou shalt lose for me one drop of blood.
Ant. I am a tainted wether of the flock,
Meetest for death,—the weakest kind of fruit   115
Drops earliest to the ground, and so let me;
You cannot better be employ'd Bassanio,
Than to live still and write mine epitaph.

Enter NERISSA[, *dressed like a lawyer's clerk*].

Duke. Came you from Padua from Bellario?
Ner. From both, my lord. Bellario greets your grace.   120
[*She presents a letter.*]

100. 'tis] *Q2, F;* as *Q; is Capell.*   101. law!] Law, *Q, F.*   107. to-day.] *Q2,
F;* to day? *Q.*   *Sal.*] *F; Salerio. Q.*   109. Padua.] *Q2, F;* Padua? *Q.*
110. letters!] letters? *Q.*   messenger!] Messenger? *Q;* Messengers. *F.*
111. Antonio!] Anthonio? *Q.*   yet!] yet: *Q, F.*   113. blood.] *Q2, F;*
blood? *Q.*   116. and] *Q, F; om. F2.*   118. epitaph.] *Q2, F;* Epitaph? *Q.*
118.] S.D., Scene II *Pope.* |*dressed . . . clerk*] *Rowe subs.; om. Q, F.*   120. From
. . . grace] *as Q; . . .* both. / My . . . *F.*   both,] *Q2;* both? *Q;* both. F.
lord.] *Blair;* L. *Q;* Lord *F;* lord: *Pope (ii).*   grace.] *Q2, F;* grace? *Q.*   S.D.]
Capell subs.; om. Q, F.

100. *'tis*] "The letters *ti* might con-
ceivably be misread as an open *a* with
an initial overhead stroke" (*N.C.S.*).
104. *Upon*] in accordance with.
112-13. *The . . . blood*] "A manifest
lie, for were it true, he had only there

and then to run a rapier through Shylock and save his friend at the cost of
being hanged for murder" (Nevill
Coghill, *Shakespeare Quarterly,* i (1948),
15). But, in performance, Bassanio's
asseveration can be accepted as whole-

Bass. Why dost thou whet thy knife so earnestly?

Shy. To cut the forfeiture from that bankrupt there!

Gra. Not on thy sole: but on thy soul (harsh Jew)
Thou mak'st thy knife keen: but no metal can,—
No, not the hangman's axe—bear half the keenness   125
Of thy sharp envy: can no prayers pierce thee?

Shy. No, none that thou hast wit enough to make.

Gra. O be thou damn'd, inexecrable dog!
And for thy life let justice be accus'd;
Thou almost mak'st me waver in my faith,   130
To hold opinion with Pythagoras,
That souls of animals infuse themselves
Into the trunks of men: thy currish spirit
Govern'd a wolf, who hang'd for human slaughter—
Even from the gallows did his fell soul fleet,   135
And whilst thou layest in thy unhallowed dam,
Infus'd itself in thee: for thy desires
Are wolvish, bloody, starv'd, and ravenous.

Shy. Till thou canst rail the seal from off my bond,
Thou but offend'st thy lungs to speak so loud: 140
Repair thy wit good youth, or it will fall
To cureless ruin. I stand here for law.

Duke. This letter from Bellario doth commend

122, 127, 139. *Shy.*] *Rowe; Iewe. Q, F.*   122. forfeiture] *Q, F; Forfeit Rowe.*
there!] there? *Q.*   123. sole . . . soul] *Hanmer;* soule . . . soule *Q;* soale . . .
soule *F.*   128. inexecrable] *Q, F;* inexorable *F3.*   dog!] dogge, *Q, F.*
134. who] *Q, F;* who, *Theobald.*   135. fleet,] *Q;* fleete; *F.*   136. layest]
Q, F; lay'st *Pope.*   dam,] *Q2, F;* dam; *Q.*   142. cureless] *Q;* endlesse
F.

heartedly sincere; Shakespeare is
taking dramatic risks in order to
accentuate the play's friendship theme.

123. *sole . . . soul*] Cf. *Rom.,* I. iv. 15
(so Theobald) and *2 H 4,* IV. v. 108 (so
Steevens).

125. *hangman's*] executioner's;
Pooler compared *Meas.,* IV. ii. 53–6.

128. *inexecrable*] i.e., that cannot be
execrated enough (so Clarendon), but
O.E.D. recorded only one other instance, as a misprint for "inexorable"
in Constable, *Diana* (1594), VIII.i.

129. *for . . . accus'd*] i.e., let executive
justice, by an injustice, take away your

life (so Capell), or, justice itself merits
accusation for permitting you to live
(so Eccles).

131. *Pythagoras*] Cf. *Tw.N.,* IV. ii.
54–7.

133–4. *thy . . . wolf*] Cf. Introduction, pp. xxiii–xxiv.

134. *who . . . slaughter*] Probably a
nominative absolute construction (cf.
Abbott, ¶376, who compared *H 8,* II. i.
42 and IV. i. 90).

140. *offend'st*] injurest; Pooler compared *All's W.,* V. iii. 55.

142. *cureless*] The word also occurs
3 H 6, II. vi. 23 and *Lucr.,* 772.

A young and learned doctor to our court:
Where is he?

Ner.   He attendeth here hard by   145
To know your answer—whether you'll admit him.

Duke. With all my heart: some three or four of you
Go give him courteous conduct to this place,
Meantime the court shall hear Bellario's letter.
[*Reads.*] *Your grace shall understand, that at the receipt of* 150
your letter I am very sick, but in the instant that your mes-
senger came, in loving visitation was with me a young doctor
of Rome, his name is Balthazar: I acquainted him with the
cause in controversy between the Jew and Antonio the mer-
chant, we turn'd o'er many books together, he is furnished 155
with my opinion, which (bettered with his own learning, the
greatness whereof I cannot enough commend), comes with
him at my importunity, to fill up your grace's request in my
stead. I beseech you let his lack of years be no impediment to
let him lack a reverend estimation, for I never knew so young 160
a body with so old a head: I leave him to your gracious accep-
tance, whose trial shall better publish his commendation.

Enter PORTIA[*, dressed like a doctor of laws*].

You hear the learn'd Bellario what he writes,
And here (I take it) is the doctor come.
Give me your hand,—come you from old Bellario?   165

Por. I did my lord.

Duke.   You are welcome, take your place:
Are you acquainted with the difference

144. to] *Q*; in *F*.   150. S.D.] *Capell*; om. *Q, F*.   *Your*] *Q, F*; Cle[rk]. *Your*
Capell; Nerissa. *Your/Sisson*.   151. in] *Q, F*; at *Rowe*.   154. cause] *Q, F*; Case
F3.   156. bettered] *Q*; bettred *Q2, F*.   162. S.D.] as *Q, F*; after l. 164 Capell;
after l. 163 N.C.S.   dressed . . . laws] Rowe subs.; for Balthazer *Q, F*.   163.
You] *N.C.S.; Duke.* You *Q, F*.   165. come] *Q*; Came *F*.   166. You are]
Q, F; Y'are *Pope*.

150–62. *Your . . . commendation*] There
is no indication that a clerk reads the
letter, for the repeated speech prefix
at l. 163 appears to be normal in this
text; cf. Introduction, pp. xvi–xvii.
For "Balthazar", cf. l. 219, note, below.
    162. S.D.] Most editors delay this

entry, but Portia's impersonation may
appear more precarious and courageous to the audience if she is not
accepted at once.
    165. *come*] Portia's *I did* suggests that
F's "Came" may be right (see also
I. ii. 57, note).

That holds this present question in the court?
Por. I am informed throughly of the cause,—
      Which is the merchant here? and which the Jew?   170
Duke. Antonio and old Shylock, both stand forth.
Por. Is your name Shylock?
Shy.   Shylock is my name.
Por. Of a strange nature is the suit you follow,
      Yet in such rule, that the Venetian law
      Cannot impugn you as you do proceed.   175
      You stand within his danger, do you not?
Ant. Ay, so he says.
Por.   Do you confess the bond?
Ant. I do.
Por.   Then must the Jew be merciful.
Shy. On what compulsion must I? tell me that.
Por. The quality of mercy is not strain'd,   180
      It droppeth as the gentle rain from heaven
      Upon the place beneath: it is twice blest,
      It blesseth him that gives, and him that takes,
      'Tis mightiest in the mightiest, it becomes
      The throned monarch better than his crown.   185
      His sceptre shows the force of temporal power,
      The attribute to awe and majesty,
      Wherein doth sit the dread and fear of kings:
      But mercy is above this sceptred sway,
      It is enthroned in the hearts of kings,   190
      It is an attribute to God himself;
      And earthly power doth then show likest God's

---

168. court?] Court. *Q*, *F*.   169. cause] *Q*, *F*; Case *F3*.   172. *Shy.*] *Rowe;*
Iew. Q, F.   176. not?] *Q2, F;* not. *Q.*   179. *Shy.*] *Q; Iew. F.*   I?] *F;* I, *Q.*

174. *rule*] order.
176. *within his danger*] in his power
(cf. *Ven.*, 639) or, in his debt (cf.
O.E.D., 1).
178. *must . . . merciful*] Portia means
either "the Jew will of course be merciful" (*N.C.S.*; cf. Abbott, ¶314), or "it's
up to him to be merciful" (so J. C.
Maxwell, privately); but Shylock
takes *must* in a compulsive sense.
H. Sinsheimer (*Shylock* (1947), p. 129)
has outlined Rabbinical teaching

which enjoins mercy on all Jews.
180–98. *The quality . . . mercy*] The
contradictory claims of mercy and
justice were often debated; e.g., many
of the ideas in this speech are found in
Seneca, *De Clementia*, i. 19 (cf. *T.L.S.*
(16 Sept. 1904)). Cf. Intro., p. l.
181. *as . . . rain*] Douce compared
Ecclesiasticus, xxxv. 20.
182. *blest*] full of blessing; cf.
"guiled" (III.ii. 97).
192–3. *earthly . . . justice*] Cf. *Tit.*,

When mercy seasons justice: therefore Jew,
Though justice be thy plea, consider this,
That in the course of justice, none of us   195
Should see salvation: we do pray for mercy,
And that same prayer, doth teach us all to render
The deeds of mercy. I have spoke thus much
To mitigate the justice of thy plea,
Which if thou follow, this strict court of Venice   200
Must needs give sentence 'gainst the merchant
    there.

Shy. My deeds upon my head! I crave the law,
The penalty and forfeit of my bond.

Por. Is he not able to discharge the money?

Bass. Yes, here I tender it for him in the court,   205
Yea, twice the sum,—if that will not suffice,
I will be bound to pay it ten times o'er
On forfeit of my hands, my head, my heart,—
If this will not suffice, it must appear
That malice bears down truth. And I beseech you   210
Wrest once the law to your authority,—
To do a great right, do a little wrong,—
And curb this cruel devil of his will.

Por. It must not be, there is no power in Venice
Can alter a decree established: 215
'Twill be recorded for a precedent,

198. thus] *Q, F;* this *Var. '85.*   200. court] *Q;* course *F.*   202. head!] head,
Q, F.   206. twice] *Q, F;* thrice *Ritson conj., Dyce (ii).*

i. i. 117–18 and *Meas.,* II. ii. 59–63.
This was a commonplace; cf. Tilley,
M898.

195–6. *in . . . salvation*] Isabella uses
the same argument in more specifically Christian terms in *Meas.,* II. ii.
73–9.

196–8. *we . . . mercy*] A reference to
the Lord's prayer and, perhaps, to
Matthew, v. 7 and *Ecclesiasticus,* xxviii.
2: "Forgive thy neighbour the hurt
that he hath done unto thee, so shall
thy sins also be forgiven when thou
prayest." Shakespeare may have intended a specifically Christian argument in order to accentuate the

nature of Shylock's claim (cf. l. 202,
note, below, and Introduction, p.
li).

199. *mitigate*] i.e., temper it with
mercy (so Pooler).

202. *My . . . head*] Henley (Var. '78)
compared *Matthew,* xxvii. 25: "His
blood be on us, and our children."

210. *bears . . . truth*] "oppresses
honesty" (Johnson).

214–15. *no . . . established*] Venice
was famed for the "inexorable admin-
istration of justice" (Z. S. Fink, *Classical Republicans* (1945), p. 43); this is
alluded to in *Il Pecorone* (cf. Appendix
I, p. 149).

And many an error by the same example
Will rush into the state,—it cannot be.
Shy. A Daniel come to judgment: yea a Daniel!
O wise young judge how I do honour thee!   220
Por. I pray you let me look upon the bond.
Shy. Here 'tis most reverend doctor, here it is.
Por. Shylock there's thrice thy money off'red thee.
Shy. An oath, an oath, I have an oath in heaven,—
Shall I lay perjury upon my soul?   225
No not for Venice.
Por.   Why this bond is forfeit,
And lawfully by this the Jew may claim
A pound of flesh, to be by him cut off
Nearest the merchant's heart: be merciful,
Take thrice thy money, bid me tear the bond.   230
Shy. When it is paid, according to the tenour.
It doth appear you are a worthy judge,
You know the law, your exposition
Hath been most sound: I charge you by the law,
Whereof you are a well-deserving pillar,   235
Proceed to judgment: by my soul I swear,
There is no power in the tongue of man
To alter me,—I stay here on my bond.
Ant. Most heartily I do beseech the court
To give the judgment.
Por.   Why then thus it is,—   240
You must prepare your bosom for his knife.

219, 222, 231, 242. *Shy.*] *Q; Iew. F.*   219. Daniel!] Daniell. *Q, F.*   220. I
do] *Q;* do I *F.*   thee!] thee. *Q, F.*   223. off'red] *Q;* offered *F.*   226. No]
Q2, F; Not *Q.*   231. tenour] *Q2;* tenure *Q, F.*   235. well-deserving]
hyphened F.   238. bond.] *Q2, F;* Bond, *Q.*   240. then] *Q2, F;* than *Q.*

---

217. *error*] i.e., injustice, or miscar-
riage of justice.

219. *Daniel*] alluding to the story of
Susannah and the Elders in the *Apo-
crypha*; *Daniel* was a "young youth"
(v. 45) and so the comparison was apt.
When Gratiano uses it (l. 336, below)
it is still more apt, for Daniel convicted
the Elders "by their own mouth".
Daniel means "God is my judge".
"Balthazar", the name Portia assumes

in disguise (cf. l. 153, above), appears
in some Bibles for Belshazzar, the
Babylonian name given to Daniel (cf.
Dan., v. i.); this means "Oh, protect the
king" (cf. *N. & Q.*, ccii (1957), 334–5).

229. *Nearest . . . heart*] When the
bond was proposed, Shylock said it
was to be taken "In what part of your
body pleaseth me"; presumably he
made the further stipulation when the
bond was prepared.

Shy. O noble judge! O excellent young man!
Por. For the intent and purpose of the law
            Hath full relation to the penalty,
            Which here appeareth due upon the bond.   245
Shy. 'Tis very true: O wise and upright judge,
            How much more elder art thou than thy looks!
Por. Therefore lay bare your bosom.
Shy.   Ay, his breast,
            So says the bond, doth it not noble judge?
            "Nearest his heart," those are the very words.   250
Por. It is so,—are there balance here to weigh
            The flesh?
Shy.   I have them ready.
Por. Have by some surgeon Shylock on your charge,
            To stop his wounds, lest he do bleed to death.
Shy. Is it so nominated in the bond?   255
Por. It is not so express'd, but what of that?
            'Twere good you do so much for charity.
Shy. I cannot find it, 'tis not in the bond.
Por. You merchant, have you any thing to say?
Ant. But little; I am arm'd and well prepar'd,—   260
            Give me your hand Bassanio, fare you well,
            Grieve not that I am fall'n to this for you:
            For herein Fortune shows herself more kind
            Than is her custom: it is still her use
            To let the wretched man outlive his wealth,   265
            To view with hollow eye and wrinkled brow
            An age of poverty: from which ling'ring penance
            Of such misery doth she cut me off.
            Commend me to your honourable wife,
            Tell her the process of Antonio's end,   270
            Say how I lov'd you, speak me fair in death:

242. judge!] Iudge, *Q*, *F*.   man!] man. *Q*, *F*.   246, 248, 252, 255, 258.
Shy.] *Q2; Iew. Q*, *F*.   247. looks!] lookes. *Q*.   251-2. It . . . flesh] *as Capell;*
one line Q, *F*.   251. balance] *Q*, *F*; Ballances *Rowe*.   252. I] *Q*, *F*; Ay, *conj.*
254. wounds] *Q*, *F*; wound *Var. '85*.   do] *Q*; should *F*.   255. Is it so] *Q*; I'
is not *F*.   259. You] *Q*; Come *F*.   268. such] *Q*, *F*; such a *F2*.

244. *Hath . . . to*] fully allows and
enforces.

247. *more elder*] For the emphatic
double comparative see Abbott, ¶11.

251. *balance*] an occasional plural
form (cf. *O.E.D.*, 2b).

257. *charity*] Meanings ranged from
"Christian love" to "relief for poor".

And when the tale is told, bid her be judge
Whether Bassanio had not once a love:
Repent but you that you shall lose your friend
And he repents not that he pays your debt.   275
For if the Jew do cut but deep enough,
I'll pay it instantly with all my heart.

Bass. Antonio, I am married to a wife
Which is as dear to me as life itself,
But life itself, my wife, and all the world,   280
Are not with me esteem'd above thy life.
I would lose all, ay sacrifice them all
Here to this devil, to deliver you.

Por. Your wife would give you little thanks for that
If she were by to hear you make the offer.   285

Gra. I have a wife who I protest I love,—
I would she were in heaven, so she could
Entreat some power to change this currish Jew.

Ner. 'Tis well you offer it behind her back,
The wish would make else an unquiet house.   290

Shy. [*Aside.*] These be the Christian husbands! I have a
        daughter—
Would any of the stock of Barrabas
Had been her husband, rather than a Christian.
We trifle time, I pray thee pursue sentence.

Por. A pound of that same merchant's flesh is thine,   295
The court awards it, and the law doth give it.

Shy. Most rightful judge!

Por. And you must cut this flesh from off his breast,
The law allows it, and the court awards it.

Shy. Most learned judge! a sentence, come prepare.   300

274. but] *Q;* not *F.*   284–5.] *as aside Halliwell.*   286. who] *Q;* whom *F.*
289–90.] *as aside Halliwell.*   291, 297, 300, 314. *Shy.*] *Rowe; Iew. Q, F.*   291.
S.D.] *after l. 293 Rowe;* om. *Q, F.*   husbands!] husbands, *Q.*   I have] *Q, F;*
I've *Pope.*   297, 309. judge!] Iudge. *Q, F.*   300, 308. judge!] Iudge, *Q, F.*

273. *love*] i.e., friend, as in *Sonn.*,   278–83. *Antonio . . . you*] The amity
xiii. 1 (so Pooler); Furness compared   between Antonio and Bassanio is fully
the use of *lover* elsewhere in this play   revealed here; cf. Introduction, pp.
(III.iv. 7 and 17).   xlv–xlvi.
    277. *with . . . heart*] "A jest like this   286. *who*] used for whom; cf. I. ii.
enhances the pathos"; cf. the death   23, and note.
scene in *John*, v. vii, and *R 2*, II. i. 73–4   292. *Barrabas*] Marlowe's Jew also
(Clarendon).   requires an unstressed second syllable.

Por. Tarry a little, there is something else,—
    This bond doth give thee here no jot of blood,
    The words expressly are "a pound of flesh":
    Take then thy bond, take thou thy pound of
      flesh,
    But in the cutting it, if thou dost shed   305
    One drop of Christian blood, thy lands and goods
    Are (by the laws of Venice) confiscate
    Unto the state of Venice.
Gra.   O upright judge!—
    Mark Jew,—O learned judge!
Shy. Is that the law?
Por.   Thyself shalt see the act: 310
    For as thou urgest justice, be assur'd
    Thou shalt have justice more than thou desir'st.
Gra. O learned judge!—mark Jew, a learned judge.
Shy. I take this offer then,—pay the bond thrice
    And let the Christian go.
Bass.   Here is the money.   315

304. Take then] *Q;* Then take *F.*   308–9. O . . . judge] *as Q, F; one line Pope.*
312. desir'st] *Q;* desirest *Q2, F.*   313. judge!] iudge, *Q, F.*   314. this] *Q,*
F; his *Q3.*

305–6. *if . . . blood*] Some critics have seen Shylock as the victim of a verbal quibble: "The Judge who admitted Shylock's right to cut a pound of flesh . . ., by that very admission recognized Shylock's right to the blood inseparable from the flesh; and he who has a right to cut a pound, may, if he pleases, take less" (R. von Ihering, tr. and quoted Furness). Haynes (*Outline of Equity* (1858), pp. 19–20) held that since blood is necessarily spilt when flesh is cut, Portia's distinction was valid only if the contract had specifically stipulated that blood should not be spilt.

Furness quoted many opinions on the case, but more important, in the play, is the fact that Portia does restore equity and the Jew's murderous schemes are foiled; her means of doing so are justified dramatically. Cf. G. W. Keeton, *Shakespeare and his Legal Prob*

lems (1930), pp. 19–20 and Introduction, p. li.

307. *confiscate*] past participle (cf. Abbott, ¶342).

310. *Is . . . law*] Two arrangements are possible: (1) this speech could complete a decasyllable with l. 309, or (2) it could be taken with Portia's following line. The second seems preferable as it marks a pause while Shylock comprehends the sudden reversal.

311–12. *For . . . desir'st*] Cf. *James,* ii. 13: "he shall have judgement without mercy, that hath shewed no mercy," and *Luke,* vi. 36–8.

314. *this*] "this" and "his" are confused elsewhere (iv. i. 30) and Q3 may be right. Malone defended Q on the grounds that Shylock was accepting Portia's specific offer of *thrice* the loan (l. 223, above) rather than Bassanio's earlier mention of *twice* (l. 206). Pooler glossed, "this that I mention"

Por. Soft!

    The Jew shall have all justice,—soft no haste!
    He shall have nothing but the penalty.

Gra. O Jew! an upright judge, a learned judge!

Por. Therefore prepare thee to cut off the flesh,—   320
    Shed thou no blood, nor cut thou less nor more
    But just a pound of flesh: if thou tak'st more
    Or less than a just pound, be it but so much
    As makes it light or heavy in the substance,
    Or the division of the twentieth part   325
    Of one poor scruple, nay if the scale do turn
    But in the estimation of a hair,
    Thou diest, and all thy goods are confiscate.

Gra. A second Daniel, a Daniel, Jew!—
    Now infidel I have you on the hip.   330

Por. Why doth the Jew pause? take thy forfeiture.

Shy. Give me my principal, and let me go.

Bass. I have it ready for thee, here it is.

Por. He hath refus'd it in the open court,
    He shall have merely justice and his bond.   335

Gra. A Daniel still say I, a second Daniel!—
    I thank thee Jew for teaching me that word.

Shy. Shall I not have barely my principal?

Por. Thou shalt have nothing but the forfeiture
    To be so taken at thy peril Jew.   340

Shy. Why then the devil give him good of it:
    I'll stay no longer question.

Por.   Tarry Jew,

316–17. Soft . . . haste] *as Capell; one line Q, F.* 316. Soft!] Soft, Q, F; *om. Pope.* 317. haste!] hast, Q, F. 319. Jew!] Iew, Q, F. judge!] Iudge. Q, F. 323. be it but] Q; be it F; be't but *Pope.* 326. do] Q, F; *om. Pope.* 329. a Daniel,] a Daniell Q, F. Jew!] Iew, Q, F. 330. you] Q; thee F. 331. pause?] pause, Q, F. thy] Q, F; the *Pope.* 336. Daniel!] Daniell, Q, F. 340. so taken] Q; taken so F. 342. longer] Q, F; longer heere in Q2.

316. *Soft*] probably an extra-metrical interjection (for other examples, cf. Abbott, ¶512).

317. *all*] nothing but.

322–8. *if . . . confiscate*] Cf. ll. 305–6, note, above.

323. *just*] exact; I. iii. 145, note and *Ado*, II. i. 375.

324–6. *in . . . scruple*] in the amount of a twentieth, or even the fraction of a twentieth. The twentieth part of a scruple is a grain.

327. *hair*] either a hair's breadth on the scale, or a hair's weight (so Clarendon).

330. *on the hip*] Cf. I. iii. 41, and note.

The law hath yet another hold on you.
It is enacted in the laws of Venice,
If it be proved against an alien,   345
That by direct, or indirect attempts
He seek the life of any citizen,
The party 'gainst the which he doth contrive,
Shall seize one half his goods, the other half
Comes to the privy coffer of the state,   350
And the offender's life lies in the mercy
Of the Duke only, 'gainst all other voice.
In which predicament I say thou stand'st:
For it appears by manifest proceeding,
That indirectly, and directly too,   355
Thou hast contrived against the very life
Of the defendant: and thou hast incurr'd
The danger formerly by me rehears'd.
Down therefore, and beg mercy of the duke.

Gra. Beg that thou may'st have leave to hang thyself,—   360
And yet thy wealth being forfeit to the state,
Thou hast not left the value of a cord,
Therefore thou must be hang'd at the state's
        charge.

Duke. That thou shalt see the difference of our spirit
I pardon thee thy life before thou ask it: 365
For half thy wealth, it is Antonio's,
The other half comes to the general state,
Which humbleness may drive unto a fine.

Por. Ay for the state, not for Antonio.

Shy. Nay, take my life and all, pardon not that,—   370
You take my house, when you do take the prop

---

349. one] *Q, F;* on *Q2.*   350. coffer] *Q, F;* coster *Q2.*   355. too,] *F;*
to *Q.*   356. contrived] *Q;* contriu'd *F.*   358. formerly] *Q2, F;* formorly *Q;*
formally *Hanmer.*   364. spirit] *Q, F;* spirits *Q2.*

348. *contrive*] plot.
349. *seize*] take possession of (a legal term).
364. *our spirit*] the "royal" plural; there is no need to adopt Q2's "spirits" (cf. ll. 16, 110, and 144 above).
365. *pardon*] remit (a penalty); cf. *Lr.,* IV. vi. 111 (so Onions).

370–3. *Nay . . . live*] Cf. *Jew of Malta,* II. i. 147–53: "I esteem the injury far less, / To take the lives of miserable men / Than be the causers of their misery. / You have my wealth, the labour of my life, / The comfort of mine age, my children's hope; / And therefore ne'er distinguish of the wrong."

That doth sustain my house: you take my life
When you do take the means whereby I live.
Por. What mercy can you render him Antonio?
Gra. A halter gratis, nothing else for Godsake!   375
Ant. So please my lord the duke, and all the court,
    To quit the fine for one half of his goods,
    I am content: so he will let me have
    The other half in use, to render it
    Upon his death unto the gentleman   380
    That lately stole his daughter.
    Two things provided more, that for this favour
    He presently become a Christian:
    The other, that he do record a gift
    (Here in the court) of all he dies possess'd   385
    Unto his son Lorenzo and his daughter.
Duke. He shall do this, or else I do recant
    The pardon that I late pronounced here.
Por. Art thou contented Jew? what dost thou say?
Shy. I am content.
Por.   Clerk, draw a deed of gift.   390
Shy. I pray you give me leave to go from hence,
    I am not well,—send the deed after me,

---

375. Godsake!] Godsake. *Q;* Gods sake. *Q2, F.*   376. court,] *Q2;* Court *Q, F.*
378. content:] *Q, F;* content *conj.*   380. Upon] *Q, F;* Until *Hanmer.*

372–3. *you . . . live*] Halliwell quoted *Ecclesiasticus*, xxxiv. 22: "He that taketh away his neighbour's living, slayeth him."

377. *quit*] remit (cf. *O.E.D.*, 4); Antonio agrees that the state should renounce its claim to half Shylock's wealth, or, perhaps, he would remit even the fine which the Duke thought of substituting for the full penalty (so Clarendon). Possibly *quit* = pay (as in *Err.*, I. i. 23); so Antonio would agree that the fine should be paid in lieu of the full penalty.

379. *in use*] in trust. This does not imply that Antonio would give or receive interest; he probably means to administer this half of the estate, giving the legitimate profits to Shylock until his death, when the property would

become Lorenzo's (cf. Halliwell). However, the terms are not clear: they could also mean that Antonio would enjoy the revenue (so Johnson), or Lorenzo (so Clarendon); the latter is unlikely in view of v. i. 291–3. In any case Antonio is generous, for he is still himself greatly in need of money (so Poel, *Westminster Review*, clxxi (1909), 59).

383. *presently*] immediately.

Christian] To become a Christian is a punishment for Jews in *The Jew of Malta* (I. ii). Halliwell quoted Coryat to the effect that the goods of a Jew were usually confiscated as soon as he became a Christian (cf. Coryat, i. 374). Cf. Introduction, pp. xl and li.

385. *possess'd*] For omission of preposition, see Abbott, ¶394.

And I will sign it.

Duke.   Get thee gone, but do it.

Gra. In christ'ning shalt thou have two godfathers,—
       Had I been judge, thou shouldst have had ten more, 395
       To bring thee to the gallows, not to the font.

                              Exit [Shylock].

Duke. Sir I entreat you home with me to dinner.

Por. I humbly do desire your grace of pardon,
       I must away this night toward Padua,
       And it is meet I presently set forth.   400

Duke. I am sorry that your leisure serves you not.
       Antonio, gratify this gentleman,
       For in my mind you are much bound to him.

                              Exit Duke and his train.

Bass. Most worthy gentleman, I and my friend
       Have by your wisdom been this day acquitted   405
       Of grievous penalties, in lieu whereof,
       Three thousand ducats due unto the Jew
       We freely cope your courteous pains withal.

Ant. And stand indebted over and above
       In love and service to you evermore.   410

Por. He is well paid that is well satisfied,
       And I delivering you, am satisfied,
       And therein do account myself well paid,—
       My mind was never yet more mercenary.
       I pray you know me when we meet again,   415

394. *Gra.*] *Q2,F; Shy. Q.*   shalt thou] *Q;* thou shalt *F.*   396. not to] *Q,F;* not *Q2.   Shylock*] *om. Q, F.*   397. home . . . me] *Q;* with me home *F.*   398. do] *Q,F; om. Q2.*   grace of] *Q, F;* Graces *Q3.*   401. I am] *Q,F;* I'm *Pope.*   403.] S.D., Scene III *Pope.*

395. *ten more*] i.e., a jury of twelve men. It was an old joke to call them godfathers; cf., for example, W. Bulleyne, *Dialogue* (1564), ed. Bullen, p. 80, and Dekker, *Seven Deadly Sins* (1606), ed. Arber, p. 2: "(like a common fellow at a Sessions) to put himselfe (as the tearme is) vpon twelue godfathers" (quoted Malone and Pooler).

396. *bring*] a quibble; a jury's verdict brought a man to the gallows, godfathers brought, or accompanied,

a convert to the font (so Clarendon).

398. *of pardon*] For the construction, cf. *Oth.*,III.iii. 212 (so Steevens).

402. *gratify*] reward: cf. *Cor.*, II. ii. 44

408. *cope*] give as an equivalent for (so Clarendon).

415. *know me*] a quibble; (1) recognize, and (2) consider this as an introduction (so Pooler, who compared Jonson, *Everyman in His Humour* (1616), III. i. 72: "pray you know this gentleman here, he is a friend of mine").

I wish you well, and so I take my leave.

Bass. Dear sir, of force I must attempt you further,—
Take some remembrance of us as a tribute,
Not as a fee: grant me two things I pray you,—
Not to deny me, and to pardon me.   420

Por. You press me far, and therefore I will yield,—
Give me your gloves, I'll wear them for your sake,
And (for your love) I'll take this ring from you,—
Do not draw back your hand, I'll take no more,
And you in love shall not deny me this!   425

Bass. This ring good sir? alas it is a trifle,
I will not shame myself to give you this!

Por. I will have nothing else but only this,
And now methinks I have a mind to it!

Bass. There's more depends on this than on the value,—   430
The dearest ring in Venice will I give you,
And find it out by proclamation,
Only for this I pray you pardon me!

Por. I see sir you are liberal in offers,—
You taught me first to beg, and now methinks   435
You teach me how a beggar should be answer'd.

Bass. Good sir, this ring was given me by my wife,
And when she put it on, she made me vow
That I should neither sell, nor give, nor lose it.

Por. That scuse serves many men to save their gifts,—   440
And if your wife be not a mad-woman,
And know how well I have deserv'd this ring,
She would not hold out enemy for ever

419. a] *Q2; om. Q, F.*   425. this!] this? *Q, F.*   426. sir?] sir, *Q, F.*
427. this!] this? *Q.*   429. it!] it? *Q.*   433. me!] me? *Q.*   442. this] *Q, F;*
the *Q2.*

422. *gloves*] probably Antonio's, for he has been asked to "gratify" Portia and *you* of l. 423 seems emphatic (so Clarendon). *N.C.S.*, however, thought Portia asks for Bassanio's gloves so that "the ring may be exposed to view"; *I'll take no more* (l. 424) may support this. Gloves were often exchanged as tokens (cf. *Troil.*, IV. iv. 73).

423. *for your love*] a customary politeness (cf. I. iii. 166), but Portia uses it

pointedly (see also *love*, l. 425).

430. *There's ... value*] i.e., more than the cost of the ring is at stake.

436. *You ... answer'd*] Cf. Heywood, *Proverbs* (1546), DI : "Beggars should be no choosers"; see also *Shr.*, Ind. i. 41–2 and Tilley, B247.

440. *scuse*] a variant form of excuse (cf. *O.E.D.*).

443. *hold out*] i.e., persist in being; cf. *Wiv.*, IV. ii. 141.

For giving it to me: well, peace be with you!
> *Exeunt [Portia and Nerissa].*

Ant. My Lord Bassanio, let him have the ring,   445
Let his deservings and my love withal
Be valued 'gainst your wife's commandement.

Bass. Go Gratiano, run and overtake him,
Give him the ring, and bring him if thou canst
Unto Antonio's house,—away, make haste. *Exit Gratiano.*
Come, you and I will thither presently,   451
And in the morning early will we both
Fly toward Belmont,—come Antonio.   *Exeunt.*

[SCENE II.—*Venice.*]

*Enter [*PORTIA *and*] NERISSA.*

Por. Inquire the Jew's house out, give him this deed,
And let him sign it,—we'll away to-night,
And be a day before our husbands home:
This deed will be well welcome to Lorenzo!

Enter GRATIANO.

Gra. Fair sir, you are well o'erta'en: 5
My Lord Bassanio upon more advice,
Hath sent you here this ring, and doth entreat
Your company at dinner.

444. you!] you. *Q, F.*   S.D.] *Capell subs.; Exeunt Q, F.*   445. Lord]
Q2; L. *Q, F.*   447. 'gainst] *Q;* against *F.*   commandement] *Q, F;*
commandment *F4.*

Scene II

Scene II] *Capell;* om. *Q, F.*   *Venice]* om. *Q, F; The same. Street before the Court
Capell; The same. A Street Malone.*   Portia *and] F;* om. *Q.*   4. Lorenzo!]
Lorenzo? *Q.*   5. o'erta'en] *Q, F;* overtaken *Malone.*   6. Lord] *Q2;* L. *Q, F.*

447. *commandement]* an old spelling
and pronunciation, as in *1 H 6,* I. iii.
20 (so Dyce).

Scene II

1. *deed]* i.e., deed of gift; there is a
pun on the word in l. 4.
3. *a day]* "Portia underrates their

eagerness" (Pooler).
5. *Fair . . . o'erta'en]* either prose (so
N.C.S.) or a short verse line with
two breaks for Gratiano to recover
his breath after running (cf. IV. i.
450).
6. *advice]* deliberation; cf. I. i. 142,
and *Gent.,* II. iv. 208.

Por.   That cannot be;
   His ring I do accept most thankfully;
   And so I pray you tell him: furthermore,   10
   I pray you show my youth old Shylock's house.
Gra. That will I do.
Ner.   Sir, I would speak with you:
   [*Aside to Portia.*] I'll see if I can get my husband's ring
   Which I did make him swear to keep for ever.
Por. Thou may'st I warrant,—we shall have old swearing   15
   That they did give the rings away to men;
   But we'll outface them, and outswear them too:
   Away, make haste! thou know'st where I will tarry.
Ner. Come good sir, will you show me to this house?   *Exeunt.*

9. His] *Q, F;* This *Q2.*   13. S.D.] *Capell subs.; om. Q, F; To Por. (at end of line)*
Pope.   18. haste!] hast, *Q, F.*   19. house?] *Q2;* house. *Q, F.*   S.D.] *F;*
om. Q.

   15. *old*] plenty of (colloquial); cf.*Ado,* v. ii. 98.

[ACT V]

[SCENE I.—*Belmont. A Grove or Green Place before Portia's House.*]

Enter LORENZO *and* JESSICA.

Lor. The moon shines bright. In such a night as this,
When the sweet wind did gently kiss the trees,
And they did make no noise, in such a night
Troilus methinks mounted the Trojan walls,
And sigh'd his soul toward the Grecian tents   5
Where Cressid lay that night.

Jes.   In such a night

ACT V

Scene I

Act v] *om. Q;* Actus Quintus *F.*   Scene I] *Rowe; om. Q, F.*   Belmont . . .
House] *Theobald; om. Q, F;* Belmont *Rowe;* Belmont. Avenue to Portia's House
Capell.   4. Trojan] *Q3;* Troian *Q, F;* Troyan *Q2.*

1-14. *In such . . . Æson*] Hunter (i.
309 ff.) detailed Shakespeare's debt to
Chaucer and Ovid. He suggested that
a folio edition of Chaucer was lying
open before him, for there he would
find Thisbe, Dido, and Medea in *The
Legend of Good Women,* immediately
preceded by *Troilus.*

1. *In . . . night*] Cf. *Wily Beguiled*
(1606), M.S.R., ll. 2173 ff.: "In such a
night did *Paris* win his love. / —In such
a night, Ænæas prou'd vnkind . . ."
Cf. Introduction, p. xxii, n. 3.

2-6. *When . . . night*] Cf. Chaucer,
Troilus and Criseyde, ed. Robinson, v.
647-75:
"And every nyght, as was his wone to
    doone,
He stood the brighte moone to
    byholde, . . .

Upon the walles faste ek wolde he
    walke,

And on the Grekis oost he wolde se,
And to hymself right thus he wolde
    talke:
'Lo, yonder is myn owene lady
    free,
Or ellis yonder, ther the tentes be.
And thennes comth this eyr, that is
    so soote,
That in my soule I fele it doth me
    boote.

'And hardily this wynd, that more
    and moore
Thus stoundemele encresseth in my
    face,
Is of my ladys depe sikes soore. . .'"

4. *Trojan*] Q's "Troian" should
probably be modernized thus, rather
than as "Troyan" (as Q2); elsewhere
in Q there is "royall" (III. ii. 238 and
IV. i. 29) and "enioynd" (II. ix. 9),
"enioyd" (II. vi. 13) and "inioying"
(III. ii. 29).

124

  Did Thisbe fearfully o'ertrip the dew,
  And saw the lion's shadow ere himself,
  And ran dismayed away.
Lor.   In such a night
  Stood Dido with a willow in her hand   10
  Upon the wild sea banks, and waft her love
  To come again to Carthage.
Jes.   In such a night
  Medea gathered the enchanted herbs
  That did renew old Æson.
Lor.   In such a night
  Did Jessica steal from the wealthy Jew,   15
  And with an unthrift love did run from Venice,
  As far as Belmont.
Jes.   In such a night
  Did young Lorenzo swear he loved her well,

11. wild sea banks] *Q*, *F*; wide Sea-banks *Rowe*; wild-sea banks *Capell*. waft
Q, *F*; wav'd *Theobald*. 17, 20. In] *Q*, *F*; And in *F2*. 17–18. In . . . well]
as *Q*, *F*; . . . did / Young . . . *Malone*. 18. loved] *Q*; lou'd *F*.

7–9. *Thisbe . . . away*] Cf. Chaucer, *Legend of Good Women*, ll. 796–812. The details, however, are not identical. The *dew* may derive from Chaucer's earlier "dew of herbes wete" (l. 775) or from "dewie grasse" in Golding's translation of Ovid, *Met.*, IV. 102 (so J. D. Wilson, *Sh. Survey*, X (1957), 22). Both Chaucer and Ovid tell of a lioness, but the former uses the masculine form occasionally (e.g. l. 829). In Gower's *Confessio Amantis* lion is used throughout. All three authorities mention the moon.

8. *saw . . . himself*] Probably the *shadow* which was cast by the moon; but *shadow* can mean reflection, and so Shakespeare might refer to the reflection of the lion in the fountain near the tomb of Ninus, which was the place of tryst (so Malone). Chaucer says the lioness came "To drynken of the welle there as she sat" (l. 808).

9–12. *In . . . Carthage*] Malone suggested that the details are from Chaucer's *Legend* of Ariadne:

"And to the stronde barefot faste she
  wente,
And cryed, 'Theseus! myn herte
  swete!...'
No man she saw, and yit shyned the
  mone, ...
She cryed, 'O turn ageyn, for routhe
  and synne!...'
Hire coverchef on a pole up steked she,
Ascaunce that he shulde it wel yse,
  ..." (ll. 2189–203).
  10. *willow*] "worne of forlorne Paramours" (Spenser, *Faerie Queene*, I. i. 9).
  11. *wild*] without bounds, unconfined (cf. C. J. Sisson and A. Brown, *M.L.R.*, xlvi (1951), 341) or, perhaps, waste, desolate (cf. II. vii. 41–2).
  waft] past tense (cf. Abbott, ¶341).
  12–14. *In . . . Æson*] The incident is not in Chaucer. In Ovid, *Met.*, vii, the herbs were gathered at full moon; Golding's version has both *enchanted herbs* and *renew*.
  15. *steal*] a quibble; she escaped, or stole away, from Shylock and took with her, or stole, money and jewels.
  16. *unthrift*] unthrifty.

Stealing her soul with many vows of faith,
And ne'er a true one.
Lor.   In such a night   20
Did pretty Jessica (like a little shrew)
Slander her love, and he forgave it her.
Jes. I would out-night you did nobody come:
But hark, I hear the footing of a man.

Enter [STEPHANO] *(a messenger)*.

Lor. Who comes so fast in silence of the night?   25
Ste. A friend!
Lor. A friend! what friend? your name I pray you friend?
Ste. Stephano is my name, and I bring word
My mistress will before the break of day
Be here at Belmont,—she doth stray about   30
By holy crosses where she kneels and prays
For happy wedlock hours.
Lor.   Who comes with her?
Ste. None but a holy hermit and her maid:
I pray you is my master yet return'd?
Lor. He is not, nor we have not heard from him,—   35
But go we in (I pray thee Jessica),
And ceremoniously let us prepare
Some welcome for the mistress of the house.

Enter [LAUNCELOT, *the*] *clown*.

20–1. In ... shrew] *as Q, F; ...* did / Pretty ... *Malone.*   21. (like ... shrew)]
Q, F.   24. Stephano] *Theobald; om. Q, F.*   a] *Q; om. F.*   26. *Ste.*] *Var.
'03 subs.; Messen. Q, F.*   friend!] friend? *Q.*   27. A friend!] A friend, *Q,
F; om. Pope.*   what friend?] *F;* what friend, *Q.*   28, 33. *Ste.*] *Var. '03
subs.; Mess. Q, F.*   34. is] *Q;* it *F*   37. us] *Q;* vs vs *F.*   38. Launcelot,
the] *om. Q, F;* Launcelot *Rowe.*

19. *Stealing*] A third sense is implied
here (cf. l. 15 above); = gain possession as in II.i. 12 (cf. *O.E.D.*, 4 f.).
24. *footing*] footsteps.
31. *crosses*] Wayside crosses were
common in England, as in Italy;
Steevens compared *Merry Devil of Edmonton* (1608), Dodsley, x. 214–15:
"But there are crosses, wife; here's one
in Waltham, / Another at the Abbey,

and a third / At Cheston; and it is
ominous to pass / Any of these without
a pater-noster."
33. *hermit*] *N.C.S.* suggested this was
a relic from an earlier play, and Johnson that Shakespeare changed his
mind during composition and left this
detail of a first idea. But it fits well with
Portia's feigned excuse for leaving
Belmont (cf. III.iv. 26–32).

Laun. Sola, sola! wo ha, ho! sola, sola!
Lor. Who calls?   40
Laun. Sola! did you see Master Lorenzo? Master Lorenzo,
    sola, sola!
Lor. Leave hollowing man,—here!
Laun. Sola! where, where?
Lor. Here!   45
Laun. Tell him there's a post come from my master, with
    his horn full of good news,—my master will be here
    ere morning.   *Exit.*
Lor. Sweet soul let's in, and there expect their coming.

39. *Laun.*] *Rowe; Clowne.* Q, F.   sola!] sola: Q, F.   ho!] ho Q.   sola!]
sola. Q, F.   41. *Laun.*] *Rowe; Clo.* Q, F.   Sola!] Sola, Q, F.   41. Master . . . Lorenzo,] *Cambridge;* M. Lorenzo, & M. Lorenzo Q; M. Lorenzo,
M. Lorenzo, Q2; M. Lorenzo, & M. Lorenzo, F; M. Lorenzo, and M. Lorenza,
F2; M. Lorenzo, and Mrs. Lorenza, F3; Mr. Lorenzo and Mrs Lorenzo? *Rowe;*
Master Lorenzo and Mrs. Lorenza? *Rowe (iii);* master Lorenzo and mistress
Lorenza? *Pope;* Master Lorenzo and Mistress Lorenzo? *Blair;* master Lorenzo,
master Lorenzo? *Delius.*   42. sola!] sola. Q, F.   43. hollowing] Q, F;
hollaing *Malone.*   here!] heere. Q, F.   44. *Laun.*] *Rowe; Clowne.* Q, F.
Sola!] Sola, Q, F.   45. Here!] Heere? Q, F.   46. *Laun.*] *Rowe; Clow.* Q, F.
48. morning.] *Rowe;* morning sweete soule. Q, F.   S.D.] om. Q, F; *Exit Clo
Capell.*   49. Sweet soul let's] Let's Q, F; Sweet soul, let's *Var. '85.*

39. *Sola . . . sola!*] Launcelot imitates the horn of the courser or *post* (so
Staunton). The cries are from hunting; in *LLL.* Costard calls "Sowla" on
exit in a hunting scene (IV. i. 151;
Quarto and Folio), and *wo ha, ho!* was
a falconer's call (cf. *O.E.D.*, 1). In
Gent., III. i. 189, Launce uses another
hunting cry.

41–2. *Master . . . Lorenzo,*] Furness
suggested that Q's "&" was a misprint for an interrogation mark;
Clarendon pointed out that *him* of
l. 46 seems to preclude reading "Mistress" for Q's second "M.".

47. *horn*] Pooler compared Dekker,
Satiro-mastix (1602), ed. Bowers, V. i.
62–3: "The king will hang a horne
about thy necke / And make a poast of
thee." "Launcelot jests by comparing
this horn to a cornucopia, or horn of
plenty" (Kittredge).

49. *Sweet soul*] Probably "the preceding passage was an insertion in the
margin, or more probably on a slip,

ending up, as was usual, with a repetition of the *following* words to show
where it was to come. . . . I suppose
that the printer finding the words repeated in the MS, omitted the second
occurrence. The compositor would
not be very likely to do this, but a
proof-reader might—or there may
have been an intermediate transcript"
(Sir Walter Greg, quoted *N.C.S.*).
Since the preceding passage provides
an entry for a clown, it has been suggested that the addition was made in
the theatre; however, in *Ed. Problem*
(1942), Sir Walter noted that it might
as easily "have been made in foul
papers" (p. 123). Before doubting
Shakespeare's authorship of this incident (as *N.C.S.*), it should be noted
that Bassanio's approach must be an-
nounced before ll. 116–18, and that
Launcelot's peculiar use of hunting cries is paralleled in *LLL.* and
Gent.

expect] await.

And yet no matter: why should we go in?   50
My friend Stephano, signify (I pray you)
Within the house, your mistress is at hand,
And bring your music forth into the air.

                                       [Exit Stephano.]

How sweet the moonlight sleeps upon this bank!
Here will we sit, and let the sounds of music   55
Creep in our ears—soft stillness and the night
Become the touches of sweet harmony:
Sit Jessica,—look how the floor of heaven
Is thick inlaid with patens of bright gold,
There's not the smallest orb which thou behold'st   60
But in his motion like an angel sings,

50. in?] *Q2, F*; in. *Q*.   51. Stephano] *Q2*; Stephen *Q, F*.   I] *Q*; om. *F*.
53. S.D.] *Johnson*; om. *Q, F; after l. 52 Theobald*.   ⎸54. bank!] banke, *Q, F*.
56. stillness] stilnes, *Q, F*.   59. patens] *Q, F*; pattents *Q2*; patterns *F2*;
patines *Malone*.

51. *Stephano*] *N.C.S.* suggested that Q's "Stephen" was a compositor's expansion of "Steph." in the copy. The metre is improved by emendation.

57. *Become*] befit.

touches] "fingering or playing of a musical instrument" as in *Gent.*, III. ii. 79; here used for notes, strains (Onions). Possibly the meaning influence, feeling (as in *Gent.*, II. vii. 18) is also implied; cf. use of the vb. at l. 76 below.

59. *patens*] shallow dishes, as used in the celebration of the Holy Communion; It. *patena* was any kind of dish (cf. Florio, *World of Words*). Dyce compared Sylvester's Du Bartas, The Fourth Day, *1st Week*, ed. 1605, pp. 125-7: "Th' Almighties fingers fixed many a million / Of golden scutchions ['*platines dorées*'] in that rich Pauilion" and "that sumptuous Canapie, / The which th' vn-niggard hand of Maiestie / Poudred so thicke with shields ['*escursons*'] so shining cleere, . . ." F's "patterns" (for which *patens* is a possible 16th-c. form) was preferred by Furness who thought it referred to the clouds, and not the stars; but cf. *Ham.*,

II. ii. 313–14: "this majestical roof fretted with golden fire" (for "fretted" = embossed, cf. *Cym.*, II. iv. 88).

60–1. *There's . . . sings*] For the music of the spheres, editors have referred to Plato, *De Republica*, x. xiv. Quintilian, *Inst.*, I. x. 12, Plutarch, *De re musica*, xliv, etc. Montaigne's account of "celestiall musicke" is particularly apposite (cf. Furness): "the bodies of it's circles, being solid smooth, and in their rowling motion, touching and rubbing one against another, must of necessitie produce a wonderfull harmonie: by the changes and entercaprings of which, the revolutions, motions, cadences, and carrols of the asters and planets, are caused and transported. But that universally the hearing senses of these low world's creatures, dizzied and lulled asleepe, . . . by the continuation of that sound, how loud and great soever it be, cannot sensibly perceive or distinguish the same" (tr. J. Florio (1603), ed. Morley, p. 42). Shakespeare may also echo *Job*, xxxviii. 7: "The morning stars sang together; the sons of God shouted for joy" (so Clarendon).

Still quiring to the young-ey'd cherubins;
Such harmony is in immortal souls,
But whilst this muddy vesture of decay
Doth grossly close it in, we cannot hear it: 65

[*Enter Musicians.*]

Come ho! and wake Diana with a hymn,
With sweetest touches pierce your mistress' ear,
And draw her home with music.   *Music.*
Jes. I am never merry when I hear sweet music.
Lor. The reason is your spirits are attentive: 70
For do but note a wild and wanton herd
Or race of youthful and unhandled colts
Fetching mad bounds, bellowing and neighing loud,
Which is the hot condition of their blood,—
If they but hear perchance a trumpet sound,   75
Or any air of music touch their ears,
You shall perceive them make a mutual stand,
Their savage eyes turn'd to a modest gaze,
By the sweet power of music: therefore the poet

62. young-ey'd] *hyphened Q3.*   ey'd] *Q; eyed F.*   63. souls] *Q, F;* sounds
Theobald.   65. it in] *Q;* in it *Q2, F;* us in it *Rowe;* us in *Rowe (iii).*   S.D.]
Malone; om. *Q, F;* Enter Musick, and Domesticks of Portia | *Capell.*   66. ho!] hoe,
Q, F.   68. S.D.] *after l. 69 Rowe;* play Musique *Q;* Play musicke *(after l. 69) F.*
69. I am] *Q, F;* I'm *Pope.*

62. *young-ey'd*] i.e., with sight ever
young; Verity compared *Ezekiel*, i. 18
and x. 12. Their power of sight is
alluded to in *Troil.*, III. ii. 74–5, *Mac.*,
I. vii. 22–4, and *Ham.*, IV. iii. 50.

63–5. *Such . . . it*] i.e., immortal souls
have this sense which appreciates the
music of the spheres; we have immortal souls like the cherubim but,
because our bodies surround the sense
with insensitive clay, we cannot hear
the celestial music. Possibly the first *it*
of l. 65 refers to man's immortal soul
and not to *harmony* (so Collier and
Dyce).

For *harmony* = power to appreciate
music, cf. *music*, l. 83 below, and T.
Bright, *Treatise of Melancholy* (1586),
Q1: "that which reason worketh by a

more euident way, that musicke as it
were a magicall charme bringeth to
passe in the mindes of men, . . . which
agreement . . . when Aristoxenes per-
ceaued, he thereby was moued to
think, that the mind was nothing else
but a kind of harmonie." The music
of the spheres is alluded to again in
Per., v. i. 231; Pericles thinks he hears
it when he has recognized Marina.

70. *spirits*] = mind, faculties of per-
ception (cf. *O.E.D.*, 17 and 18).

72. *race*] herd or stud.

colts] Malone compared *Tp.*, IV. i.
175–8.

77. *mutual*] common; cf. *MND.*, IV.
i. 121.

79. *poet*] perhaps Ovid (*Met.*, x and
xi).

Did feign that Orpheus drew trees, stones, and floods, 80
Since naught so stockish, hard, and full of rage,
But music for the time doth change his nature,—
The man that hath no music in himself,
Nor is not moved with concord of sweet sounds,
Is fit for treasons, stratagems, and spoils,   85
The motions of his spirit are dull as night,
And his affections dark as Erebus:
Let no such man be trusted:—mark the music.

Enter PORTIA *and* NERISSA.

Por. That light we see is burning in my hall:
How far that little candle throws his beams!   90
So shines a good deed in a naughty world.
Ner. When the moon shone we did not see the candle.
Por. So doth the greater glory dim the less,—
A substitute shines brightly as a king
Until a king be by, and then his state   95
Empties itself, as doth an inland brook
Into the main of waters:—music—hark!
Ner. It is your music (madam) of the house.
Por. Nothing is good (I see) without respect,—

---

80. floods,] floods. *Q*, *F*.   81. stockish, hard,] *F*; stockish hard *Q*.   82. the]
Q; om. F.   87. Erebus] *F2;* Terebus *Q;* Erobus *F*.   88. S.D.] *Q, F; at a
distance (added) Johnson.*   90. beams!] beames, *Q, F*.   92. candle.] *Q2;*
candle? *Q, F*.   97. hark!] harke. *Q, F*.   97.] S.D., *Musicke. (at end of line)
F*.   98. your . . . the] *Q, F;* the . . . your *Rowe*.   house.] *Q2, F;* house? *Q*.

---

81. *stockish*] "blockish, unfeeling"
(Onions).

83. *The . . . himself*] like Cassius (cf.
Cæs., I. ii. 204) and Shylock (cf. II. v.
29–36).

85. *spoils*] acts of plunder and
rapine; cf. *H 5*, III. iii. 32.

86. *motions . . . night*] Cf. Angelo:
"one who never feels / The wanton
stings and motions of the sense"
(*Meas.*, I. iv. 58–9). For *motions* = im-
pulses, cf. *Oth.*, I. iii. 335; for *dull* =
inert, drowsy, cf. *John*, III. iv. 109, and
Wint., I. ii. 421.

87. *Erebus*] a place of nether dark-
ness, on the way to Hades. *N.C.S.* noted

that Q's error might be due to the
occasional similarity of "E" and "T"
in Elizabethan secretary hand.

91. *So . . . world*] Cf. *Matthew*, v. 16:
"Let your light so shine before men,
. . ." (quoted Halliwell).

naughty] wicked, worthless; cf. III. ii.
18.

92–3. *When . . . less*] Cf. *LLL.*, IV.
iii. 230–1 and New Arden edn, note.

97. *main of waters*] ocean.

98. *music*] musicians; cf. *H 8*, IV. ii.
94.

99. *Nothing . . . respect*] i.e., nothing
is absolutely good, but only relatively
good as it is modified by circumstan-

Methinks it sounds much sweeter than by day.   100
Ner. Silence bestows that virtue on it madam.
Por. The crow doth sing as sweetly as the lark
When neither is attended: and I think
The nightingale if she should sing by day
When every goose is cackling, would be thought   105
No better a musician than the wren!
How many things by season, season'd are
To their right praise, and true perfection!
Peace!—how the moon sleeps with Endymion,
And would not be awak'd!   [*Music ceases.*]
Lor.   That is the voice,   110
Or I am much deceiv'd, of Portia.
Por. He knows me as the blind man knows the cuckoo—
By the bad voice!
Lor.   Dear lady welcome home!
Por. We have bin praying for our husbands' welfare,
Which speed (we hope) the better for our words: 115
Are they return'd?

100. day.] *Q2;* day? *Q, F.*   101. that] *Q, F;* the *Rowe (ii).*   madam.] *Q2,
F;* madam? *Q.*   106. wren!] Renne? *Q, F.*   108. perfection!] perfection:
Q, F.   109. Peace!—how] *Pope;* Peace, how *Q, F;* Peace, hoa! *Malone.*
110. awak'd!] awak'd. *Q, F.*   S.D.] *F;* om. *Q.*   111. deceiv'd,] deceau'd *Q,
F.*   112–13. He . . . voice] *as Q;* . . . the / Cuckow . . . *F; as prose F2.*   113.
voice!] voyce? *Q, F.*   home!] home? *Q, F.*   114. bin] *Q;* bene *F.*   husbands' welfare] *Q, F;* husband health *Q2.*

ces (so Johnson; cf. *O.E.D.,* Respect,
6 and 7a), or, perhaps, nothing is
good without the thought to make
it so (so Staunton; for *respect,* cf. I. i.
74).
    103. *When . . . attended*] i.e., when
both are alone (cf. *Tw.N.,* I. v. 111);
most editors take attended = listened
to (cf. *Cym.,* I. vi. 142).
    104. *if . . . day*] Here, and in *Lucr.,*
1142, Shakespeare writes as if the
nightingale did not sing by day (so
Pooler).
    107. *season*] favourable occasion.
    109. *Peace*] possibly, to the musi-
cians (so Malone; cf. F's S.D.), or to
Nerissa; but it might be an exclamation (see next note).
    109–10. *how . . . awak'd*] Portia

draws attention to Jessica lying en-
tranced with Lorenzo on the moonlit
bank (R. David *(S.S.,* v (1952), p. 124)
noted the effectiveness of this interpretation on the stage), or, possibly,
it is a personified equivalent of l. 54
above ("How sweet the moonlight
sleeps . . ."). Malone's emendation is
supported by *Rom.,* IV. v. 65 and *AYL.,*
v. iv. 131; *how* was often equivalent to
"ho!" (cf. II. vi. 25).
    109. *Endymion*] Selene (Diana), en-
amoured of his beauty, caused him to
sleep for ever on Mount Latmos.
    112–13. *cuckoo . . . voice*] Cf. *LLL.,*
v. ii. 908–12: "The cuckoo . . . Mocks
married men . . ."
    114. *bin*] an unaccented form of
been.

Lor.   Madam, they are not yet:
But there is come a messenger before
To signify their coming.
Por.   Go in Nerissa.
Give order to my servants, that they take
No note at all of our being absent hence,—   120
Nor you Lorenzo,—Jessica nor you.   [*A tucket sounds.*]
Lor. Your husband is at hand, I hear his trumpet,—
We are no tell-tales madam, fear you not.
Por. This night methinks is but the daylight sick,
It looks a little paler,—'tis a day,   125
Such as the day is when the sun is hid.

Enter BASSANIO, ANTONIO, GRATIANO, *and their
followers.*

Bass. We should hold day with the Antipodes,
If you would walk in absence of the sun.
Por. Let me give light, but let me not be light,
For a light wife doth make a heavy husband,   130
And never be Bassanio so for me,—
But God sort all: you are welcome home my lord.
Bass. I thank you madam,—give welcome to my friend,—
This is the man, this is Antonio,
To whom I am so infinitely bound.   135
Por. You should in all sense be much bound to him,
For (as I hear) he was much bound for you.
Ant. No more than I am well acquitted of.
Por. Sir, you are very welcome to our house:

118. coming.] *Q2,F;* comming? *Q.*   in] *Q, F; om. Pope.*   121. S.D.] *F; om.*
Q.   132. you are] *Q, F;* y'are *Q2.*

121. S.D. tucket] flourish on a trumpet.

122. *his trumpet*] Each person might have his own trumpet-call; cf. *Lr.*, II. iv. 185–6, and *Oth.*,II. i. 180.

124. *This night . . .*] Portia changes the subject abruptly, and "talks of the weather," in order to appear unconcerned when Bassanio enters.

127–8. *We . . . sun*] Bassanio has overheard Portia's last speech. Malone paraphrased: "If you would always

walk in the night, it would be day with us, as it now is on the other side of the globe."

129. *light . . . light*] The quibble was common. Portia also twists the proverb, "A good wife makes a good husband" (Tilley, W351; so H. T. Price).

132. *sort*] dispose of.

136. *in all sense*] (1) in all reason, or (2) in every sense of the word (for the sing. form cf. *Mac.*, v. i. 28).

It must appear in other ways than words,   140
Therefore I scant this breathing courtesy.
Gra. [*To Nerissa.*] By yonder moon I swear you do me wrong,
In faith I gave it to the judge's clerk,—
Would he were gelt that had it for my part,
Since you do take it (love) so much at heart.   145
Por. A quarrel ho, already! what's the matter?
Gra. About a hoop of gold, a paltry ring
That she did give me, whose posy was
For all the world like cutler's poetry
Upon a knife, "Love me, and leave me not."   150
Ner. What talk you of the posy or the value?
You swore to me when I did give it you,
That you would wear it till your hour of death,
And that it should lie with you in your grave,—
Though not for me, yet for your vehement oaths,   155
You should have been respective and have kept it.
Gave it a judge's clerk! no—God's my judge—
The clerk will ne'er wear hair on's face that had it.
Gra. He will, and if he live to be a man.
Ner. Ay, if a woman live to be a man.   160
Gra. Now (by this hand) I gave it to a youth,
A kind of boy, a little scrubbed boy,
No higher than thyself, the judge's clerk,

142. S.D.] *after l. 143 Rowe; om. Q, F.* 146. ho, already!] hoe already, *Q ,F.*
148. give] *Q , F;* give to *Var. '93 conj., Collier* (ii). 148, 151. posy] *Q;* poesie
Q2, F. 151. value?] valew: *Q, F.* 152. give it] *Q2, F;* giue *Q.* 153. your]
Q; the *F.* 157. clerk!] Clarke: *Q, F.* no . . . judge] *Q;* but wel I
know *F.*

141. *breathing*] i.e., of mere breath or
words; cf. ii. ix. 90 and *Mac.*, v. iii. 27:
"mouth-honour, breath."

142. *moon*] Cf. *Rom.*, ii. ii. 109:
"swear not by the moon, the incon-
stant moon."

148. *posy*] "A short motto, originally
a line or verse of poetry, and usually in
patterned language, inscribed on a
knife, within a ring, . . . etc." (*O.E.D.*).

150. *leave*] part with; cf. ll. 172 and
196 below, and *Gent.*, iv. iv. 79: "It
seems you loved not her, to leave her
token." The *posy* applies to the gift and
the giver.

152. *it*] Emendation seems necessary for both sense and metre.

153. *your*] Furness noted the frequent use of *you* and *your* in this speech;
he preferred F, but pointed out that
Q's repetition might be purposeful.

156. *respective*] careful.

162-4. *A . . . boy*] "This description
seems to leave Nerissa speechless for
the moment; it is resented, l. 261"
(Pooler).

162. *scrubbed*] stunted (Steevens);
cf. Cotgrave, Marpaut, "An ill-
fauoured scrub, a little ouglie, or
swartie wretch."

A prating boy that begg'd it as a fee,—
I could not for my heart deny it him.   165
Por. You were to blame,—I must be plain with you,—
To part so slightly with your wife's first gift,
A thing stuck on with oaths upon your finger,
And so riveted with faith unto your flesh.
I gave my love a ring, and made him swear   170
Never to part with it, and here he stands:
I dare be sworn for him he would not leave it,
Nor pluck it from his finger, for the wealth
That the world masters. Now in faith Gratiano
You give your wife too unkind a cause of grief,   175
And 'twere to me I should be mad at it.
Bass. [*Aside.*] Why I were best to cut my left hand off,
And swear I lost the ring defending it.
Gra. My Lord Bassanio gave his ring away
Unto the judge that begg'd it, and indeed   180
Deserv'd it too: and then the boy (his clerk)
That took some pains in writing, he begg'd mine,
And neither man nor master would take aught
But the two rings.
Por.   What ring gave you my lord?
Not that (I hope) which you receiv'd of me.   185
Bass. If I could add a lie unto a fault,
I would deny it: but you see my finger
Hath not the ring upon it, it is gone.
Por. Even so void is your false heart of truth.
By heaven I will ne'er come in your bed   190
Until I see the ring!
Ner.   Nor I in yours

166. to] *Q;* too *Q2, F.*   169. so riveted] *Q, F;* riveted *Pope;* riveted so *Capell.*
175. a] *Q, F;* om. *Walker conj., Dyce (ii).*   177. S.D.] *after l. 178 Theobald;*
om. *Q, F.*   191. ring!] ring? *Q.*   191–2. Nor . . . mine] *as Q; one line*
F.

166. *to blame*] In this phrase, *to* was
often "misunderstood as *too*, and
blame taken as adj. = blameworthy,
culpable" (*O.E.D.*, 6, which quoted
1 H 4, III.i. 177).
169. *so*] Dyce thought this was
repeated by mistake from l. 167
above, but *riveted* may be equivalent to only two syllables.
172. *leave*] Cf. l. 150 above, note.
175. *too . . . cause*] Abbott (¶462)
wished to elide *too un-*, but both syllables may be emphatic (Walker compared *Lr.*, III. iv. 73, for "únkind");
a is, perhaps, an error.
176. *And*] if.

Till I again see mine!
Bass.   Sweet Portia,
  If you did know to whom I gave the ring,
  If you did know for whom I gave the ring,
  And would conceive for what I gave the ring,   195
  And how unwillingly I left the ring,
  When nought would be accepted but the ring,
  You would abate the strength of your displeasure.
Por. If you had known the virtue of the ring,
  Or half her worthiness that gave the ring,   200
  Or your own honour to contain the ring,
  You would not then have parted with the ring:
  What man is there so much unreasonable
  (If you had pleas'd to have defended it
  With any terms of zeal) :—wanted the modesty   205
  To urge the thing held as a ceremony?
  Nerissa teaches me what to believe,—
  I'll die for't, but some woman had the ring!
Bass. No by my honour madam, by my soul
  No woman had it, but a civil doctor,   210
  Which did refuse three thousand ducats of me,
  And begg'd the ring,—the which I did deny him,
  And suffer'd him to go displeas'd away,
  Even he that had held up the very life
  Of my dear friend. What should I say sweet
      lady?   215
  I was enforc'd to send it after him,
  I was beset with shame and courtesy,
  My honour would not let ingratitude
  So much besmear it: pardon me good lady,

192. mine!] mine? *Q*.   198. displeasure.] *Q2;* displeasure? *Q*, *F*.   201. contain] *Q*, *F*; retain *Pope*.   206. ceremony?] *Q2;* ceremonie: *Q*, *F*.   208. ring!] ring? *Q*, *F*.   209. my honour] *Q*. mine honor *F*.   211. Which] *Q*, *F*; Who *Pope*.   215. lady?] *Q2, F;* Laay. *Q*.

199. *virtue*] power, efficacy; cf. *John*, v. vii. 44, and *H 8*, v. iii. 99. For the *virtue*, cf. iii. ii. 171-4.

201. *contain*] retain; cf. *Sonn.*, lxxvii. 9.

205-6. *wanted . . . urge*] i.e., so lacked moderation that he would have urged. The lax construction "is due to the intervening parenthesis" (Clarendon); Q's colon is retained to mark this.

206. *ceremony*] sacred thing, symbol; cf. *Meas.*, ii. ii. 59-61.

210. *civil doctor*] doctor of civil law. There may also be a pun on *civil* = well-bred, polite (cf. *O.E.D.*, 9).

For by these blessed candles of the night,   220
Had you been there, I think you would have begg'd
The ring of me to give the worthy doctor.

Por. Let not that doctor e'er come near my house—
Since he hath got the jewel that I loved,
And that which you did swear to keep for me,   225
I will become as liberal as you,
I'll not deny him any thing I have,
No, not my body, nor my husband's bed:
Know him I shall, I am well sure of it.
Lie not a night from home. Watch me like Argus,— 230
If you do not, if I be left alone,
Now by mine honour (which is yet mine own),
I'll have that doctor for my bedfellow.

Ner. And I his clerk: therefore be well advis'd
How you do leave me to mine own protection.   235

Gra. Well do you so: let not me take him then,
For if I do, I'll mar the young clerk's pen.

Ant. I am th'unhappy subject of these quarrels.

Por. Sir, grieve not you,—you are welcome notwithstanding.

Bass. Portia, forgive me this enforced wrong,   240
And in the hearing of these many friends
I swear to thee, even by thine own fair eyes
Wherein I see myself—

Por.   Mark you but that!
In both my eyes he doubly sees himself:

220. For] *Q;* And *F.*   222. doctor.] *Q2;* Doctor? *Q,F.*   232. yet mine] *Q,F;*
yet my *Pope.*   233. that] *Q;* the *F.*   my] *Q2,F;* mine *Q.*   239. Sir . . . not-
withstanding] *as Q; . . .* you, / You . . . *F.*   you are] *Q, F;* you're *Dyce (ii).*
242. even] *Q, F;* ev'n *Pope.*   243. myself—] my selfe.— *F2;* my selfe. *Q, F.*
that!] that? *Q, F.*   244. my] *Q, F;* mine *F2.*

220. *blessed . . . night*] Cf. *Rom.,* III.v.
9, *Mac.,* II. i. 5, and *Sonn.,* xxi. 12 (so
Malone).

226. *liberal*] a quibble: (1) free in
giving, and (2) licentious (cf.II. ii. 176,
note).

230. *Argus*] Cf. Ovid, *Met.,* i and S.
Bateman, *Golden Book* (1577), A4^v:
"The Poets feigne that *Argus* the Sonne
of *Aristor,* had an hundred eyes, of al
which, only two did sleepe by course,
so that he was not to be taken withal a

sleepe: So subtil was *Argus,* that what
fraude soeuer was imagined, hee had
policie to defende it."

233. *my*] "mine" was normally used
only before vowels (cf. *O.E.D.,* and
Abbott, ¶237); the compositor could
have caught *mine* from the preceding
line.

234. *advis'd*] cautious.

237. *pen*] Cf. the use of "pike",
*2 H 4,*II. iv. 55, and "weapon", *Rom..*
I. iv. 166.

In each eye one,—swear by your double self,   245
And there's an oath of credit.
Bass.   Nay, but hear me.
Pardon this fault, and by my soul I swear
I never more will break an oath with thee.
Ant. I once did lend my body for his wealth,
Which but for him that had your husband's ring   250
Had quite miscarried. I dare be bound again,
My soul upon the forfeit, that your lord
Will never more break faith advisedly.
Por. Then you shall be his surety: give him this,
And bid him keep it better than the other.   255
Ant. Here Lord Bassanio, swear to keep this ring.
Bass. By heaven it is the same I gave the doctor!
Por. I had it of him: pardon me Bassanio,
For by this ring the doctor lay with me.
Ner. And pardon me my gentle Gratiano,   260
For that same scrubbed boy (the doctor's clerk)
In lieu of this, last night did lie with me.
Gra. Why this is like the mending of highways
In summer where the ways are fair enough!
What, are we cuckolds ere we have deserv'd it?   265
Por. Speak not so grossly,—you are all amaz'd;
Here is a letter, read it at your leisure,—

---

249. his] *Q;* thy *F.*   257. doctor!] Doctor. *Q, F.*   258. me] *Q;* om. *F.*
264. where] *Q, F;* when *Collier (ii).*   enough!] enough? *Q.*   265. it?] *Q2;*
it. *Q, F.*

246. *oath of credit*] laughingly ironical; *double* (l. 245) may mean either
two-fold or deceitful (so Pooler).

249. *wealth*] welfare, prosperity, as
in *Ham.,* IV. iv. 27; Steevens quoted the
English *Litany*: "In all time of our
tribulation; in all time of our wealth."
See also, Introduction, p. lvii.

250. *Which*] referring to *my body,* or
his wealth, or, probably, the whole
transaction which has been alluded to.

251. *miscarried*] Cf. earlier uses, II.
viii. 29, and III. ii. 314.

262. *In lieu of*] in return for.

263–4. *Why . . . enough*] For a wife

to take a lover to bed while her husband is still lusty and amorous is like
the mending of highways in summer;
Gratiano implies that there is justification for doing so when the husband
is old and impotent (so E. Schanzer,
privately). For *highway* in similar contexts, cf. *Rom.,* III. ii. 134: "a highway
to my bed." For *where =* when, Pooler
compared *AYL.,* II. iii. 60.

266. *grossly*] There is, perhaps, a
double meaning: (1) stupidly (cf.
John, III. i. 163, and "gross", *R 3,* III. vi.
10), and (2) indelicately, licentious-
ly.

It comes from Padua from Bellario,—
There you shall find that Portia was the doctor,
Nerissa there her clerk. Lorenzo here   270
Shall witness I set forth as soon as you,
And even but now return'd: I have not yet
Enter'd my house. Antonio you are welcome,
And I have better news in store for you
Than you expect: unseal this letter soon,   275
There you shall find three of your argosies
Are richly come to harbour suddenly.
You shall not know by what strange accident
I chanced on this letter.

Ant.   I am dumb!
Bass. Were you the doctor, and I knew you not?   280
Gra. Were you the clerk that is to make me cuckold?
Ner. Ay, but the clerk that never means to do it,
    Unless he live until he be a man.
Bass. Sweet doctor, you shall be my bedfellow,—
    When I am absent then lie with my wife.   285
Ant. Sweet lady, you have given me life and living;
    For here I read for certain that my ships
    Are safely come to road.
Por.   How now Lorenzo?
    My clerk hath some good comforts too for you.
Ner. Ay, and I'll give them him without a fee.   290
    There do I give to you and Jessica
    From the rich Jew, a special deed of gift
    After his death, of all he dies possess'd of.
Lor. Fair ladies, you drop manna in the way
    Of starved people.
Por.   It is almost morning,   295
    And yet I am sure you are not satisfied
    Of these events at full. Let us go in,

272. even but] *Q;* but eu'n *F.*   273. Enter'd] *Q;* Entred *Q2, F.*   279.
dumb!] dumb? *Q.*   281. cuckold?] *Q2;* cuckold. *Q, F.*   282. Ay,] I, *Q2, F;*
I *Q.*   284. Sweet doctor,] (Sweet Doctor) *Q, F.*   286. Sweet lady,] *Q2;*
(Sweet Lady) *Q, F.*   296. I am] *Q, F;* Ime *Q2.*

278-9. *You . . . dumb*] "This beauti-   cized by some pundits" (*N.C.S.*).
ful example of Shakespeare's dramatic   286. *living*] possessions.
impudence has been severely criti-   288. *road*] anchorage.

And charge us there upon inter'gatories,
And we will answer all things faithfully.
Gra. Let it be so,—the first inter'gatory   300
That my Nerissa shall be sworn on, is,
Whether till the next night she had rather stay,
Or go to bed now (being two hours to day):
But were the day come, I should wish it dark
Till I were couching with the doctor's clerk.   305
Well, while I live, I'll fear no other thing
So sore, as keeping safe Nerissa's ring.   *Exeunt.*

FINIS

308. inter'gatories] *F;* intergotories *Q;* interrogatories *F3.*   300. inter'gatory] *F;* intergory *Q (incorrect);* intergotory *Q (correct);* interrogatory *F3.*   303. bed] *Q;* bed, *F.*   305. Till] *Q, F;* That *Q2.*

298. *charge . . . inter'gatories*] Witnesses at court were called to answer upon oath (*charge us*) a series of questions (interrogatories).

307. *ring*] a bawdy pun; Partridge (*Shakespeare's Bawdy* (1947), p. 179) compared the use of "circle" in *Rom.,* II. i. 24.

TRANSLATION FROM THE FIRST STORY
OF THE FOURTH DAY OF SER GIOVANNI,
IL PECORONE

There lived in Florence a merchant, called Bindo, of the Scali family, who had visited Tana and Alexandria several times and had been on all the long voyages which are made on business. This Bindo was very rich and had three fine, manly sons, and when he came close to death, he called the two eldest and made his will in their presence, bequeathing all he had in the world to these two heirs, and to the youngest he bequeathed nothing. When this will had been made, the youngest son, called Giannetto, heard of it and went to the bedside and said to him, "Father, I am amazed at what you have done—not mentioning me in the will." The father replied, "Giannetto, there is no creature living to whom I wish better fortune than to you, and therefore I do not wish you to stay here after my death, but I want you to go to Venice to your godfather, Ansaldo, who has no child and has often written asking me to send you to him. Moreover, I may say that he is now the richest of the christian merchants. Therefore, I want you to go, as soon as I am dead, and to take this letter to him—then, if you know how to behave, you will become a rich man." The son answered, "Father, I am ready to do whatever you command"; and thereupon he gave him his blessing and, in a few days, he died, and all the sons mourned him greatly and paid all the proper honours to his body.

Then a few days afterwards the two brothers called for Giannetto, and told him, "Brother, it is true that our father made a will and left us his heirs and made no mention of you: nevertheless, you are still our brother and you shall not want until we are in want." Giannetto replied, "I thank you, my brothers, for your offer; but, for my part, I am resolved to seek my fortune elsewhere, and so do you stay and possess the blessed inheritance which is yours by right." The brothers, seeing that he had made up his mind, gave him a horse and money to spend. Giannetto took leave of them and went to Venice, and came to Ansaldo's counting house and presented the letter which his father had given him just before his death. As he read the letter, Ansaldo knew that this young man was the son of his dearest friend Bindo; and when he had read it, he embraced him at once, saying, "Welcome my dear godson, whom I have longed for so much": and immediately he asked after Bindo, and Giannetto replied that he was dead: so, with many tears, he embraced and kissed Giannetto and said, "The death of Bindo grieves me very much, for he helped me to get a great part of my possessions; but the joy I have from you is so great that it allays that grief." He led him to his house and ordered his factors, partners, grooms, servants, and everyone in his house that Giannetto should be obeyed and served better than himself. And at once he entrusted to him the keys of all his ready money, and said, "My son, spend this and clothe and shoe yourself to your own liking, and keep open house to the townspeople, and make yourself known: I leave it to you to do as you think best, and the more you get the goodwill of everyone, the dearer you will be to me."

Now Giannetto began to get acquainted with the gentlemen of Venice, to pay court, to entertain and give presents, to keep servants and buy good horses, and to attend jousts and revelry at which he excelled, being skilled, magnanimous, and courtly in all things; he knew how to act with honour and courtesy on all occasions, and always he paid more honour to Ansaldo than if he had been an hundred times his father. And he bore himself so wisely with all kinds of people, that almost the whole of Venice, seeing such discretion, together with such charm and infinite courtesy, wished him well, and men and women loved him greatly: Ansaldo could think only of him, he was so pleased with his style and manner of living. There was hardly a single festivity in Venice to which Giannetto was not invited, he was so esteemed by all.

Now it happened that two of his close friends intended to go in two ships with merchandise to Alexandria as they were accustomed to do every year, and thereupon, they spoke to Giannetto, saying, "You would do well to amuse yourself at sea with us, to see the world and particularly Damascus and its neighbourhood." Giannetto replied, "Certainly, I would go willingly if my father Ansaldo will give me leave." They answered, "We will so arrange it with him, that he will be content." And they went to Ansaldo immediately, and said, "We want to ask if you would be content to allow Giannetto to come with us to Alexandria in the spring, and provide him with some kind of ship so that he may see a little of the world." Ansaldo said, "I am content, if it pleases him." "Sir," they replied, "it does please him." Then Ansaldo at once prepared a very fine ship, and loaded it with merchandise, dressed it with flags, and fitted it with as many arms as were needed. And after it was ready, Ansaldo ordered the captain and all the crew to do everything that Giannetto commanded, and to take care of him: "I do not send him," he said, "for the profit I wish him to make, but to see the world at his pleasure." And when Giannetto was about to embark, all Venice was gathered to see him because it was a long time since such a beautiful and well-furnished ship had sailed from that city. And everyone was sorry at his departure; and he took leave of Ansaldo and all his friends, and they put out to sea, hoisted sail, and made for Alexandria in the name of God and good fortune.

Sailing together for some days, the three friends in their three ships, it happened early one morning that Giannetto saw a bay with a fine harbour and asked the captain what it was called; he replied, "Sir, that place belongs to a widowed lady who has ruined many gentlemen." "In what way?" said Giannetto. "Sir," he replied, "she is a fine and beautiful lady, and she has made a law: whoever arrives here must sleep with her, and if he can enjoy her, he must take her for wife and be lord of the seaport and all the surrounding country. But if he cannot enjoy her, he loses everything he has." Giannetto thought for a moment, and said; "Do everything you can and make for that harbour." The captain said, "Sir, mind what you say, for many have gone there who have been robbed of everything." "Do not trouble yourself about that," said Giannetto, "do what I bid you." And so it was done and immediately they changed direction and slipped into the port so that the friends in the other ships knew nothing of it.

In the morning, news spread that this fine ship had come into port, so that everyone came to see it; and at once the lady was told, and she sent for Giannetto who waited on her forthwith, and greeted her with a low bow; and she took him by the hand and inquired who he was and from whence he came, and if he knew the custom of the country. Giannetto replied that he did and that he had come for no other reason. Then she said, "You are a hundred times welcome"; and that day she paid him very great honour, and ordered barons, counts, and many knights who were her subjects, to attend on him. The courtly behaviour of Giannetto pleased all the nobles, in that he was well bred, agreeable, and of good conversation; everyone was delighted with him and there was dancing, singing, and feasting at court the whole day in honour of Giannetto: and everyone would have been well pleased to have him for their lord.

Night coming on, the lady took him by the hand and led him to her chamber and said, "I think it is time to go to bed." "Lady, I am at your service," replied Giannetto; and at once two damsels

entered, one with wine and the other with sweet-meats. The lady
said, "I know you must be thirsty, so take a drink." Giannetto took
some sweet-meats and drank some wine, which was prepared in
such a way that it induced sleep; and he did not know this and took
half a cup, since he found it to his taste; and at once he undressed
and went to bed, and as soon as he reached it, he fell asleep. The
lady lay down by his side, and he did not wake at all until late in the
morning and past nine o'clock. But the lady rose early and ordered
the ship to be unloaded, which was found to be full of rich and good
merchandise. After nine o'clock, the maid-servants came to Giannetto's bed and told him to rise and be gone, for he had lost the ship
and everything in it; and then he was ashamed and saw that he had
acted with great foolishness.

The lady gave him a horse and money to spend, and he departed
sad and sorrowful, and went on his way towards Venice; when he
arrived he dared not return home for shame, but went at night to
the house of a friend, who was amazed to see him and said, "Alas
Giannetto, what is the matter?" And he replied, "My ship struck a
rock at night and was broken in pieces and everything destroyed
and scattered; I held on to a piece of wood which cast me ashore and
so I have come over land and am here." Giannetto stayed several
days in this friend's house, who went one day to visit Ansaldo and
found him very melancholy. Ansaldo said, "I am very much afraid
that my son is dead or that the sea has brought him ill fortune, so
that I have found no rest—so great is the love I bear him." The
young man said, "I can tell you news of him; he has been shipwrecked and lost everything, but he himself is safe." "Praise be to
God," said Ansaldo, "if he is saved, I am satisfied; the loss of the
ship does not worry me. Where is he?" The young man replied,
"He is at my house." And immediately, Ansaldo started out and
ran to meet him, and when he saw him, he embraced him and said,
"My son, there is no need for you to be ashamed because of me; it
is quite common to lose ships at sea, and do not alarm yourself on
that account, my son; since you have received no hurt, I am content." And he took him home, comforting him all the way.

The news spread throughout Venice, and every one was sorry
for the loss Giannetto had sustained. Shortly afterwards his companions returned from Alexandria very rich, and when they
arrived, they asked after Giannetto and were told everything.
Then they ran at once to embrace him, asking, "How did you part
from us and where did you go, that we could know nothing of you,
and sailed to and fro all that day, and could not see you or understand where your ship had gone; we were so grieved that through-

out the voyage we could not enjoy ourselves, believing that you were dead." Giannetto replied, "A contrary wind blew up from a certain bay, which drove my ship straight up against a rock close to the shore; I hardly saved myself and everything was wrecked." Giannetto made this excuse in order not to disclose his fault. And they made merry with him, thanking God that he was spared, and saying, "Next spring, God willing, we will make up for what you have lost this time; and therefore let us devote ourselves to enjoyment without melancholy." So they gave themselves to pleasure and happy days, as they used to do before. But still Giannetto thought of nothing but of how to return to the lady, thinking and saying, "I must marry her or die"; and so he could not be merry. Therefore Ansaldo often said to him, "Do not be down-hearted, we have enough to be able to live very comfortably." "Dear sir," replied Giannetto, "I shall not be satisfied until I make this voyage again." Ansaldo, seeing his desire, when the time came, provided another ship with more merchandise than the first and of greater value, putting the best part of his wealth into it. His companions, when they had prepared their ship with things necessary for their trade, put out to sea with Giannetto, hoisted sail, and went on their way. Sailing for several days, Giannetto was always on the look out for the lady's seaport, which was called the port of the lady of Belmonte. Coming one night to the entrance of this port, which was in a great bay, Giannetto recognized it at once, and shifting the sails and the helm, he entered so secretly that, once more, his friends in the other ships did not know he was missing.

Waking next morning and looking down on the harbour, the lady saw the ship's flags flying and recognized it at once; and she called her maid and said, "Do you know those flags?" "Madam," said the maid, "it is the ship of the young man who came last year and made us so rich with his cargo." "You are right," said the lady, "and certainly he must be in love with me, for no one has ever returned a second time." The maid said, "I have never seen a more courteous or agreeable man." The lady sent many pages and servants to him, who served him with great ceremony; and he treated them cheerfully and well, and came to the castle and presented himself to the lady. And when she saw him, she embraced him most joyfully and he very courteously returned the embrace: and the whole day was spent in feasting and revelry, for she had sent for many lords and ladies who came to the court to celebrate in honour of Giannetto: and because of his charm and courtesy all the noblemen regretted that he was not their lord; and all the ladies were enamoured of his dancing; he appeared so comely that they all thought he was the son of some great man. And seeing that night was coming, the lady took Giannetto by the hand and asked him to go to bed; and when they were seated in the chamber, the two damsels came with wine and sweet-meats, and having eaten and drunk of them, they went to bed; and as he lay down, Giannetto fell asleep. The lady undressed and lay down at his side, and, to put it briefly, he did not wake the whole night. And when morning came, the lady got up and at once ordered his ship to be stripped. When it was passed nine o'clock, Giannetto awoke and looked in vain for the lady; he raised himself up and saw that it was late; he got up and felt ashamed of what had happened. He was given a horse and money to spend, and told to be gone; and shamefully he left directly, being sad and down-hearted, and for many days he did not stop until he arrived at Venice; and by night he went to his friend's house, who was astonished beyond measure when he saw him and asked what was the matter. Giannetto replied, "I am undone; cursed be my fortune which brought me to this place." "You may well curse your fortune," said his friend, "for you have ruined Ansaldo who was the greatest and richest of christian merchants, and the shame of this is greater than the loss." Giannetto lived secretly for many days in his friend's house, not knowing what to do or say, and almost thought of returning to Florence without seeing Ansaldo; however he decided to go to him, and he did so. When Ansaldo saw him, he stood upright, and embraced him and said, "Welcome, my son." And with tears Giannetto embraced him. When he heard everything, Ansaldo said, "How is it, Giannetto? do not give yourself over to melancholy; since I have you again, I am satisfied. We still have enough to live quietly. The sea enriches some men, others it ruins."

The news spread throughout Venice and everyone was concerned for Ansaldo, and was grieved at the loss he had suffered; and he had to sell many of his possessions to pay the creditors who had provided the goods. Then Giannetto's friends returned from Alexandria very rich, and when they arrived at Venice, they were told that Giannetto was returned and had lost and wrecked everything, at which they were astonished, saying, "This is the strangest thing that could happen"; and they went to Ansaldo and Giannetto, and said very kindly, "Do not be dismayed, next year we will travel on your behalf; in a way, we are the cause of your loss, for at the beginning we advised Giannetto to come with us. Therefore do not fear, as long as we have possessions, use them as your own." Ansaldo gave them thanks and said that he had still enough to live on. But day and night Giannetto thought of this and he could not be joyful; when Ansaldo asked him what was the matter, he answered, "I shall not be satisfied until I have regained what I have lost." "My son," said Ansaldo, "I do not want you to go any more; it will be better to stay here, content with the little we have, than for you to venture forth again." Giannetto replied, "I am determined to do all in my power to go—for I am ashamed to live in this way."

When Ansaldo saw that he was resolved, he began to sell all that he had in the world and to equip another ship for him: and so he did, he sold all he had and provided a fine ship with merchandise: and, because he lacked ten thousand ducats, he went to a Jew of Mestri and borrowed them on condition that if they were not repaid the next June on St John's day, the Jew might take a pound of flesh from whatever part of his body he pleased. Ansaldo agreed, and the Jew had a bond drawn up and witnessed with all necessary form and ceremony; and then he counted him ten thousand golden ducats, with which Ansaldo provided what the ship lacked; and although the other two were fine, this third ship was finer and better equipped. So the friends equipped their two ships, with the intention that whatever they gained would be for Giannetto. And when the time came to depart, Ansaldo said to Giannetto, "My son, you are going and know the bond to which I agreed, I beseech you if misfortune comes to you, that you will be pleased to return so that I may see you before I die—then I will depart contented." Giannetto replied, "Ansaldo, I will do everything that I think will please you." Ansaldo gave him his blessing, and so they took their leave and set out on their voyage.

The two companions watched Giannetto's ship carefully all the time, and Giannetto was always thinking of how to slip into the port of Belmonte. He prevailed with one of the sailors to sail the ship by night into the port of the lady. When morning lightened, the friends in the other ships looked around and could see nothing of Giannetto's ship and said to themselves "Truly he has bad luck," and they decided to continue their course, wondering greatly.

When the ship came into the port, everyone ran from the castle to see it, hearing that Giannetto had returned and marvelling greatly at it and saying, "He must be the son of some great man, since he comes here every year with so much merchandise and such fine ships; would to God he were our master"; and so he was visited by all the great ones, both nobles and the knights of that land, and the lady was told how Giannetto had come into the harbour: so she opened a window of the palace and saw the beautiful ship and recognized the flags and made the sign of the cross, saying, "Certainly, this is a great undertaking—this is the man who has left such wealth in this country": and she sent for him.

Giannetto went to her with great show of affection, and they greeted each other, and he bowed; and all the day was spent in joy and feasting; and a great tournament was held in honour of Giannetto and many lords and knights jousted that day, and Giannetto wished to joust also, and did miracles, so well did he with lance and horse; and his deportment so pleased all the noblemen, that they all wished to have him as their lord.

When the time came to go to rest, the lady took Giannetto by the hand and said, "Let us go to rest"; and when he was passing the door of the chamber, one of the lady's maids, who was sorry for Giannetto, put her mouth to his ear and whispered, "Pretend to drink, but do not drink tonight." Giannetto understood what she said, and having entered the chamber the lady said, "I know you are thirsty, and I want you to drink before you go to bed"; and immediately two damsels who looked like angels, came with wine and sweet-meats in the usual way, and offered him a drink. "Who can refuse to drink when the two damsels are so beautiful?" said Giannetto, whereupon the lady smiled. Giannetto took the cup, and seemed to drink, pouring the wine into his breast, and the lady believed that he had drunken and said to herself, "You must bring another ship, for you have lost this one."

Giannetto went to bed feeling clear-headed and in good spirits, and it seemed a thousand years before the lady came to bed; and he comforted himself by thinking that he had certainly caught her, that he had found a different way of doing things. And so the lady would come to bed sooner, he began to pretend to snore and be asleep. Therefore the lady said, "This will do," and at once undressed and came to bed to Giannetto; he lost no time, but as soon as the lady was in bed he turned towards her, and embraced her and said, "Now I have what I desired so much" and therewith he gave the satisfaction of wedlock, and all night long she lay in his arms; and the lady was highly pleased with him, and rose early in the morning and sent for all the lords and knights, and many other citizens and told them, "Giannetto is your lord, and therefore celebrate." Immediately the news spread through the whole land, the people crying, "Long live our lord! Long live our lord!" and bells and music sounded in joy; and many barons and counts who were not at the castle, were sent for saying, "Come to see your lord"; and so a great and wonderful celebration was started. And when Giannetto came from the chamber he was knighted and placed in the chair of state, and the sceptre was put in his hand and he was proclaimed sovereign with great pomp and glory. And when all the lords and ladies were come to the court, he married the lady with high ceremony and great joy that cannot be told or imagined, for all the nobles and gentlemen of the land came to the feast to be joyful, to joust, combat, dance, sing, and make music, with everything else that belongs to such an occasion.

Giannetto was magnanimous, and began by giving gifts of silk and other rich things which he had brought with him, and grew in manhood and made himself respected by administering justice to all kinds of people: and so he continued in this rejoicing and happiness and never gave a thought to poor Ansaldo who had given his bond to the Jew for ten thousand ducats. Then one day, when Giannetto was at the window of the palace with his wife, he saw a company of men pass through the square bearing burning torches in their hands as if they were going to present an offering. Giannetto asked what this meant. The lady replied, "It is a company of craftsmen going to make their offerings at the church of St John, because it is his feast-day today." Giannetto instantly remembered Ansaldo and having left the window he sighed heavily and turned pale, and walked about the room for a long time, deep in thought. The lady asked him what had happened. Giannetto answered that it was nothing. But she began to question him, saying, "Certainly, something has happened to you and you do not wish to tell me"; and she so pressed him that Giannetto told her how Ansaldo was bound for ten thousand ducats and that the time for repayment was expired this very day, "Wherefore," he said, "I am distressed that my father should die because of me, for if the debt is not repaid today, he must lose a pound of his flesh." "Sir," the lady said, "to horse immediately and journey there by land, it is quicker than by sea, and take what companions you wish and take a hundred thousand ducats, and do not stop until you are in Venice; and if he is living, bring your father here." Thereupon Giannetto at once had trumpets sounded, and mounted with twenty followers and, taking plenty of money, he set out for Venice.

When the limit of the bond was expired, the Jew caused Ansaldo to be seized and insisted on taking a pound of flesh; and Ansaldo besought him to delay his death a few days so that if his Giannetto returned, he could at least see him. The Jew said, "I am willing to grant what you ask about the respite, but if he comes a hundred times, I intend to take the pound of flesh according to the bond." Ansaldo answered that he was content.

The whole of Venice talked of this affair and all were distressed; and many merchants joined together to pay the money, but the

Jew would have none of it, but rather he wished to commit this murder so that he could say that he had killed the greatest of the christian merchants. Now it happened that while Giannetto was pressing forward to Venice, his lady quickly followed him dressed as a lawyer and with two attendants. Arriving in Venice, Giannetto went to the Jew's house and joyfully embraced Ansaldo, and then said to the Jew that he would give him the money and as much more as he cared to demand. The Jew replied that he did not want the money since it was not paid at the appointed time, but that he would take a pound of flesh: and this brought about a great controversy, and everyone blamed the Jew; but since Venice was a place where the law was enforced, and the Jew had his right fully and publicly, no one dared to speak against him, they could only entreat. So all the merchants of Venice came to entreat the Jew, but still he was more determined than ever. Therefore Giannetto offered him twenty thousand and he would not have it; then he advanced his offer to thirty thousand, and then to forty, and then to fifty, and finally to a hundred thousand ducats; then the Jew said, "Understand this: if you were to offer more ducats than this city is worth, it would not satisfy me: I would rather have what my bond says is mine."

And as they were in this debate, the lady, dressed as a lawyer, arrived in Venice, and dismounted at an inn: and the innkeeper asked one of the servants who this gentleman was. The servant had been taught by the lady what he must answer to this question, and he replied, "This gentleman is a lawyer, returning home from his studies at Bologna." The innkeeper, hearing this, treated him respectfully, and the lawyer, when he was seated at table, asked the innkeeper how his city was governed. The host replied, "Sir, the law has become too strict!" "How is that?" said the lawyer. "I will tell you," continued the host: "a young man, called Giannetto, came here from Florence, to a relation called Ansaldo, and he behaved so well and pleasingly that the men and women of this place were devoted to him. Never before had such a pleasing youth come to this city. Now on three occasions this relation of his fitted out three ships for him, all of very great value and each time they met with disaster; and he did not have enough money for the last ship, so Ansaldo borrowed ten thousand ducats from a Jew, on condition that if he had not repaid the debt by St John's day the following June, the said Jew could take a pound of flesh from what part of his body he pleased. Now this fortunate young man has returned and has offered a hundred thousand ducats for the ten thousand, and the base Jew will not take them; and all the good people of this place have come to entreat him, but it is of no use." The lawyer replied, "This controversy is easily settled." "If you will take the trouble to settle it, so that this good man may not die," said the host, "you will win the gratitude and love of the most noble young man who was ever born, and that of every person in this place."

Then the lawyer had it proclaimed everywhere, that every one who had a dispute to settle should come to him: so Giannetto was told that a lawyer was come from Bologna who could decide all disputes. Therefore Giannetto said to the Jew, "Let us go to this lawyer." The Jew agreed but added that come what might, he would have what the bond said was his by right. And when they came before the lawyer and paid him due respect, the lawyer recognized Giannetto, but Giannetto did not know him, because his face was stained with certain herbs. Giannetto and the Jew each told their demand and duly set forth their difference before the judge. He took the bond and read it, and then said to the Jew, "I would have you take these hundred thousand ducats, and set free this good man, who will always be obliged to you." The Jew replied, "I will do no such thing." "It will be better for you," said the lawyer. But the Jew would not consent at all. And they agreed to go to the proper court for such cases and the lawyer spoke for Ansaldo and said, "Let the man be brought forth"; and he was fetched and the lawyer said, "Come now, take a pound of flesh where you will, and do your deed." Then the Jew ordered him to be stripped naked, and took a razor in his hand which he had got for the purpose. Then Giannetto turned to the lawyer, and said, "Sir, this is not what I asked of you." "Be calm," replied the lawyer, "he has not yet cut his pound of flesh." Yet the Jew was about to start. Then the lawyer said, "Take care what you do; for if you take more or less than a pound, I shall have your head struck off. Moreover, I tell you that if one drop of blood is spilt, I shall have you put to death, for your bond does not mention the shedding of blood, but expressly says that you may take a pound of flesh, neither more nor less. And if you are wise, you will take great care what you do." And he sent at once for the executioner, and the block and axe, and said, "As soon as I see one drop of blood spilt, I will have your head struck off." The Jew began to fear, and Giannetto to take heart. And after much argument the Jew said, "Sir, you are wiser than I, so give me the hundred thousand ducats and I am satisfied." The lawyer said, "I will have you take a pound of flesh according to your bond, for I will not give you a farthing; why did you not take the money when I offered it?" The Jew came down to ninety thousand, and then to eighty, but the lawyer remained resolute. Giannetto told the lawyer to give him what he asked so that Ansaldo might be freed, but the lawyer said, "I advise you to leave it to me." Then the Jew said "Give me fifty thousand," and the lawyer replied that he would not give him the smallest coin that he had ever had. The Jew went on, "At least give me my ten thousand ducats, and a curse be on you all." "Do you not understand me?" said the lawyer, "I will give you nothing; if you will take what is yours, do so—if not, I will protest and have your bond annulled."

Everyone present rejoiced greatly at this, and jeered at the Jew, saying, "He who thought to ensnare others, is caught himself." Then the Jew, seeing he could not do what he had wished, took the bond and tore it in pieces in a fury, and so Ansaldo was released and Giannetto took him home in great joy; and straightway he took the hundred thousand ducats and went to the lawyer and found him in his room preparing to depart. Then Giannetto said to him, "Sir, you have done me the greatest service I have ever known, and so I wish you to take this money, since you have well earned it." The lawyer replied, "I thank you, Giannetto, but I have no need of it; keep it, so that your lady may not say that you have squandered it." "By my troth," said Giannetto, "she is so generous, kind, and good, that if I were to spend four times this amount, she would not mind; she wanted me to take away much more than this." The lawyer asked if he was happy with his lady and Giannetto replied, "There is no one in the world I hold as dear; she is so wise and beautiful that Nature could not make a better. If you would do me the favour of coming to visit her, you will be amazed at the honour she will show to you, and you will see whether I speak the truth." "I may not come with you," replied the lawyer, "for I have other things to do; but since you speak so well of her, pay her my respects when you meet." "It shall be done," said Giannetto, "but I wish you would accept some money." While he was speaking, the lawyer noticed a ring on his finger, and said to him, "I would have this ring, I do not want any money." "That will content me," Giannetto replied, "but I give it unwillingly, for my lady gave it to me, telling me to wear it always for her love: and if she sees me without the ring she will think that I have given it to some other woman and so be angry with me and think I love another—and yet I love her better than I love my self." "It seems certain that she loves you well enough to believe what you say;" rejoined the lawyer, "tell her that you have given it to me. But perhaps you wish to give it to some former mistress here in Venice." Giannetto replied, "So great is the love and trust I have for her that I would not exchange her for any woman in the world—she is so perfectly beautiful in every way."

So he drew the ring from his finger and gave it to the lawyer, and they embraced and saluted each other. The lawyer begged a favour and Giannetto agreeing, he said, "Do not linger here, but return at once to your lady." "It will seem a thousand years till I see her," replied Giannetto, and so they took leave of each other.

The lawyer took ship and went his way: and Giannetto gave banquets and gifts of horses and money to his friends, and the celebrations continued several days, and he kept open house; and then taking Ansaldo with him, he took leave of the Venetians, and many of his old friends accompanied him on his way; practically everyone wept for love at his departure, he had given such pleasure to everyone while he had been in Venice; and so he left and returned to Belmonte.

The lady had arrived some days previously and gave out that she had been at the baths, and having resumed her woman's dress she had great preparations made and the streets hung with tapestries, and ordered many companies of armed men to prepare themselves. And when Giannetto and Ansaldo arrived, all the nobles and the whole court went out to meet them, crying, "Long live our lord! long live our lord!" And as they landed, the lady ran to embrace Ansaldo but she pretended to be cross with Giannetto, although she loved him better than she loved her self. Great celebrations were made by all the nobles and ladies who were there, with jousting, combat, dancing, and singing.

When Giannetto saw that his wife did not receive him with her accustomed kindness, he went apart and called her and asked what was the matter, and tried to embrace her. The lady said, "I have no need of these caresses, for I know, well enough, that you have found your former mistresses in Venice." Giannetto began to justify himself, when the lady said, "Where is the ring I gave you?" He answered, "What I expected has happened, for I said you would think badly of me. But I swear to you by the faith I have in God and in you, that I gave the ring to the lawyer who won the suit for me." The lady said, "I swear to you by the faith I have in God and in you, that you gave it to some woman—I know this to be so; are you not ashamed to swear as you have?" "I pray God to strike me dead if I do not speak the truth," Giannetto rejoined, "and if I spoke not to the lawyer as I have told you, when he asked for the ring." The lady said, "You should have stayed in Venice and sent Ansaldo to me, while you enjoyed yourself with your mistresses, for I hear that they all wept when you left." Giannetto burst into tears, and in great sorrow, cried, "You swear that which is not true, and cannot be true." Then the lady seeing his tears, which cut to the heart, ran at once to embrace him, laughing heartily: and she showed him the ring and told him everything—what he had said to the lawyer, how she herself was the lawyer, and in what manner he had given her the ring. Then Giannetto was greatly astonished; and finding it all true, he was full of joy. When he left the chamber he told the story to his nobles and friends, and this adventure increased the love between this pair. Afterwards Giannetto called the damsel who had advised him not to drink the wine that night, and gave her in marriage to Ansaldo; and so they lived in happiness and joy all the days of their life.

APPENDIX II

THE BALLAD OF *GERNUTUS*[1]

A new Song:
Shewing the crueltie of *Gernutus* a Iew, who lending to a Merchant a hundred Crownes, would have a pound of his flesh, because he could not pay him at the day appointed.
To the Tune of *Black and Yellow*.

IN *Venice* Towne not long agoe
   a cruell Iew did dwell,
Which lived all on Usurie,
   as *Italian* writers tell.

Gernutus called was the Iew,
   which never thought to die,
Nor never yet did any good
   to them in streetes that lye.

His life was like a Barrow Hogge,
   that liveth many a day,
Yet never once doth any good,
   untill men will him slay.

Or like a filthy heape of dung,
   that lyeth in a hoord;
Which never can doe any good,
   till it be spred abroad.

So fares it with this Usurer,
   he cannot sleepe in rest,[2]
For feare the theefe doth him pursue,
   to plucke him from his nest.

His heart doth thinke on many a wile,
   how to deceive the poore;
His mouth is almost full of mucke,
   yet still he gapes for more.

1. Reprinted from the Bodleian copy, Wood, 401 (101); it was "Printed at London by *E.P.* for *I. Wright*, / dwelling in Gilt-spur-street." The Pepys copy (from another edition) is reprinted in *The Pepys Ballads*, ed. H. E. Rollins, i (1929), 18–23.

In this and subsequent appendices, footnotes draw attention to incidental parallels in *The Merchant of Venice*. Editorial corrections to the text of these reprints are within square brackets.

2. II. v. 16–18.

His Wife must lend a shilling,
    for every weeke a penny,
Yet bring a Pledge that's double
    worth,
    if that you will have any.

And see (likewise) you keepe your
    day,
    or else you loose it all:
This was the living of his Wife,
    her Cow she doth it call.

Within that Citie dwelt that time
    a Merchant of great fame,
Which being distressed in his need,
    unto *Gernutus* came:

Desiring him to stand his friend,
    for twelve moneth and a day,
To lend to him an hundred Crownes,
    and he for it would pay

Whatsoever he would demand of
    him,
    and Pledges he should have:
No (qd. the Iew with fleering lookes)
    Sir, aske what you will have,

No penny for the loane of it
    for one yeere you shall pay;
You may doe me as good a turne,
    before my dying day.

But we will have a merry ieast,[1]
    for to be talked long:
You shall make me a Bond (quoth
    he)
    that shall be large and strong.

And this shall be the forfeiture,
    of your owne flesh a pound:
If you agree, make you the Bond,
    and here's a hundred Crownes.

The second part of the Iewes crueltie, setting forth the mercifulnesse of the Iudge towards the Merchant. To the same Tune.

*W*Ith right good will, the Merchant
    said,
    and so the Bond was made.
When twelve moneth and a day
    drew on,
    that back it should be payd,

The Merchants ships were all at
    Sea,
    and Money came not in;
Which way to take, or what to doe,
    to thinke he doth begin

And to *Gernutus* straight he comes,
    with cap and bended knee;
And sayd to him of curtesie,
    I pray you beare with mee.

My day is come, and I have not
    the Money for to pay:
And little good the forfeiture
    will doe you, I dare say.[2]

With all my heart, *Gernutus* said,
    command it to your minde;
In things of bigger weight then this,
    you shall me readie finde.

He goes his way: the day once past,
    Gernutus doth not slacke
To get a Serieant presently,
    and clapt him on the backe.

And layd him into Prison strong,
    and sued his Bond withall;
And when the iudgement day was
    come,
    for iudgement he doth call.

The Merchants friends came thither
    fast,
    with many a weeping eye;
For other meanes they could not
    finde,
    but he that day must dye.

1. I. iii. 141.   2. III. i. 45–6.

Some offered for his hundred
    Crownes
  five hundred for to pay;
And some a thousand, two, or
    three,
  yet still he did denay:

And at the last, ten thousand
    Crownes
  they offered him to save.
Gernutus said, I will no Gold,
  my forfeit I will have,

A pound of flesh is my desire,
  and that shall be my hyre.
Then said the Iudge, yet good my
    friend
  let me of you desire,

To take the flesh from such a place,
  as yet you let him live:
Doe so, and loe an hundred
    Crownes
  to thee here will I give.

No, no (quoth he) no iudgement
    here,
  for this it shall be try'de;
For I will have my pound of flesh
  from under his right side.

It grieved all the companie
  his crueltie to see,
For neither friend nor foe could
    helpe,
  but he must spoyled bee.

The bloudie Iew now readie is,
  with whetted blade in hand,[1]
To spoyle the bloud of Innocent,
  by forfeit of his Bond.

And as he was about to strike
  in him the deadly blow:
Stay (quoth the Iudge) thy
    crueltie,
  I charge thee to doe so.

1. IV. i. 121.

Sith needs thou wilt thy forfeit have,
  which is of flesh a pound;
See that thou shed no drop of bloud,
  nor yet the man confound,

For if thou doe, like murtherer,
  thou here shalt hanged bee:
Likewise of flesh see that thou cut
  no more then longs to thee.

For if thou take either more or lesse,
  to the value of a Mite,
Thou shalt be hanged presently,
  as is both Law and right.

Gernutus now waxt frantick mad,
  and wotes not what to say:
Quoth he at last, ten thousand
    Crownes
  I will that he shall pay,

And so I grant to set him free:
  the Iudge doth answere make,
You shall not have a penny given,
  your forfeiture now take.

At the last he doth demand,
  but for to have his owne:
No (quoth the Iudge) doe as you list
  thy Iudgement shall be showne.

Either take your pound of flesh (qd
    he)
  or cancell me your Bond:
O cruell Iudge, then quoth the Iew,
  that doth against me stand.

And so with griped grieved minde
  he biddeth them farewell:
All the people prays'd the Lord,
  that ever this heard tell.

Good people that doe heare this
    Song,
  for truth I dare well say,
That many a wretch as ill as he
  doth live now at this day,

That seeketh nothing but the spoyle of many a wealthie man,	From whom the Lord deliver me, and every Christian too,
And for to trap the innocent, deviseth what they can.	And send to them like sentence eke, that meaneth so to doo.

FINIS

Appendix III

EPITOME OF BOOK III OF ANTHONY MUNDAY, *ZELAUTO* OR *THE FOUNTAIN OF FAME* (1580).[1]

The Amorous lyfe of *Strabino* a *Scholler, the braue behauiour of* Rodolfo a martiall Gentleman,[2] and the right reward of Signor Truculento a Vsurer.

*THe Recordes of aun*cient antiquitie, vnfoldeth in apert, and liuely manner the happy and prosperous estate, of the florishing and famous Cittie *Verona*, whose *Accademies* so woorthily gouerned, and the Schollers so effectually instructed: that it caused Syr *Vincentio* of Pescara, to sende his sonne *Strabino*, there to be trayned vp in such vertuous educations: as was meete for one of his tender time. This *Strabino*, a gallant & lusty youth, of forme well featured, of audacitie expert, in manners well nurtured, but from Martiall affayres wholy enclined, & to looue one seuerely enthraled: fel at length in acquayntaunce with one *Rodolfo*, a Gentlemans sonne of the Cittie, who more vsed the Schole for his pleasure, then any profite, more for a pastime to talke & conferre with his freendes: then for any minde he bare to his booke. And this *Rodolfo* was one that greatly gaue himselfe to Martiall exercises, a disdayner of looue, and a reiecter of the company of Women. Betweene these twayne were ioyned such a league of Amytie: that neyther bitter blastes should procure the breach thereof, nor any accident whatsoeuer, mooue them to mislike one of the other, but euen brotherlyke were vnited, tyll terme of lyfe were vtterly expired. *Strabino* vsually frequenting the house of his freend and brother *Rodolfo*, who had a Sister in all

1. Reprinted from the Bodleian copy, Douce MM474. Narrative links between the passages reprinted from the novel are within square brackets.
2. I. ii. 109.

poynts so well proportioned: that the lookes of her Amorous countenaunce, infected in the heart of *Strabino*, such a restlesse rage, a
torting torment, a Feuer so fantasticall: that none but only shee
must be the curer thereof. Now are his bookes reiected, and his
fancie followed: his study banished, & the Gentlewoman dutifully
serued Who (alas) although he were her superior: of her was re-
garded, as her farre inferior. He lykes, he looues, he sues, he serues,
he runnes, he waytes: she lowres, she frownes, she disdaynes, and
vtterly reiecteth his company. Which when he sawe, that his proffered paynes were esteemed as trifles, his continuall courtesie, re-
garded as lyght as a feather, and his affectioned seruice, cleane cast
out of memorie: walked into the feeldes, . . . [and there he dis-
coursed with himself, bewailing his ill fortune but saying:] She is
the Saint whome I serue, she is the Goddesse whome I adore, . . . [1]
[At last he determined to make his suit to her, and he found her,]
sitting at her Sampler in the garden: [and taking fresh heart he sat
down by her. He complained of the ill-usage men received from
women:] In fayth, then fare well frost, more such haue we lost. . . .
A colde sute, and a harde penniwoorth haue all they that traffique
for such merchandize. [2]

[He continued in such terms until Cornelia, the lady, guessed
that he was crossed in love, and offered her counsel and help. Their
conversation proceded courteously, and with Cornelia's encouragement Strabino at length confessed his love. She did not answer
directly and he resumed:] Why Lady (quoth he) doo you mis-
doubt of my bountifull behauiour? or y^t I am such a one as regar-
deth not my honesty? Thinke you if I would make my choyse, I
could not haue as good as you, or if my minde had beene so
adicted, ere this I could not haue beene sped? thinke you all
Women are of your minde? or that they will dislyke vpon no occasion? No credit me, *Cornelia* (I speake *Bona fide*) if my stomacke had
serued: I could haue beene soone suffised, and if all Women were of
your minde: I should haue but a colde sute with my wooing. [3] But
belyke you are betrothed already: and that makes you so dayntie,
if you be tell me, that I may loose no more labour. [4] [She assured him
that she was not betrothed, and shortly made excuse to enter the
house and break off the conversation.

Strabino returned to his chamber and gave himself up to melancholy and love-sickness. Rodolfo, his friend, was unable to comfort
him and as soon as he was alone he wrote a letter to "his sweete
Saint". Rodolfo soon rejoined him and the two set out together for

1. i. i. 120, ii. vii. 40, etc.   2. ii. vii. 73–5, and i. ii. 68.
3. ii. vii. 73.   4. ii. vii. 74.

Ruscelli's house, that is, to the house of the father of Cornelia and Rodolfo.

The narrative here breaks off, to tell of old Signor Truculento, "an extorting Vsurer", who] smoutched vp him selfe in his Fustian slyppers, and put on his holy day hose, to come a wooing to Mistresse *Cornelia*. The olde horson would needes be lusty, and to cheerishe vp his churlishe carkase, would get him a wanton Wife.[1] And though I say it, he was as well made a man, and as curious in his quallities: as euer an olde Horse in this towne, when he is gnabling on a thystle. This carpet Knight, hauing pounced himselfe vp in his perfumes, and walking so nice on the ground, that he would scant bruse an Onion: comes to the house of *Signor Ciorolamo Ruscelli*, bringing with him a verie costly Cuppe, wherein was about fiue hundred Crownes. When he was come into the presence of the Gentleman, he sayd Syr, as one right glad to heare of your health, and willing besides to woorke your well fare: I am come to see how it fareth with you; because that long tyme I haue beene desirous. First Syr, this Cuppe I freely giue you, and these fiue hundred Crownes, I frankly bestowe on you, besides if you pleasure me in my reasonable request: you shall finde me your freend in more then I wyll speake of.

The Gentleman amazed at *Truculentos* lyberalytie, who before would scant bestowe on him selfe a good meales meate for expence of money:[2] made him this aunswere. I can not chuse Syr, but consider well of your courtesie, and lykewise esteeme of your bountifull beneuolence, vndeserued of my part to be so rytchly rewarded: considering my countenaunce to you hath beene small. And if your request be so reasonable as you seeme to affyrme, & that it lyeth in me to bring the same to effect: doubt not that I will make you any denyall, since you haue gratified me with so great a gyft. [With this Truculento made suit for the hand of Cornelia and Ruscelli,] hauing well lystened this newe come wooers tale, and seeing at what marke he leueld his looue, he beeing one him selfe that preferred money before manly modestie, coyne before courteous ciuillitie, and rytches before any vertuous action, besides, ouercome with the costlynesse of the Cuppe, out of measure contented with the fiue hundred Crownes: Furthermore he thought, if he matched his daughter with him: she would soone send him to Church, and then should she swym in her golden bagges: was verie lothe to send away such a sweete Suter, thinking it rare to haue a rytcher: wherefore to *Truculento* [he made kind answer.

Cornelia was brought before them and her father told her of

1. III. i. 32.   2. II. ii. 101-2.

Truculento's suit. . . .] *Cornelia* somewhat mooued at this made matter, and nothing contented with her Fathers choyse, all her senses distracted with this sodayne motion: yet tooke corrage to aunswere the matter in this sort. Deere Father, it is the duty of the Chylde to be obedient to her Parentes preceptes: and it is the Fathers fame to haue his Chylde vertuously nurtured, I confesse it is my part to obay your graue aduise: and it ought to be your care to see me meetely matched. If then your care be no better bestowed: my dutie must be as much neglected, though your will be to see me carelesly cast away, if it lye in me, I am to preuent it. . . . Wyll you for money marrie me to a myser? Wyll you for wealth wedde me to a Wyttoll? And wyll you for rytches so lyttle regard me? Shall I for a lyttle vaine glorie[,] forsake vertue? Shall I for paltrie pride run headlong to hell? Shall I for mortall muck, forsake immortality?

[Ruscelli tried to reassure Truculento but he soon left the house which Rodolfo and Strabino even then were approaching. On the way, Strabino had told his friend that it was his sister whom he loved and Rodolfo had promised all possible help. They found Cornelia in the garden, "sad and sorowfull"; she told them what had passed and of her resolve never to marry the old miser. Strabino then presented his letter and when she had read it and considered his constancy, Cornelia pledged herself to him, and sealed their love with a kiss.

Then Cornelia propounded a plan to "deceyue" her father. If they acted in this way, she said:] my Father shall glue his consent: and the olde worldly wretch [be] serued in his right kinde. First, Brother you shall goe with *Strabino* to *Truculentos* house, and there on your credite, take vp a great summe of money, as much as you shall thinke good, then go you into *La strada di San Paolo*, and buy the Jewell which my Father hath long had such great affection to, the which will so win him: that I dare warrant none but you shall haue me to his Wife. For the payment therof you shall not neede greatly to accoumpt: for that you shall referre vnto me, but this way I thinke you shall soonest speede, and this way I warrant you shall gayne no nay.

[This was agreed upon and when the two friends came to Truculento's house they found him] sitting at his doore verie soly-tarie: *Rodolfo* in the freendlyest fashion saluteth him, and flattering the foole, thus frameth his tale. Woorthy Syr, if I say otherwayes then beseemes me: I hope you wyll beare with me, and if I speake as affection serues me: I doubt not but you wyll deeme all at the best: [with such a preamble, he assured the miser that he was "the only man must matche" with his sister. Truculento was highly pleased and offered his service to Rodolfo, who with further flattery asked for a loan of four thousand ducats on behalf of his friend, for one month only; if the debt is not paid by that time, the miser was assured,] he is willing to forfayte his patrimony, and besydes the best lym of his body.

Freend *Rodolfo* (quoth *Truculento*) the world is so wretched now a dayes, & diuers of ye people so pinched by pouerty: that many will borrow, but slack payment is made, then if we exact the Law to the vttermost: we are accoumpted couetous carles, worldly wretches, and such like, which makes me so lothe to lende: for I care not for dealing in ye trade any more. What pleasure were it to me to maime or mangle this Gentleman for mine owne: truly I had rather if I could well spare so much, to giue it him outright, so should I sustayne no reproch my selfe: nor he be endamaged in ye distresse of the law. Yet for your sake, I care not if I lende him so much: so that you wyll stande bound vnto mee, as straytlie as hee shall.

Syr (quoth *Rodolfo*) for the credit of the Gentleman, I dare wage all that I am woorth, ... Well (quoth *Truculento*) this is the bonde, if by the first day of the month ensuing, the whole sum be not restored: eache of your Lands shall stand to the endamagement, besides the losse of bothe your right eyes, are you content to stand to this bargayne? Yea (quoth they bothe) and that right wyllingly.

With that he departed to fetche the money, then quoth *Strabino* to his freende. Dyd euer man see a more extorting villayne then this? Is not our Landes sufficient to glut vp his greedinesse? But that each of our eyes must stand to the hazard? Oh myserable myser, oh egregrious cormorant, surely the iust iudgement of God, wyll reward him for his wickednesse. Well, cease (quoth *Rodolfo*) no more woordes, *Lupus est in fabula*, little sayd is soone amended. [And so the bargain was made, and they received the four thousand ducats, together with a gift of forty ducats for Cornelia.

The following morning the two friends met to buy the jewel and present it to Ruscelli. During the night Rodolfo had had a "dream", or so he called it, and as they took] theyr way downe by *Signor Truculentos* doore, where he sawe the Saint sitting which all night was in his vision, no further could he goe he was so faynt, but stoode leaning on the brest of his freend *Strabino*, at last he burst foorth in these woordes, saying.

O my *Strabino*, but that you are my freend, and one whom I doo highly make accoumpt of: I should doubt to discouer the cause of my dollor, ... [and with that, he acknowledged that he was in love. For fear of being suspected, they walked away, and then Strabino rallied his friend, and told him,] I knowe it is *Truculentos* Daughter whome you desire, and she it is must cease your sorrowes: let vs first ende the matter we haue in hande, and then you shall see how I wyll compasse this geere. [So they purchased the jewel and presented it to Ruscelli, receiving in return his assurance;] demaund of me what you shall deeme expedient, and I vow to the vttermost to graunt your request. [Strabino then asked for Cornelia as his wife, and when Ruscelli demurred, he held him to his bargain assuring him that] the patrimony my Parentes dooth allowe me, is more then the dowrie you wyll make to her mariage. Againe, if my lyberalitie, of you be dyslyked, and the niggardly sparing of a worldly wretch[, such as Truculento,] so much commended: I perceyue you preferre rytches before a noble minde, and accoumpt more of vanitie, then you doo of vertue. . . . neuer disprayse lyberalitie, which is the cheefe ornament of a noble minde: but hate that worldly pleasure, enemie to all vertuous actions. I content my selfe to stand to her gentle iudgement, if she doo not regard me: I am content you shall refuse me, and if she lyke me not: I will let her alone. [Ruscelli agreed to this and when Cornelia had chosen Strabino for husband, he was forced to pronounce them man and wife and allow them to fix an early date for the nuptials.

Shortly after, Rodolfo and Strabino went to Truculento's house,] and who should open the doore but *Brisana* his Daughter, the Mistresse of *Rodolfo*, whome he saluted in very freendly sort. But euen so willing as he was to haue her to his Wife: she was as desirous to haue him to her Husbande. Heere was hote looue on bothe sides, and each of them so farre in: that it was vnpossible for eyther to gette out. *Rodolfo*, he in secrete telles *Truculento* such a flattering tale in his eare, howe his Sister had calmed her courage, and was content to stand to her Fathers appointment: that the day after the debt was discharged the mariage should be made, so he for ioy of these newcome tydinges: ioyneth them bothe hand in hand, to marie when they will, & God giue them much ioy. Heere were mariages soone made, and Wiues soone wonne, . . . Nowe is *Rodolfo* returned reioysing, and *Strabino* right glad of his good succcesse, *Truculento* presently hyes him to horsebacke, to goe wyll all his freendes, to meete at his mariage.

When *Signor Ruscelli* knew how his sonne had spedde, and by so fine a drift had deceyued *Truculento*: the next morning marieth his sonne, and *Truculentos* Daughter together, and *Cornelia* and *Strabino* in the selfe same sort. [But when Truculento] is returned from bydding his Guestes, and hath heard of the hap which chaunced in his absence, he comes as one bereft of his wyttes, or as a man feared out of his fiue sences [, and complained to Ruscelli, and swore revenge. But Ruscelli was unconcerned, saying:] If you set not a poynt by vs: we care not a pyn for you, if we may haue your good will so it is: if not, keepe your winde to coole your Pottage.

This aunswere made *Truculento* more mad then he meant to be, and he flung foorth of doores in such a fume: as though all the Towne would not haue helde him.

On the morrow, he caused *Strabino* and *Rodolfo* to be summoned to appeere before the Iudge, for the payment of the money, which when *Cornelia* and *Brisana* perceyued: they willed their Husbandes in nothing to doubt, for that by their industrie they should be discharged. *Cornelia* apparelleth her selfe all in blacke like a Scholler, and *Brisana* attyreth her selfe in the same sorte. After dinner they appeered before the Iudge, where *Truculento* appealed against them in this order ...

*M*Ost magnificent Iudge, tyme was (quoth *Truculento*) when firme affection, and pure zeale of freendshippe, mooued me to minde the destitute estate of these two Gentlemen, when as either they had not money to their contentment: or wanted such necessaries, as then was to them needefull. At which tyme (as the Lambe endaungered by the rauenous Woolfe, flyeth for sauegard to his folde, [1] or as the Ship abiding the hazard of Fortune, and fearing the emminent daunger, posteth to some Porte, or hasteth to some Hauen in hope of succour): Euen so these twayne repayred to me, who beeing sufficiently stored of that which they wanted, and besides, willing to pleasure them, to their greater profite: committed to their custody, a certayne summe of money, which amounteth vnto fowre thousand Crownes. Nowe theyr necessite indifferently satisfied, and they beeing bound to delyuer the summe at a certayne daye: they haue broken theyr promise, which is open periurie, and falsyfied theyr faythes, in not restoring the money. Wherefore, that all Gentlemen may be warned by such wylfull offenders, and that God may be glorified in putting them to punishment: I haue thus determined how the debt shall be discharged. The rendring of the money I doo not accoumpt of, ne wyll I be pleased with twise as much restored: the breach of the Lawe I meane to exact, and to vse rygor, where it is so required.

The forfayture of theyr Landes, is the one part of the penaltie, the losse of theyr right eyes the whole ingenerall, now remembring the wofull estate of theyr solitarie wiues, how in depriuing theyr substaunce, they might be pinched by penurie: I let theyr Landes remayne vnto them in full possession, whereon heereafter they may liue more honestly I clayme theyr right eyes for falsifying theyr

faith: to mooue others regard howe they make lyke rechlesse promises. So shall Iustice be ministred without partialytie, they rightly
serued for infringing theyr fidelity: and my selfe not thought to
deale with crueltie.

Thus haue you heard the cause of my comming: now giue iudgement as your wisedome shall thinke most expedient. My freends
(quoth the Iudge) heere is no place to deale with partialitie, heere
is no roome where falsehood should be frequented, nor time in this
place to deferre in trifling affayres: but heere is simply Iustice to be
aduaunced, wrong righ[t]ly reuenged, and mercie mildly main-
tayned. Wherfore, ere I beginne to deale in this diuersitie, or that I
seeme to contend about this controuersie: I exhort you each one to
exempt double dealing, to flye forged fraude, & to minister nothing
malitiously, but on each cause to way the matter aduisedly. Consider you come to deale in matters of conscience, matters of your
owne mayntenaunce, and such thinges whereon your credite consisteth, now you are not for freendshippe to further falsehood, ne
yet for malice to touch an vntrueth, but euen to deale so directly,
to frame your matters so faithfully, and to vse your selues heere so
vprightly: that not so much as a motion be made of any misorder.
But euery one to aunswere as occasion is offered, so helpe you God
and the contentes of this booke, wherat they all kissed the booke.
And then the Iudge called *Strabino*, to shewe in what sort, and after
what order the money was borrowed, and what promise there was
betweene them.

Most mightie Iudge (quoth *Strabino*) trueth neuer defameth his
Maister, right repelleth all proffered wrong, and vpright dealing
disdayneth all forged fraude, wherefore, neyther fearing the force
of his reuenging rigor, nor yet dismaying at ought that is doone:
I will tell my tale, reporting nothing but trueth, and clayming no
other courtesie then my desertes shall deserue.

Trueth is, my Father fayling to send me such money, as serued to
the mayntenaunce of my studious exercise, and besides, wanting
wherewith to deale in waighty affayres: my freend & I came vnto
this Caterpyller, (so rightly may I call him, neyther defacing his
lycentious lyuing, condempning his practised science, and cunning
handy craft, nor yet inuaying against any of his honest behauiour:
but commending his cut throate[1] conditions, in pinching the poore,
to fyl vp his own poutch.) Beeing come to this aforesayd woorme of
the world, (who eateth so many to the bare bones, out of Lands and
lyuing, to glut his greedy desire) we desired a certayne summe of
money, which is no lesse then him selfe hath confessed, for a

1. 1. iii. 106.

monthes space, and then to restore the same to the vnrightfull owner, who binding vs straytly in the losse of our Landes, and of each our right eyes: lent vs this aforesayd sum. Now in deede, we not minding the so short restoring of his due debt, for that necessary occasions was partly our hinderaunce: haue indamaged our selues in two dayes more, then the limmited time did amount vnto, for which time we will allow him to the vttermost he can aske, & his money to haue when him pleaseth. Now if your wisdome dooth not thinke we deale with him honestly and well: we will stand to what effect it shall like you to bring it.

My freend (quoth the Iudge) your reply is reasonable, you confesse your selfe indebted in that which he hath demaunded, and yeeld that you haue broken the band, wylling to make an amends, insomuch that you will satisfie the vttermost, which he may seeme to sue for: I can not chuse but accoumpt your woordes of good credite, in that your dealing dooth demonstrate no other. Now *Truculento*, you see the Gentleman graunteth him selfe guilty, since his earnest affayres dyd hinder the repayment of your debt to you due, now he hath the whole ready to restore, and beside, ouer & aboue this sum: will content you to the vttermost it shall please you to request. In my opinion you can reasonably require no more, if you doo: you shall but seeme to shame your selfe.

Syr (quoth *Truculento*) he that before my face will vse such terrible tauntes, behinde my backe, would gladly brew my bane, he that in my presence will so spightfully reprooue me: in my absence would hang me if it were in his possibilitie. Dooth he demerit fauour: that so frowneth on his freend? Can he clayme any courtesie: that abuseth him selfe so disorderly? Or can he once pleade for pittie: that standeth in so great a presumption? Or you my Lord, desire me deale gently: with one who respecteth not gentillitie? No, the money is none of mine, ne will I haue it, his Landes I respect not, ne care I for them, and now his submission I way not, ne will I accept of it. You my Lord shall rather reape reproche by pleading on his part: then gayne any credite in maintayning so carelesse a creature. I driue my whole action to this issue, I plead my priuiledge vnto this poynt, & to this clause I am seuerely bent: I will haue the due which breach of promise dooth deserue, I will exempt all courtesie: and accoumpt of cruelty, I wyll be pleased with no ritch reward whatsoeuer, no pitty shall preuayle, rigor shall rule, and on them bothe I will haue Lawe to the vttermost.

Why *Truculento* (quoth the Iudge) respect you cruelty: more then Christian ciuillitie, regard you rigor more then reason. Should the God aboue all Gods, the Iudge aboue all Iudges, administer desert, which your sinnes hath deserued? If his fatherly affection, if his mercifull myldnesse, if his righteous regard, dyd not consider the frayltie of your fleshe, your promptnes vnto peryll, and your apt-nes vnto euyll: how mightie were the myserie, which should iustly fall vpon you? Howe sharpe the sentence that should be pronounc-ed against you, and howe rigorous the reuenge, which should right-ly reward you?[1] Is this the looue you beare to your brother? Is this the care you haue of a Christian? The Turke, whose tyranny is not to be talked of: could but exact to the vttermost of his crueltie.[2] And you a braunche of that blessed body, which bare the burden of our manifolde sinnes: howe can you seeme to deale so sharply with your selfe? seeing you should vse to all men: as you would be dealt with-all. Yet to let you haue the lybertie of your demaund in Lawe, and you to stand to the Iustice which heere I shall pronounce, let first your right eye be put foorth in theyr presence: and then shall they bothe abide lyke punishment.

For since neyther the restoring of your debt wyll suffice you, nor yet the lyberall amendes they are content to make you: I deeme it expedient you should be pertaker of theyr paynes, so shall you knowe if you demaund a reasonable request. Howe say you, will you stand to the verdict pronounced: or take the rewarde which they haue promised.

My Lord (quoth *Truculento*) neyther doo I deserue to abide any such doome, nor they woorthy to be fauoured with any such freend-shippe, I may lawfully alleadge that you permit partiality: & that you deuide not each cause indifferently, for to what ende should you seeme to satisfie me with their woordes: when your selfe per-ceyues how they are found faultie? And what vrgeth you to vse such gentle perswasions: when you see your selfe they deserue no such dealing? If I had wylfully offended in any such cause, and wytting-ly broken in such sort my bonde: I would be contented you should deliuer me my deserts, so that you dyd minister nothing but Iustice.[3] And wherefore should you seeme to demaund the losse of my eye who haue not offended: for sauegarde of their eyes that haue so trecherously trespassed? I am sure I go not beyond the breache of my bande, nor I desire no more then they haue deserued. Where-fore obiect no more matters, whereby to delude me, nor impute no occasions to hinder my pretence, I craue Iustice to be vprightly vsed, and I craue no more, herefore I will haue it.[4]

Indeede my freends (quoth ye Iudge) who seeketh the extremitie, & vrgeth so much as his wilfull minde dooth commaund him: his commission is very large, & his request not to be refused. Wherfore, since neither pittie can preuaile, nor freendly counsayle perswade: you must render the raunsome that he dooth require, for we cannot debarre him in these his dealings, nor we can not chuse but giue our consentes. Therfore if you haue any that will pleade your case in Law: let them speake & they shall be heard, to further your safety as much as we may.

My Lord (quoth *Rodolfo*) theyr courtesie is ouermuch that will kneele to a Thystle, and theyr beneuolence bountifull that will bowe to a Bramble: Euen so we are farre foolishe to craue courtesie of such a cut throate,[1] and more wytlesse then wyse to meddle with such a worldly wretch. If there be no remedy: we knowe the vtter-most of our paynes, yet we craue that these our Attorneyes, may haue such lybertie as Lawe will permit.

With that *Truculento* fared like a fiend, and curssed and banned like a Diuell of hell, (quoth he) my Lord, you deale with me dis-courteously: when the Lawe is come to the passe to let them haue theyr Attorneyes.

Syr (quoth the Iudge) you haue vsed all this whyle your Attorneyes aduise, and they haue aunswered simply of them selues, now since you the Plaintife haue had this prerogatiue: it is reason the Defendaunts should demaund their due. It may be that their Attorneyes may put you to such a plundge: that you shall haue small occasion to bragge of your bargayne: wherefore let them speake.

Then *Brisana* (*Truculentos* Daughter) began in this order to pleade for her auayle. Admit my Lord (quoth she) that I come to such a person as this partie, to borrow ye lyke sum of money, binding me in ye selfe same band, to restore the money to the same party of whome I had it. Well, the time expyred, I come to deliuer the due to the owner, he being not at home, nor in the Citty, but ridden foorth, and vncertaine of his comming: I returne home to my house, and he him selfe comes out of the Countrey as yesterday. Now he vpon some seuerall spight or malicious intent: sueth me in the Lawe, not demaunding his due, nor I knowing of his ariuall. Am I to be condempned for breaking the Lawe: when the partie him selfe hath deferred the day?

How lyke you this geere *Truculento*? you haue now an other Pigeon to pull, and heere is one wiser then you were beware. Can you condempne this partie, not demaunding you due, nor beeing at home when it might haue beene discharged? And making the bande to be restored to your selfe?

My Lord (quoth *Truculento*) though I was not at home: my house
1. 1. iii. 106.

was not emptie, and though I was away, if it had beene restored: it stoode in as good effect as if it had beene payd to me. Wherefore it is but follie to frame such an allegation: for my Receyuer in my absence dooth represent my selfe.

Well (quoth *Brisana*) admit your seruaunt in your absence, standeth in as full effect as your selfe, and admit the debt had beene discharged to him, if wylfulnesse had allured your seruaunt to wandering, and that he had departed with the debt he receyued: you returne and finde it styll in your booke, neither marked nor crossed, as if payment had not beene made, you wyll let your seruaunt slyp with his offence: but you wyll demaund the debt agayne of me.

Tush (quoth *Truculento*) this is but a tryfle, and your woordes are now to be esteemed as winde, you should haue restored the summe to my seruaunt: and I would not haue troubled you in any such sort, for there is no man that vseth such follie: but he will see the booke crossed before he depart. Therefore you doo but trouble tyme with mentioning such matters: for your redemption is neuer the neere.

Well then Syr (quoth she) you will thus much allow, that at the deliuery: the bande should be restored, and if I had delyuered the money to your seruaunt: I should haue respected my bande tyll yesterday, for your seruaunt had it not to delyuer: and I would not pay it before I had my bande. Ah *Signor Truculento* (quoth the Iudge) he toucheth you to ye quick now, how can you reply to this his demaund? In deede I confesse (quoth he) my Cubborde kept the bande tyll I returned, but yet noting the receyt in the booke, would haue beene sufficient tyll my comming home.

With that *Cornelia* stepped vp, saying, Since (*Signor Truculento*) you will neyther allowe the reasonable aunsweres he hath made, nor be content to abide my Lord the Iudges verdict: receyue the raunsome you so much require, and take both their eyes, so shall the matter be ended. But thus much (vnder verdict of my Lord his lycence) I giue you in charge, and also especially notifie, that no man but your selfe shall execute the deede, ne shall you craue any counsayle of any the standers by. If in pulling foorth their eyes, you diminshe the least quantitie of blood out of their heads, ouer and besides their only eyes, or spyll one drop in taking them out: before you styrre your foote, you shall stand to the losse of bothe your owne eyes. For that the bande maketh mention of nothing but their eyes, and so if you take more then you should, and lesse then you ought: you shall abide the punishment heere in place pronounced. Nowe take when you will, but beware of the bargayne.

Truly (quoth the Iudge) this matter hath beene excellently handled, it is no reason if you haue your bargayne: that you should hinder them with the losse of one droppe of blood, wherefore I pronounce no other Iudgement, shall at this tyme be ministred.

Now was *Truculento* more mad that he could not haue his hearts desire, for that he knewe he must needes spyll some blood, it could not be otherwyse chosen, wherefore he desired he might haue his money, and so let all other matters alone. Nay (quoth yᵉ Iudge) since you would not accept of it when it was offered, nor would be contented with so large a promise: the money shall serue to make them amendes, for the great wrong which you would haue offered. Thus in my opinion is Iudgement equally vsed, and neyther partie I hope will be miscontented.

Truculento seeing there was no remedy, and that all the people praysed the Iudgement so woorthily: accepted *Rodolfo* for his lawfull sonne, and put him in possession of all his lyuinges after his disease.[1] Thus were they on all partes verie well pleased, and euerie one accoumpted him selfe well contented.

Appendix IV

DECLAMATION 95 OF *THE ORATOR* (1596),
"WRITTEN IN FRENCH BY ALEXANDER SILVAYN, AND ENGLISHED BY L. P[IOT]."[2]

Of a Jew, who would for his debt haue a pound of the flesh of a Christian.

A *Iew vnto whom a Christian Marchant ought nine hundred crownes, would haue summoned him for the same in Turckie: the Merchant because he would not be discredited, promised to pay the said summe within the tearme of three months, and if he paied it not, he was bound to giue him a pound of the flesh of his bodie. The tearme being past some fifteene daies, the Iew refused to take his money, and demaunded the pound of flesh: the ordinarie Iudge of that place appointed him to cut a iust pound of the Christians flesh, and if he cut either more or lesse, then his owne head should be smitten off: the Iew appealed from this sentence, vnto the chiefe iudge, saying:*
IMpossible is it to breake the credite of trafficke amongst men

1. IV. i. 384–6.   2. Reprinted from the British Museum copy.

without great detriment vnto the Commonwealth:[1] wherfore no man ought to bind himselfe vnto such couenants which hee cannot or wil not accomplish, for by that means should no man feare to be deceaued, and credit being maintained, euery man might be assured of his owne; but since deceit hath taken place, neuer wonder if obligations are made more rigorous & strict then they were wont, seeing that although the bonds are made neuer so strong, yet can no man be very certaine that he shal not be a loser. It seemeth at the first sight, that it is a thing no lesse strange then cruel, to bind a man to pay a pound of the flesh of his bodie, for want of money: Surely, in that it is a thing not vsuall, it appeareth to be somewhat the more admirable, but there are diuers others that are more cruell, which because they are in vse seeme nothing terrible at all: as to bind al the bodie vnto a most lothsome prison, or vnto an intollerable slauerie,[2] where not only the whole bodie but also al the sences and spirits are tormented, the which is commonly practised, not only betwixt those which are either in sect or Nation contrary, but also euen amongst those that are all of one sect and nation, yea amongst neighbours and kindred, & euen amongst Christians it hath ben seene, that the son hath imprisoned the father for monie. Likewise, in the Roman Commonwealth, so famous for laws and armes, it was lawfull for debt, to imprison, beat, and afflict with torments the free Cittizens: How manie of them (do you thinke) would haue thought themselues happie, if for a small debt they might haue ben excused with the paiment of a pound of their flesh? Who ought then to maruile if a Iew requireth so small a thing of a Christian, to discharge him of a good round summe? A man may aske why I would not rather take siluer of this man, then his flesh:[3] I might alleage many reasons, for I might say that none but my selfe can tell what the breach of his promise hath cost me, and what I haue thereby paied for want of money vnto my creditors, of that which I haue lost in my credit: for the miserie o[f] those men which esteeme their reputation, is so great, that oftentimes they had rather indure any thing secretlie then to haue their discredit blazed abroad, because they would not be both shamed and harmed. Neuerthelesse, I doe freely confesse, that I had rather lose a pound of my flesh, then my credit should be in any sort cracked: I might also say that I haue need of this flesh to cure a friend of mine of a certaine maladie, which is otherwise incurable, or that I would haue it to terrifie thereby the Christians for euer abusing the Iewes anie more hereafter: but I will onelie say, that by his obligation he

1. III. ii. 277–8, III. iii. 27–31, and IV. i. 38–9.   2. IV. i. 90–8.
3. IV. i. 40–2.

oweth it me. It is lawfull to kill a souldior if he come vnto the warres
but an houre too late, and also to hang a theefe though he steale
neuer so little: is it then such a great matter to cause such a one to
pay a pound of his flesh, that hath broken his promise manie times,
or that putteth another in danger to lose both credit & reputation,
yea and it may be life and al for greife? were it not better for him to
lose that which I demand, then his soule, alreadie bound by his
faith? Neither am I to take that which he oweth me, but he is to
deliuer it me: And especiallie because no man knoweth better then
he where the same may be spared to the least hurt of his person, for
I might take it in such a place as hee might thereby happen to lose
his life: what a matter were it then, if I should cut of his priuie
members, supposing that the same would altogether weigh a iust
pound? Or els his head, should I be suffered to cut it off, although
it were with the danger of mine owne life? I beleeue I should not;
because there were as little reason therein, as there could be in the
amends wherevnto I should be bound: or els if I would cut off his
nose, his lips, his eares, and pull out his eies, to make of them altogether a pound, should I be suffered? Surely I thinke not, because
the obligation dooth not specifie that I ought either to chuse, cut,
or take the same, but that he ought to giue me a pound of his flesh.
Of euery thing that is sold, he which deliuereth the same is to make
waight, and he which receiueth, taketh heed that it be iust: seeing
then that neither the obligation, custome, nor law doth bind me to
cut, or weigh, much lesse vnto the aboue mentioned satisfaction, I
refuse it all, and require that the same which is due should bee
deliuered vnto me.

The Christians Answere.

IT is no strange matter to here those dispute of equitie which are
themselues most vniust; and such as haue no faith at all, desirous
that others should obserue the same inuiolable, the which were yet
the more tollerable, if such men would bee contented with reasonable things, or at the least not altogether vnreasonable: but what
reason is there that one man should vnto his own preiudice desire
the hurt of another? as this Iew is content to lose nine hundred
crownes to haue a pound of my flesh, whereby is manifestly seene
the antient and cruell hate which he beareth not only vnto Christians, but vnto all others which are not of his sect: yea, euen vnto
the Turkes, who ouerkindly doe suffer such vermine to dwell
amongst them, seeing that this presumptuous wretch dare not
onely doubt, but appeale from the iudgement of a good and iust
Iudge, & afterwards he would by sophisticall reasons prooue that

his abhomination is equitie: trulie I confesse that I haue suffered
fifteene daies of the tearme to passe, yet who can tell whether he or
I is the cause thereof, as for me I thinke thàt by secret meanes he
hath caused the money to bee delaied, which from sundry places
ought to haue come vnto me before the tearm which I promised
vnto him; Otherwise, I would neuer haue been so rash as to bind
my selfe so strictly: but although he were not the cause of the fault,
is it therefore said, that he ought to bee so impudent as to goe about
to prooue it no strange matter that he should be willing to be paied
with mans flesh, which is a thing more natural for Tigres, then
men, [1] the which also was neuer heard of: but this diuell in shape of
a man, seeing me oppressed with necessitie propounded this accursed obligation vnto me. Whereas hee alleageth the Romanes for an
example, why doth he not as well tell on how for that crueltie in
afflicting debtors ouer greeuously, the Commonwealth was almost
ouerthrowne, and that shortly after it was forbidden to imprison
men any more for debt. To breake promise is, when a man sweareth
or promiseth a thing, the which he hath no desire to performe,
which yet vpon an extreame necessitie is somewhat excusable; as
for me, I haue promised, and accomplished my promise, yet not so
soone as I would; and although I knew the danger wherein I was to
satisfie the crueltie of this mischeeuous man with the price of my
flesh and blood, yet did I not flie away, but submitted my selfe vnto
the discretion of the Iudge who hath iustly repressed his beastli-
nesse. Wherein then haue I falsefied my promise, is it in that I
would not, (like him) disobey the iudgement of the Iudge? Behold
I will present a part of my bodie vnto him, that he may pay himselfe, according to the contents of the iudgement, where is then my
promise broken? But it is no maruaile if this race be so obstinat
and cruell against vs, for they doe it of set purpose to offend our
God whom they haue crucified: and wherefore? Because he was
holie, as he is yet so reputed of this worthy Turkish nation: but
what shal I say? Their own bible is full of their rebellion against
God, against their Priests, Iudges, & leaders. What did not the
verie Patriarks themselues, from whom they haue their beginning?
They sold their brother, and had it not been for one amongst them,
they had slaine him euen for verie enuie. How manie adulteries and
abhominations were committed amonst them? How manie mur-
thers? *Absalon* did not he cause his brother to be murthered? Did
he not persecute his father? Is it not for their iniquitie that God hath
dispersed them, without leauing them one onlie foot of ground?
If then, when they had newlie receiued their law from God, when

1. III. ii. 273-5.

they saw his wonderous works with their eies, and had yet their Iudges amongst them, they were so wicked, What may one hope of them now, when they haue neither faith nor law, but their rapines and vsuries? And that they beleeue they do a charitable work, when they do some great wrong vnto anie that is not a Iew? It may please you then most righteous Iudge to consider all these circumstances, hauing pittie of him who doth wholy submit himselfe vnto your iust clemencie: hoping thereby to be deliuered from this monsters crueltie.

Appendix V

EXTRACTS FROM HISTORY 32 OF *GESTA ROMANORUM*, TRANSLATED AND "NOW NEWLY PERVSED AND CORRECTED BY R. ROBINSON" (1595).[1]

[To secure peace with the Emperor of Rome, the King of Ampluy sent his only daughter to marry the Emperor's only son. The ship in which she travelled was shipwrecked and she was swallowed by a whale which, being wounded, came to the seashore. Here the princess was rescued by an Earl named Pyrris.]

And when she was thus deliuered, shee told him foorthwith whose daughter shee was, and how shee had lost all his goods in y ͤ sea, and how shee should haue bene married vnto the Emperours son. And when y ͤ Earle heard this [hee] was right glad, wherefore hee comforted hir the more, and kept hir still with him till she was well refreshed. And in the meane time hee sent messengers to the Emperour, letting him to wit how this knights daughter was saued. Then was the Emperour right glad of hir sauety and comming, & had great compassion on hir, saying: A good Mayde for the loue of my sonne thou hast suffered much woe, neuerthelesse if thou be worthy to be his wife soone shal I proue. And when he had thus sayd, hee let bring foorth three vessells, the first was made of pure Gold well beesette with precious stones without and within, full of dead mens bones, and therevpon was engrauen this posey. *Who so chooseth mee shall finde that he deserueth.*

The second vessell was made of fyne siluer, fylled with earth and wormes, and the superscription was thus. *Who so chooseth me shall*

1. Reprinted from the Bodleian copy, Douce R4.

finde that his nature desireth. The third vessell was made of Lead, full within of precious stones, and therevpon was insculpt[1] this posey. *Who so chooseth mee, shall finde that God hath disposed for him.*

These three vessells the Emperour shewed to the Mayden and sayde. Loe here daughter, these bee noble vessells, if thou choose one of these wherin is profit to thee and to other the*n* shalt thou haue my son. And if thou choose that wherin is no profit to thee nor to none other, sothly thou shalt not wed him.

When the Mayden saw this, shee lift vp hir hands to God and sayde. Thou Lord which knowest all things, graunt mee grace this houre so to choose, that I may receiue the Emperours sonne. And with y[t] shee beeheld the first vessell of gold which was grauen royally, & reade this superscription. *Who so chooseth mee. &c.* saying thus. Though this vessel be full precious and made of pure gold, neuerthelesse know not I what is within, therefore my deere Lord this vessell will I not choose.

And then behelde shee the second vessell that was of pure siluer, and reade the superscription, *who so chooseth me, shall finde that his nature desireth.* Thinkeing thus within hir selfe, if I choose this vessell, what is within I know not, but well I wot there shall I finde that [na]ture desireth, & my nature desireth the lust of the flesh, and therefore this vessell will I not choose.

When she had seene those two vessells, & giuen an answere as touching two of the*m*, shee beeheld the third vessell of lead, & read the superscription, *who so chooseth me, shall finde that God hath disposed.* Thinking within hir selfe this vessell is not passing riche, ne thorowly precious, neuerthelesse the superscription faith, who so chooseth mee, shall finde that God hath disposed, & without doubt God neuer disposed any harme, therefore as now I will choose this vessell, by the leaue of God.

When the Emperour saw this, he said, O good Mayden, open thy vessell, for it is full of precious Stones, and see if thou hast well chosen or no. And when this yong Lady had opened it, she found it full of fine gold and precious stones, lyke as the Emperour had foretold hir beefore.

And than sayd the Emperour, O my deere daughter, because thou hast wisely chosen, therefore shalt thou wed my sonne. And when he had so said, he ordained a marriage, and wedded them together with great solempnitie, & much honour, and so continued to theyr liues ende.

I. II. vii. 57.

[Extract from "The Morall"]

The Emperour sheweth this Mayden three vessells, that is to say, God putteth before man life & death, good and euill, & which of these that he chooseth hee shall obtaine. Therefore saith *Sampson: Ante hominem mors & vita.* Death and lyfe is sette before man, choose which him lyst. And yet man is vncertaine whether he bee worthy to choose lyfe beefore death.

By the first vessell of golde full of dead mennes bones we shall vnderstand some worldly men, both mightie men & riche, which outwardly shine as golde in riches and pomps of this world.

Neuerthelesse within they be full of dead mennes bones, that is to saye, the workes that they haue wrought in this world bene dead in the sight of god thorough deadly sinne. Therefore if any man choose such life he shall haue that he deserueth, that is to say, hell. And such men be like toumbes that be white and roially painted and arayed without and couered with cloth of gold and silke, but within there is nothing but dry bones.[1] By the second vessell of siluer we ought to vnderstand some Justices & wise men of this world which shine in faire speach but within they be full of wormes[2] and earth, that is to saye, theyr faire speach shall auaile them no more at the day of iudgement, than wormes of earth, and paraduenture lesse, for than shall they suffer euerlasting paine, if they dye in deadly sinne.

By the third vessell of lead full of golde and precious stones, we ought to vnderstand a simple life and a poore, which the chosen men choose, that they may be wedded to our blessed Lorde Jesu Christ by humilitie and obeysance, and such men beare with them precious stones, that is to saye, faith and hir fruitfull workes, pleasinge to God: by the which at the iudgement day they be espoused to our Lord Jesu Christ and obtaine the heritage of heauen, vnto the which bring vs he that dyed on the Crosse. Amen.

1. II. vii. 69.   2. II. vii. 69.